THE PERIOD SHIP HANDBOOK 2

THE PERIOD SHIP HANDBOOK 2

Keith Julier

NAVAL INSTITUTE PRESS
Annapolis, Maryland

© 1995 by Keith Julier

All rights reserved. No part of this publication may be reproduced in any form, by print, photography, microfilm or any other means without written permission from the publisher.

First published in Great Britain by Nexus Special Interests.

Published and distributed in the United States of America and Canada by the Naval Institute Press, 118 Maryland Avenue, Annapolis, Maryland 21402-5035.

Library of Congress Catalog Card Number: 95-71690

ISBN 1-55750-673-6

This edition is authorized for sale only in the United States and its territories and possessions and Canada.

Printed and bound in Great Britain.

Contents

List of colour plates		6
Introduction		7
Chapter 1	The Expanding Tool Box	9
Chapter 2	Kit Selection	11
Chapter 3	The Royal Yacht *Caroline* 1749	13
Chapter 4	The French Frigate *La Renommée* 1793	35
Chapter 5	An Armed Pinnace Circa 1803	53
Chapter 6	A 15th-Century Portuguese Caravel	65
Chapter 7	The Three-Masted Schooner *Sir Winston Churchill*	75
Chapter 8	A Portuguese Bomb Ship *Lancha Bombardiera* 1798	83
Chapter 9	The Clinker Built Rowing Boat *Holly*	93
Chapter 10	The Hermaphrodite Brig *Le Hussard* 1848	101
Chapter 11	The Yacht *Britannia* 1893	109
Chapter 12	A Frontiersman Canoe	117
Chapter 13	The Rate system	123
Chapter 14	More Modelmaking Techniques	125
Chapter 15	The Planking of Period Ship Models	129
Conclusion		137
Bibliography		139
Index		141

List of Colour Plates

(Between pages 64 to 65)

The Royal Yacht Caroline 1749

The French Frigate *Renommée* 1793

An Armed Pinnace circa 1803

A 15th-Century Portuguese Caravel

The Three-Masted Schooner *Sir Winston Churchill*

A Portuguese Bomb Ship *Lanchia Bombardiera* 1798

The Clinker Built Rowing Boat *Holly*

The Hermaphrodite Brig *Le Hussard* 1848

The Yacht *Britannia* 1893

A Frontiersman Canoe

Introduction

Modelmaking is an on-going hobby and, once bitten with the making of period ship models, you do not easily let it fall by the wayside. You learn about so many things in the early years, not only about the practical craftsmanship involved, but the history and the people who made it. What a waste to acquire knowledge and then let it fall into disuse.

Apparently useless pieces of information seem to stay with you. For instance, George Parkin Christian, the great-grandson of Fletcher Christian, leader of the *Bounty* mutineers, sailed as First Mate on the American whaler *Charles W. Morgan* on its 21st voyage starting in December 1895. I say *apparently* useless, but it is those little tit-bits of information which help to paint the whole worthwhile picture for the modelmaker. I, for one, am convinced that these odd bits of information help you to make a better model because they tend to make you feel a part of the ship itself.

Like the first *Period Ship Handbook*, this volume also uses kits as a basis for discussion and demonstration of modelmaking techniques. Because you are building a kit, it doesn't mean that you have to forego the interesting research, although a lot has probably been done for you by the kit manufacturer. But, bearing in mind that at the time of writing, there are no major English companies in the market place, some of the accuracy of that research may sometimes be a bit suspect; the original translation from official records into the manufacturer's language, then the re-translation into English for the kit, are areas where facts and figures can go astray. I have often found research material confusing in English of the day, so I guess a degree of forgiveness for the foreign manufacturer is in order in that respect.

However, while the written word may be subject to misinterpretation, drawings and draughts are a universal language and inaccuracies in this area should not occur. Unfortunately, they sometimes do, hence the need for your own bit of research if you want to be sure that you are building something akin to the original design.

Remember, kits always come on the market as a commercial enterprise and, as such, are not often likely to directly produce a museum quality model. Nevertheless, with your own research and ingenuity, many of them do provide a very sound basis for that sort of standard. Scratch-builders, of course, do not have the same problems, the entire result is totally dependent upon their own research and craftsmanship. They can be more selective in their choice of materials and, indeed, choice of subject, not being confined to the kit manufacturers catalogues. Unfortunately, not everyone has the facilities for scratch-building, and kits, with their pre-cutting and fittings, are the only way many modellers can fulfil their hobby.

I have worked in both disciplines. *Once you are set up*, there isn't much in it with regard to cost. However, working independently is far more satisfying – you can work with higher quality materials and you have total responsibility for the outcome. But I never knock the kit *per se*, it fills an absolutely essential niche in the market place and permits the hobby to flourish and develop, as many models in national and club exhibitions bear witness. No kit is perfect. Some deserve more adverse criticism than others, but I always try to make my comments fair and constructive. If, at the end of the day, what is available doesn't satisfy your needs, then you either have to do an improver's job on the kit or build entirely from scratch. Kits that fall from favour don't sell well and, in a competitive market, poor sales are often the hotline back to the manufacturer.

Again, in this volume, the kits chosen cover vessels of various types and periods, varying degrees of difficulty for the modeller and, thus, a fairly comprehensive range of modelmaking techniques. Kits produced by Panart, Mamoli, Billing, Artesania Latina and Euromodel-Como are featured here, and are joined by comparative newcomers to these shores, Artenaval of Portugal and Kish Model Boats of Ireland.

I am once again indebted to Dennis Horne at Euro Models of Twickenham for his assistance with the *Royal Caroline*. John Cundell at *Model Boats* magazine continues to be a source of help and inspiration and all the brilliant photography of the finished models is once again the work of Manny Cefai.

Unfortunately, my wife can no longer actively participate in my modelmaking activities, or the preparation of the written word. Nonetheless, her advice on sail making, together with her general support and encouragement, have been vital factors in the making of the models and the production of this, my second volume on the subject of model boat building.

CHAPTER 1

The Expanding Tool Box

Having collected together the basic essentials for model-making, it is then time to think about how you can improve your modelmaking performance by the addition of more sophisticated tools. These perhaps fall into the category of *wants* rather than *needs* and what you choose will largely depend upon your skills with basic tools and, of course, the depth of your pocket.

Basic Tools

We have all *heard* about the model built on the dining-room table with just glue, sandpaper and a razor blade. If you have actually *seen one*, I have no doubt that you will very quickly get the basic tools to hand before you start, unless you are a dedicated masochist, that is! Here then, is a list of those items that can be considered as essential and without which you are not going to get very far.

- Modelling knife with a selection of blades
- Razor saw
- Fine nosed pliers
- Side cutters
- Lightweight hammer
- David plane or similar
- Selection of twist drills up to about 3mm diameter
- Pin chuck up to 3mm capacity
- A selection of small electricians' crocodile clips

You should be able to manage most kits with those tools, albeit that things might be made easier if a few more items were to hand.

Extending the Tool Box

The most useful addition is undoubtedly a 12v power drill. There are several good ones on the market and making a suitable choice is not too difficult. However, what is most important is the choice of the transformer to go with it. Make sure that you think about what other tools you may wish to run off it in the future and buy one that will provide enough oomph!

A small wood-turning lathe that may draw 8 to 10 amps for adequate performance is one such tool. This piece of equipment will certainly take the slog out of tapering masts and spars and provide a facility for making many other fittings as well.

Another very handy piece of kit, and one that I now find I can't do without, is the disc sander. This permits accurate square ending and facing, with an integral work table that provides both accuracy and safety. Chamfering, shaping corners and edges become an absolute doddle.

The combination of jig saw and fret saw is also quite a worthwhile addition to the toolkit. Not quite so important if you are only going to build kits with the usual provision of pre-cut parts, but extremely useful for the scratch-builder. For serious fret-work in any quantity, then the stand-alone powered fret saw or vibro-saw is probably the better bet.

For the more dedicated there are circular saw benches, orbital sanders, drill stands, etc. – the choice is wide and dependent on your own particular needs.

At the other end of the price scale, the simple cabinet-makers' scraper can take a lot of the laborious work out of final hull shaping. These come in several shapes and, once you have got the hang of applying them at the correct angle, they can shift surplus material at quite an acceptable rate.

Plank bending equipment of some sort is also a worthwhile investment, but be careful what you buy. Some of the products available are gimmicky and fairly useless, others are pretty expensive. I always keep an Amati plank nipper to hand which I find most useful for general plank bending but you have to bear in mind that this always marks the inside of the bend. So what can be used for bends where the inside is exposed to view? Well, before you go and spend a lot of cash on one of the more expensive special benders, consider the lowly electric jug/kettle. You can get about 10″ of wetted length with strips of wood standing down the spout which can be brought back to the boil as often as is necessary. It won't be much good for making the workroom tea without regular cleaning, but it's a lot cheaper than some of the proprietary equipment!

Finally, I would mention an item that, instead of cutting or sanding timber, sucks it up! The rechargeable mini vacuum cleaner is a very practical way of keeping the mess under control and is one that is in constant use in my workroom. It is also much easier than its full-size counterpart for retrieving bits accidentally sucked up!

Tool Condition

Tools need to be maintained in proper condition if they, and you, are going to produce the best results. Cutting tools should initially be ground to the correct angles, then kept in good trim by the use of an oil stone. Once you have got the hang of using a stone, you can save yourself quite a bit of cash by sharpening the replacement blades for your craft knife too!

Drills, particularly the small sizes we normally use for this type of model boat building, can prove to be a bit of a problem when it comes to sharpening. Obviously, drills kept solely for use in wood will not need attention very often but, when they do, it is well worth getting them professionally serviced. Of course, if you have the right equipment in your own workshop, and have the cutter grinding expertise to use it, so much the better. But beware of the drill grinding devices that are used in conjunction with a power drill. They are usually made from moulded plastic and may well be accurate enough for larger drills, but I found them fairly useless for the smaller sizes.

Consumables

There is a whole range of adhesives and sticky stuff in general available today that, with the right selection, will virtually stick anything to everything. The two major factors to consider when buying glue are (a) will it stick the materials that need to be stuck together and (b) is it safe to use in the environment in which you are going to work? You'll get no thanks at all for using cellulose in the confines of a small kitchen and will probably finish up not feeling very well either. Some of the contact adhesives are particularly nasty in this respect.

Abrasive papers come in a vast range of types and grades and, as with adhesives, the choice is largely concerned with buying the right ones for the job in hand. Incidentally, glasspaper does not last forever and, contrary to what some modellers seem to think, worn coarse grade paper does not equate to a finer grade. If you note the feel of new paper when rubbing down, you will soon recognise when it loses its cut; it slides across the surface without apparently doing very much. The cut on even the finest grades can be felt when the paper is new. Abrasive paper can produce a large amount of dust when, for instance, rubbing down a large planked hull. So it is always advisable to use a mask when sanding, and the aforementioned mini vacuum cleaner is a great asset after you have finished.

Finishes

There is not usually too much colouring to contend with on period ship models, and where colour is needed, the use of acrylic paint is recommended. It covers extremely well, flows nicely off the brush, and can be easily cleaned in water afterwards.

White stuff, that witches' brew used as anti-fouling below the waterline of many period vessels, can be very nicely simulated by the use of some of the many shades of white to be found in those small sample, or colour tester, pots produced by some of the major paint manufacturers. They usually contain more than enough for at least one model and don't break the bank either.

Matt, satin and gloss varnishes are ideal for the natural wood areas and, again, the acrylic types have much to offer. However, beware! If you have used a contact adhesive to lay very thin planks, try any acrylic varnish on a test piece before applying to the model. Some have a penetrating effect which can destabilise the adhesive below with devastating results.

I have also found that oil-based paints are preferable to acrylics when it comes to the use of metallic media. Many of the applications involve a dry-brushing technique and the acrylics that I have so far used tend to have an inadequate viscosity.

Incidentally, while talking about brushing techniques, do not waste your money on cheap brushes – buy the best that you afford. Then, provided that you look after them, which means keeping them properly clean, they will last a lifetime.

CHAPTER 2

Kit Selection

It is unfortunate that virtually all of the better quality kits available in the United Kingdom today are the products of overseas manufacturers. I am not going to get into a discussion as to the whys and wherefores of this sad state of affairs, but suffice to say that it seems quite deplorable that modelmakers in a country like ours, with its great sea-faring traditions, have to rely on imported kits. However, we have to be realistic, and if you have to build kits rather than scratch-build, for whatever reason, then there are accordingly a few things that have to be taken into consideration.

Materials are seldom a major problem in kits from the reputable producers. Both quality and quantity are usually of a very acceptable standard. Fittings sometimes need some modification due to the fact that, in many cases, they are taken from standard catalogues and you get the nearest one in the box. Anchors, pumps, gun carriages and capstans are typical of this category but, more often than not, they are quite readily put to rights.

Drawings and instructions vary in quality. The drawings themselves are usually well draughted and, although some notes are often left in the manufacturer's own language, it is usually very apparent to what they refer although occasionally you may need the relevant dictionary. Instructions are usually in English, in some cases sparse and sometimes not too well translated, leaving much to the interpretation and ingenuity of the modelmaker. But, there again, in other instances, not only is the correct sequence of building shown, but also the recommended techniques involved.

So, what are the key elements in kit selection? Obviously, the first thing to do is to decide what vessel you want to build. That's the easy bit, but now you have to ask yourself, how big and what scale? These questions are not quite so easily answered and often involve a compromise between what detail you want to show as a modelmaker and what you are going to do with the model when it is finished. Is your sideboard really the right place for a 48″ long model of the *Victory* and, even if it is, have you got room enough on your workbench to conveniently build it?

Having got that far, you look around for the right kit, assuming that you wish to build from a kit rather than from scratch. Catalogues from the major manufacturers are very nice, but expensive, particularly if you are just looking for a specific vessel. In this instance, the lists put together by the main stockists are often a good bet, listing as they do a wide range of manufacturers' products. A telephone call will also usually bear fruit; many of them are run by, or employ, enthusiasts who are willing to give help and advice as well as take your money.

When you have homed in on a likely kit, try to get a look at it. The obvious reason for this is to see just what you are getting for your money. But, just as important, it gives you the opportunity to see whether or not it is within your capabilities, either as a craftsman or because of limited facilities. If you are building for the first time, do not be over-ambitious. Far too many kits are bought and never finished for this reason or, if completed, do not give satisfaction and put the builder off for life. Stick to something that will give you a challenge – that's what modelling is all about – but make sure that the challenge is a reasonable one. The instruction manual and drawings are a good guide to complexity and difficulty. You can nearly always get a good idea from them whether you are in the right league. One or two A4 sheets of instructions can be bad news if you are a newcomer to the hobby. In the more comprehensive manual, look for clear rigging instructions and see if there is a belaying diagram among the sheets of drawings. Without these, a beginner could be in a bit of trouble.

As I said earlier, material quality is not usually a problem. A fair selection of fittings is a good sign as is a range of different coloured rigging threads. Remember, if it is all one colour (usually white), somewhere along the way you are going to have to dye some of it, again not good news.

Don't be put off if the picture on the box shows sails. If you don't fancy the needlework, don't fit them, just remember to adjust the position of the yards accordingly. It also saves you quite a bit of rigging. A lot of modelmakers will tell you that sails cover up a much of the craftsmanship of the main part of the model, which is why they don't fit them. I wonder! But beware, there are some craft that look positively wrong without sails. The Thames barge is an obvious example and the Portuguese Caravel, discussed herein, is another.

So, in summary, decide on your subject and scale, make sure that the kit you choose is reasonably within your capabilities and then go ahead and enjoy yourself.

CHAPTER 3

The Royal Yacht *Caroline* 1749

Anyone in industry today, reading about the circumstances surrounding the conception and building of the *Royal Caroline*, must be only too aware that things haven't changed much during the past 250 years. The Admiralty requested the submission of plans by the Surveyor of the Navy and various Master Shipwrights in June 1749. Some pressure for urgent action must have been put behind the requests, since the order was actually placed against an approved design just two months later. The same cry, still heard today, was "We want it yesterday", and Deptford yard was told to have the vessel ready for a journey to Holland by His Majesty King George ll during the following spring. Again, like today, costs escalated during building and there were delays in completion — so much so, that the ship undertook that first royal trip in an unfinished state.

Having done a little bit of research into the *Royal Caroline*, I have to confess that I was completely thrown by some of the salient dates. Plans requested June 1749, order placed August 1749 and then the Captain's log records the launch date as January 1749! However, a very helpful lady at the National Maritime Museum ultimately came up with the solution – Calendar Reform; the year end at that time was March. Thus, what is recorded as January 1749 was, in our modern calendar terms, January 1750.

Built in the fashion of the day, she was planked and decked entirely in English oak and was probably one of the most ornate vessels of its size ever built in an English dockyard.

When the King died in 1760, his grandson became George lll and the yacht was re-christened *Royal Charlotte* in honour of his intended bride, the German princess Charlotte von Mecklenburg-Strelitz.

The vessel was finally broken up in 1820.

The Kit

Panart has produced a kit which provides all of the ornamentation and high class materials and fittings to build a model 815mm long. The frames and all of the other ply parts have been accurately laser cut. Strip material is excellent in terms of constant thickness and matching colour. The ornamentation comes as a complete set of castings already gilded and packed in a cleverly thought-out way that identifies each piece and its place on the model.

The multilingual manual provides a step-by-step list of instructions which is supplemented by well-detailed drawings showing all the various stages of construction although, I have to say, things are a little weak on the masting and rigging. Obviously, a lot of planning has gone into this kit and it makes a potentially difficult subject within the scope of anyone with say a two or three previous models under their belt.

However, once again in one of my reviews, I have to complain that there is no provision in the kit for a stand. I have never understood the thinking behind this omission, particularly in a kit of this high quality.

Built straight from the box you get a very attractive and detailed model, but it is also an excellent kit to buy as a foundation for a model with that something extra special in the way of greater detail and accuracy. Having done some basic research I found that most of the essential information available was to be found summarised in *The Royal Yacht Caroline 1749*, a book in the Anatomy of the Ship series from Conway Maritime Press. There were several quite significant differences between the documented description and the kit, nearly all concerned with the masting and rigging. As far as was possible I decided to be guided by the book and, with the exception of requiring an additional twelve 5mm deadeyes, all of the differences were accommodated with the contents of the kit. Those that I did choose to do I have described in the salient parts of this review.

Tools

This is not a beginner's kit and, therefore, it will be anticipated that you have a good low-voltage electric drill, a razor saw, modelmakers' plane, a light hammer and some device for plank bending together with a basic set of needle files. A disc sanding unit with support table will be a great asset although not an absolute essential. You will also need to be able to firmly hold the model during the course of construction. The usual selection of abrasive papers will be required and a supply of white PVA and cyanoacrylate adhesives, together with a handful of small electricians' crocodile clips. Various shapes of forceps, crochet hooks and cutters will be needed for rigging. There are no sails to make in this kit, so you can forget the sewing machine and inevitable bribe for the operator!

Building the Hull – Stage One

The construction follows the familiar frames slotted into false keel method (Fig. 3.1). The accuracy of the laser cut parts means that little preparatory work is required before assembly can begin. However, do read the total instructions first to familiarise yourself with the sequence of events and have at least one dry run before picking up the glue pot. It is absolutely essential to make sure that when all the parts come together, the edges of the frames and associated beams that later support the decks, are in correct alignment. I found that virtually no corrective work was necessary to attain this condition but, all the same, check it out before you commit the glue! I would suggest that the transom sub-assembly not be glued in place until the fitting of the after deck. The rake of the transom unit relative to the other frames makes the fitting of the deck a mite awkward if it has been glued first and set.

The drawings indicate that the first two frames at the front end have their edges bevelled to conform to the natural curve of the hull such that the planking will sit flat across the edges. In fact, I found that a better seating was attained by treating the first three frames at the bow and the last two at the stern.

Panart advise as to the sequence of laying the planks and it works very well, no undue twists or severe bends. In fact, the first planking is quite a simple job (Fig. 3.2). A plank nipper is all that is needed to comfortably bend the strips. All planks should be glued edge to edge and pinned to each frame. Advance reading of the instructions showed that the tops of some frames above deck level had to be removed at a later stage of construction, thus at these points the planks should not be glued to the frames.

When the adhesive has thoroughly cured and all of the fixing pins removed, the first planking should be rubbed down so as to attain a fair surface with no ridges or bumps. A cabinet-maker's scraper is a good tool to start off with, followed by a couple of grades of abrasive paper. A dead smooth finish is not necessary. In fact, if you are going to use contact adhesive for the second planking, a better key is provided by a surface produced with a medium grade of abrasive paper.

The second planking follows the same sequence as the

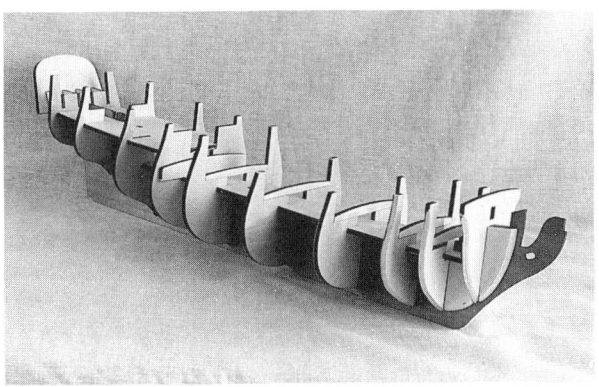

Fig. 3.1 The basic hull construction.

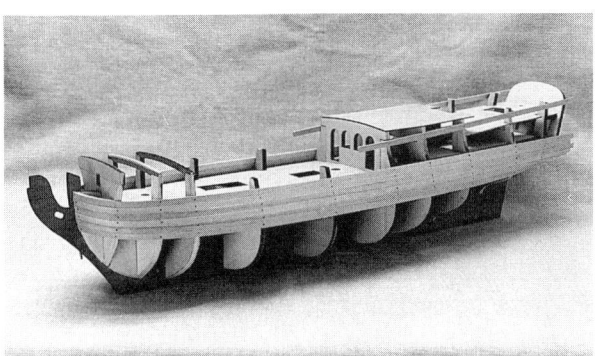

Fig. 3.2 The start of the first planking.

first but with 1mm thick strips instead of 1.5mm. A point to watch here is one of colour. The strips provided were a pretty good match but, nonetheless, there were some a shade darker than the rest. If you find the same situation, keep the darker ones for below the waterline. The visible planking was a light oak by all accounts and, since the lower hull is painted with anti-fouling white stuff, the selective choice of colour in the planking strips fulfils the condition.

There is not too much bevelling and tapering to do, but that which is necessary must be done accurately if the final result is to look right. Particular attention is required to the angle and bevel on the bow end of each plank so that it fits tight up against the stem. As I mentioned earlier, I found that a contact adhesive was probably the best for the second planking; Dunlop Thixofix is particularly good in that it is a gel and does not string. I started by rubbing a coat of it in to the entire hull; this primed and sealed the surface and ensured that the second planking sat firmly down. Each plank was laid starting at the stem, ensuring that a little over-bend was induced by the plank nipper to avoid any adverse spring in the strip which might prevent the plank from seating properly.

Provided that a fair surface was attained when rubbing down the first planking, and that you have all the second planking seating flat throughout, there is little to do in the way of heavy work to finish. Once you are satisfied with the finish, it is worth giving the whole outside of the hull a coat of matt varnish. This with help protect it

The Royal Yacht *Caroline* 1749

Fig. 3.3 The complete hull carcase.

while you proceed with the later stages of construction. It also prevents the natural oils from the fingertips marking the surface — marks that can sometimes be very difficult to remove. This completes the basic hull carcase construction (Fig. 3.3).

Building the Hull – Stage Two

The next operation is to remove the tops of the frames above deck level. A razor saw or a similarly small, fine-toothed tool is definitely required to do this safely, particularly those frames under the beams that are to support the forecastle deck. Having got all of these pieces out of the way, the decks can be planked and the insides of the bulwarks lined. These surfaces are to be finished in matt red and, bearing in mind the later deck clutter, this is the prime opportunity to do this particular bit of painting, before putting the forecastle deck in place. Also, don't forget to accurately mark and cut the hole in the forecastle deck for the foremast. Again this is best done before installation.

While talking about the forecastle area, all of the drawings show a rectangular aperture through the front bulkhead to take the bowsprit. When facing the bulkhead with the vertical strips of walnut, it is necessary to recognise that the section of the bowsprit is circular. It is probably best to completely plank over the rectangle and drill a new hole, then file out to suit final size and angle required.

Having done that, put the model to one side and make yourself a stand. This is something that will become increasingly essential as you proceed with the construction. The design has to be functional and cosmetic, but don't overdo the latter such that the stand draws the eye away from the model. To be able to hold the hull in an upright position when viewed fore and aft, and with the waterline parallel to the base of the stand when viewed from the side, will help enormously when marking the waterline ready for painting on the white stuff.

Panart give you a very useful thick card template in the kit for marking out the position of all the cut-outs on the sides of the hull, gunports, windows etc. together with the top profile line of the bulwarks (Fig. 3.4). A useful point to make at this stage is that it is worth checking the relative levels of the rails and the ornamental strakes. Study of the side elevation drawing will show that the distance between the various levels is controlled by the width of the etched brass ornamental strips. This may entail some very minor adjustment to the top rail profile line due to variations in construction techniques.

The card template aligns with the edges of the upper and forecastle decks and should be pinned or clipped in place while a sharp pencil is used to mark the various features on to the surface of the hull. This ensures that both size and position are easily made identical both sides, although the size of each aperture so marked is somewhat smaller than required. The drawings indicate the finished sizes and each aperture should be carefully opened out with a scalpel (Fig. 3.5).

Making the windows is a bit of a fiddly job, but the sequence of assembly of each frame as given can be followed quite satisfactorily, with one exception. Because the area around each window aperture is not flat, you will find it easier to keep the canopy sub-assembly separate from the lower frame and bars (Fig. 3.6), until actually bringing them together when fixing to the hull sides (Fig. 3.7).

The very small section of materials used needs a fine sharp scalpel to keep cut ends square in order to give the adhesive the largest possible area for adhesion. Superglue is fine, providing that you remember that it will soak through 1 × 1mm strip. I cut a panel from the lid

Fig. 3.4 The card template clipped in position.

Fig. 3.5 Windows and gunports.

Fig. 3.6 Keep canopies and frames separate until assembly. A simple cutting jig keeps frames identical in shape and size.

Fig. 3.7 Assembling windows to hull.

of an empty icecream box to work on; cyano doesn't adhere to this and thus helps to make life a little easier. All these minor problems aside, the major difficulty is making the windows all identical. Because of their small proportions, the smallest difference sticks out like a sore thumb. I made some simple cutting jigs (again see Fig. 3.6), similar to those shown on the drawings, for cutting the deck planks in order to get lengths of similar parts the same. Finally, due to the fact that the canopy is made up from a combination of strip and ply materials, I chose to paint the whole assembly with Humbrol Matt Brown No. 110 to cover the ply laminations.

The rails are added next. Take care to ensure that you have the correct 2mm overlap all round so that the decorative trim can be properly blended later on. The wider rail across the top of the transom is definitely not easy to make from the 8 × 2mm strip supplied unless you have some good plank bending kit. An alternative method is to laminate some 6 × 1mm in two layers to give a covering 12 × 2mm, then trim the edges to suit to get back to the required 8mm width.

From what reading I have done, most sources suggest that the two main wales were painted black. If you wish to follow this suggestion, paint the wales before assembly (Fig. 3.8). This avoids the difficulties of keeping the paint off of the surface of the hull.

To complete the second stage of hull construction, you now have to make the quarter galleries. I started to make the first of the two assemblies in accordance with the procedure outlined on the drawing which involves building up the structure on the hull. Personally, I found this quite awkward and abandoned this for the alternative method of building each unit on the bench. One of the problems that I found was the shape of the glazing units. Because they are pressed from the sheet, they have a draft angle on each surface which does not permit full coverage of the window apertures with a glazed surface. This cannot be avoided if you build the galleries up on the hull because the structure is built around the glazing piece and it is therefore trapped. Having built the structure on the bench, I was able to cut three individual pieces of clear sheet from the kit (there is plenty supplied), and fit them tight up against the inside of the window frames. The bench method also allows you to keep the completed quarter galleries to one side (Fig. 3.9), while the rest of the hull construction proceeds. They are rather vulnerable if assembled to the hull at this stage.

Fig. 3.8 The painted wales in place.

Fig. 3.9 The complete quarter galleries.

Building the Hull – Stage Three

This part of the construction involves the making of over forty details, each being a mini-project in itself. The decoration and ornamentation are also included in this section. In addition to the windows and doors in the front bulkhead of the main cabin to make and fit, there are bitts, the capstan, pin racks, pumps, gratings, skylight, guns, anchors, etc. The majority of these items are relatively simple to make but there are several which are worthy of some comment. While I do not see any reason to make these parts in any particular order, you will need to adopt an assembly sequence that does not restrict access or make things difficult for further work on fitting out or rigging. Three items particularly come to mind, the pumps, the sheet bitt gallows assembly and the stove chimney stack on the forecastle deck. All of these items, if assembled at this stage, would inhibit access for rigging later on.

The rudder assembly (Det. 1)

From the drawing, mark the position of the rudder hinges on to the hull and fix in place. You also need to cut an aperture in the transom to take the upper end of the rudder.

With regard to the rudder itself, the edges should be faced with spare 0.5 × 4mm strip to cover the visible laminations of the ply. It further adds to the appearance if you lightly score the side faces to represent the various pieces of timber from which the rudder was made.

Ideally, the pins that fit through the hinge units should be soft soldered into the rudder half of the hinge. Most important of all, each of the hinges that fix to the front edge of the rudder should be housed in pockets to minimise the gap between the rudder and the stern post on the hull. If you make the pockets 10mm long and fit the hinge at the top of the aperture, you will find that the rudder will assemble without trouble.

Finally, the drawings indicate that the top of the rudder should be pared down to 3mm diameter. Bearing in mind that the rudder is cut from 4mm ply, this produces a very weak spindle on which to fit the tiller head!

A better alternative is to cut off the top of the rudder, drill a hole 2mm diameter and fit a spindle made from 3mm dowel suitably reduced at one end.

Painting the hull

Having assembled the rudder, I decided to paint the underside of the hull. It permits several coats to be applied and dry while all of the various other bits and pieces are being made. The anti-fouling, or white stuff, can be well represented by using Dulux Barley White Colour Matcher. These small pots are inexpensive and really do the job well, giving a slightly off-white effect that looks far better than pure white.

The cabin doors and windows

As with the side windows, I found that these features were best made on the bench rather than directly on to the hull. This provides a much better chance of positioning the glazing bars accurately and without marking the clear material with adhesive. The canopies were kept separate, painted (Humbrol Matt No. 110) to hide the ply laminations and assembled to the face of the bulkhead last. Before gluing these in place, check that the relative alignment of their tops is correct and adjust as necessary. This is important because the ornamental strip that trims the upper part of the bulkhead comes fairly close to the tops of the canopies and any misalignment of the canopies will show up.

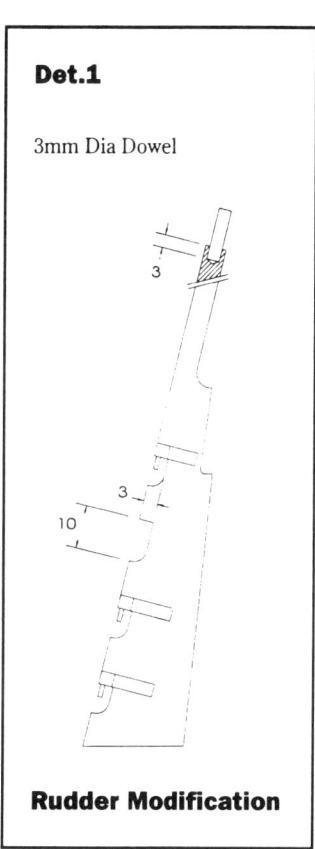

The ornamentation

The fine scroll work comes from an etched brass sheet. I applied these to the model as it became convenient during the construction. I don't think it matters whether you paint them before or after you cut them out. Do watch for the sharp edges that will slice into the pads of your fingers if you aren't careful. I chose to use Humbrol 5025 Matt Blue Acrylic paint which was right for colour and makes brush cleaning easy. It also rubs off the raised surfaces easily to leave gold ornamentation on a blue background.

On the subject of brush cleaning, whether you use oil-based or acrylic paints, after conventional cleaning try using a drop of hair shampoo on the brush and rinse out. You really can wash and go back to the bench with a squeaky clean brush!

With regard to the decorative figures on the sides of the vessel, there are certain alignments that are controlled by the line of the rail on the bulwarks of the after deck (Fig. 3.10). Thus, it is not a bad idea to start by running the wooden trim as a continuation of this rail to the upper portion of the side windows, then forward and down to the front of the amidships bulkhead, where it terminates in line with the upper main deck rail. The etched brass decorative strips can then be cut and fixed. Before adding the smaller of the two sizes of brass rail to the lower edge of the strips, the quarter gallery assemblies should be fixed in place together with the brass canopies on top. The brass rail is not a continuous piece, there being short sections to fit between the windows and either side of the quarter galleries. Therefore it is important to make sure that when eyeing the finished effect along the length of the hull, that each separate piece follows the same line. Note too, that the section of the brass rail is heavier on one edge to that on the other. The heavy edge should be at the top throughout the model.

The gunport surrounds should be fitted next followed by the wider brass rail (Fig. 3.11). The line of this strip is governed by the edge of the peak deck from where it continues parallel to the upper rails previously fitted, finishing at the stern. When satisfied that all of the alignments are correct, the space between the two brass rails can be painted blue and the remainder of the ornamentation fitted.

Fig. 3.11 Gunport surrounds and wider brass rail in position.

Fig. 3.10 Note that rail on afterdeck controls position of lower rail below ornamental strip.

The stern decoration is quite straightforward, but adhering to the sequence of application that follows will help. First fix the two lowest transverse rails and then the curved rail around the top of the transom. Next put the two outer decorative figures in place and paint the whole intermediate space blue. Paint the main etched brass panel and drill the holes for the outer two lanterns and fix in position, followed by the central and upper figure group (Fig. 3.12).

Fig. 3.12 The stern ornamentation.

A cosmetic point here; Panart suggest that the glazed part of the windows be painted white, but when you look at the transparent glazing of the quarter galleries and side windows, you will see that the effect is far from white. I chose to use gloss black tinged with dark brown and found that it gave a very reasonable match and certainly looked a lot less artificial.

The two remaining figure groups are a bit of a pain in that they have to sit on a curved surface either side of the stern post. The curve has to be very gently coerced into the group, not the easiest of jobs since the castings are fairly thick in places. In fact, because of this, a little bit of judicious filing can be done to supplement the bending.

The headrails and figurehead

The fitting of these rails is probably the most difficult part of the whole project, so do not start without giving the task a bit of thought. Again, sequence is the key to success remembering that throughout the construction identical but opposite hands have to be made and fitted in matching attitudes; all designed to test your patience, temper and vocabulary! I found the following procedure quite successful.

First, fix the figurehead in position. The jaws of the casting needed to be gently closed in to match the thickness of the stem. Make sure that it is assembled so that there is sufficient space for the rails fixing points behind the figurehead casting. The curved cheek castings can then be fixed relative to the figurehead and the lower main wale, and the pieces with the two hawse holes glued in place (Fig. 3.13). It is important that each stage is immediately repeated on the opposite side of the hull.

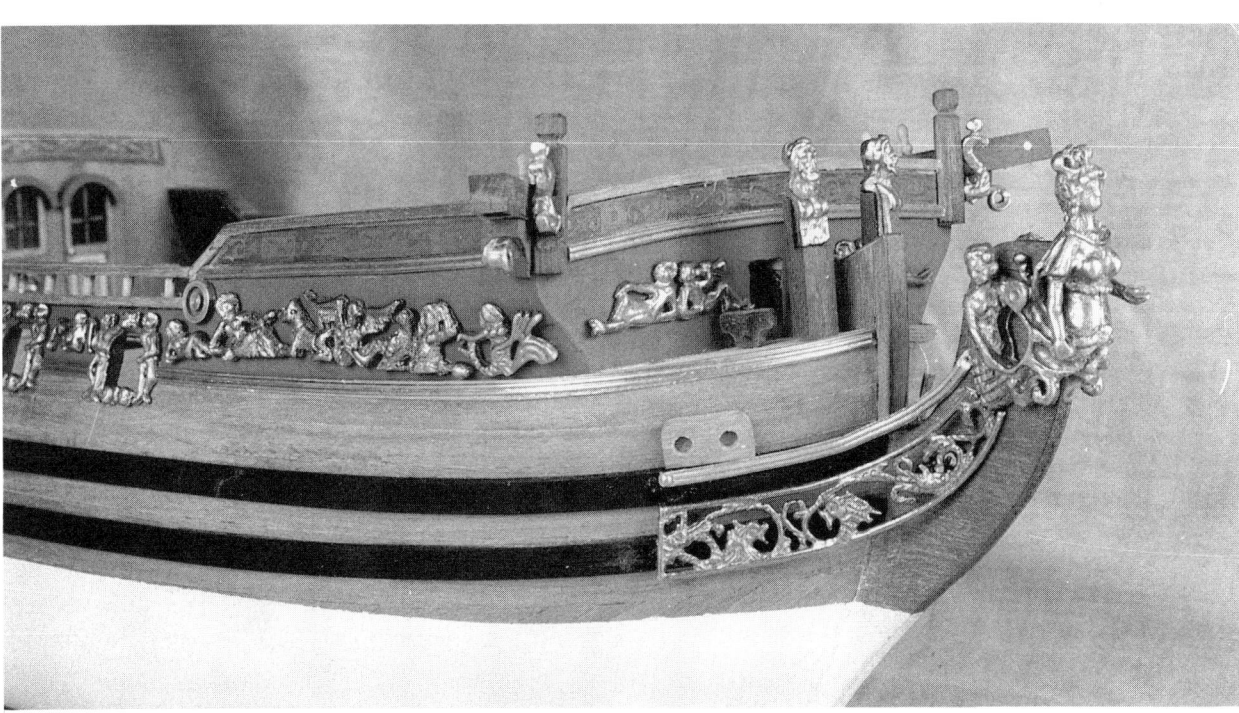

Fig. 3.13 The hawse holes, figurehead and cheek castings in place.

The lower headrails are next. Form one side to the shape required, then make a matching opposite hand (or as near as possible). Fix one side in position using pins and adhesive and offer up the opposite side to see whether any minor adjustment is required to attain a correct and matching attitude to the other side. You need to look from the sides, the top and the front, to be certain before fixing the second side. Now fit the middle rails from the cathead knee to the stem following the same procedure and using the lower rails as a comparative line to get the alignment correct.

The three head timbers should now be slotted and assembled to the two lower rails, remembering to also file in the slot for the top rail. File the depth of the slots as an adjustment to attain the correct splay of these pieces and sight down from the top and in from the front to ensure that the attitudes are matching side to side. Finally, the top rails should be formed and fitted to complete the whole headrail assembly (Fig. 3.14).

Fig. 3.14 The complete head rail assembly.

The anchors (Det. 2).

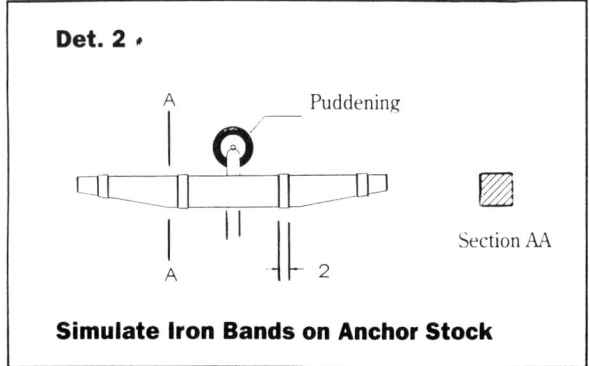

The anchor stocks come from the 5mm ply sheet and will inevitably finish up with all the laminations showing. You have two alternative options; either paint them with Humbrol No. 110 or similar, or make them from something in your scrap box. The other point for nitpickers is that the stocks are shown rope bound, whereas I am pretty certain that they should have iron bands or, in the case of my model, strips cut from the black page of an old photograph album. Finally, bind the anchor rings with thread (the puddening) for that extra touch of realism.

The pumps (Det. 3)

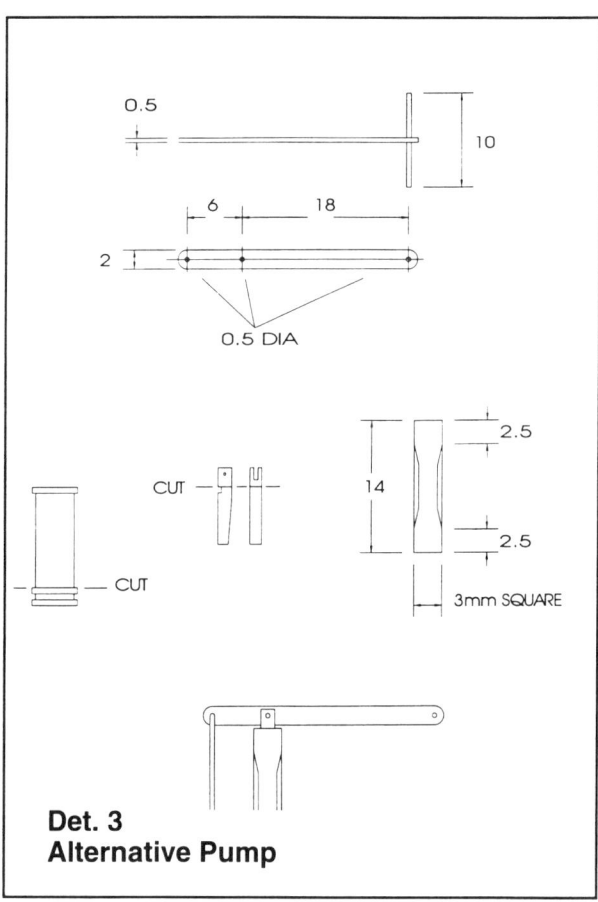

Det. 3
Alternative Pump

The parts in the kit are from a standard range of fittings and represent a conventional elm tree pump. If you consult Conway's Anatomy of a Ship series for the *Royal Caroline*, you will see that while the design of the pump is basically the same as that portrayed in the kit, the application is somewhat different. The pivot for the handle is on a separate post, the cylinder is, for the most part, below deck level and the handle is fitted with a crossbar. I chose to use this latter design for the model and it can be done by modifying the parts provided in the kit and using a couple of pieces of scrap strip material.

Drill the given cylinder right through and cut off the bottom section. Carefully cut the clevis from the end of the small wooden bracket provided and use superglue to attach it to the top of a square section post 15mm long.

The handle is cut 2mm wide from 3mm × 0.5mm strip and is drilled with three holes 0.5mm diameter. The crossbar is a piece of wire 0.5mm dia.

Ladders

These are the usual kit type assemblies and present no problems. However, do remember to make up two additional units to those shown on the drawings and place them inside the bulwarks at the two boarding points. I am sure that His Majesty would have objected to jumping down to deck level! There are enough pieces in the kit provided that you don't scrap any.

Gratings

There is not much to say about these apart from that on all the drawings that I have seen for the *Caroline*, the anchor ropes stow below deck via two cut-outs at the aft end of the bigger of the two hatches (Fig. 3.15), and not through the holes shown on Panart drawings. This is easy enough to modify if you so wish.

Remember too, that the gratings comprised two main parts – the ledges, which ran athwartships and the battens, which ran in grooves on top of the ledges fore and aft. Thus, it is the battens which you should see in their entirety on the model.

The spiral staircase

There are several points to make here. The Panart method of making them works wonderfully well and is worth remembering for any future projects. However, again referring to the drawings seen during my initial research, none of them show two spiral staircases, only one on the port side.

The kit also omits to show, or describe, the access to the lower deck staircase that is situated between the spiral staircase and the main deck bulkhead. This is below the small platform from which the small ladder leads to the upper deck (Fig. 3.16). Fortunately for the modelmaker, the access is through a door which is quite easily made up from scrap material, thus avoiding having to cut any additional apertures in the main deck. This access housing does, however, have to be duplicated on the starboard side (Fig. 3.17), but without the spiral staircase and short ladder.

Fig. 3.16 The spiral staircase.

Fig. 3.15 Ladders and hatches.

The Period Ship Handbook 2

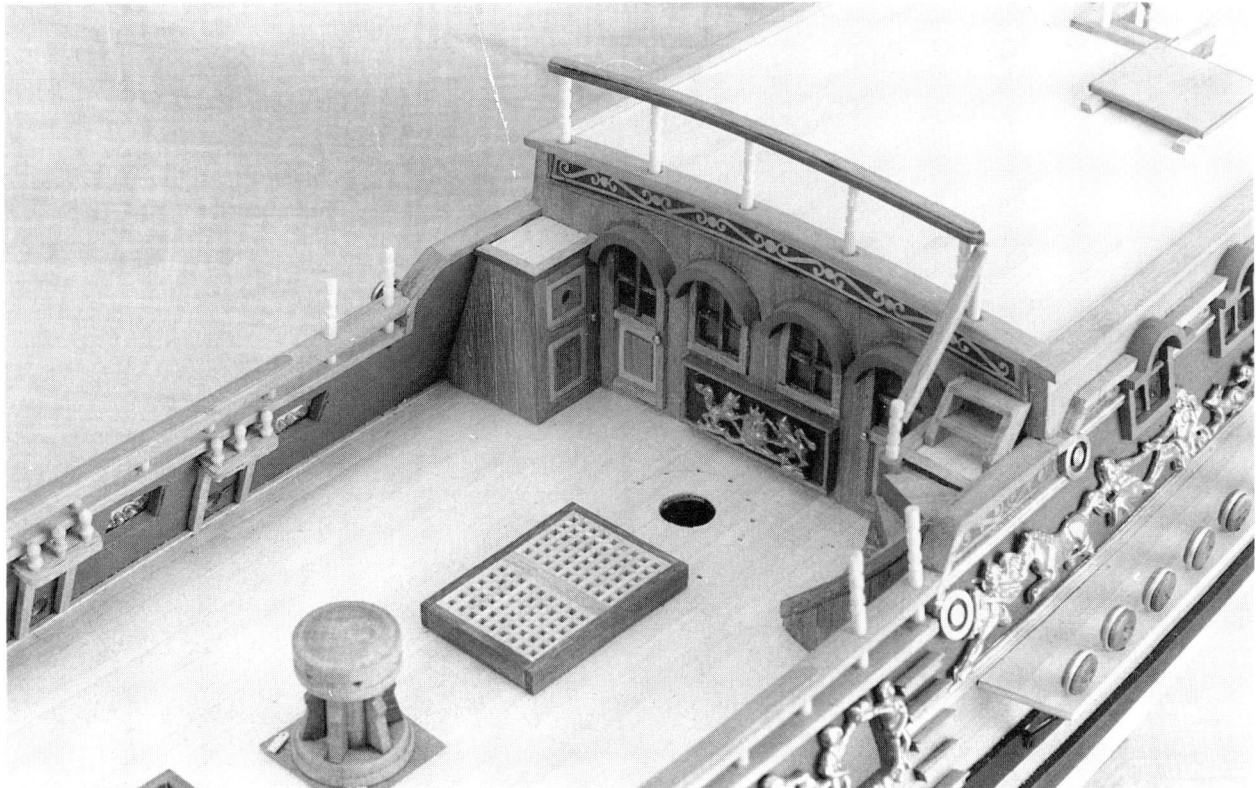

Fig. 3.17 The starboard side lower deck access housing.

The capstan

To add a little bit of extra detail, cut two small pieces of 0.5mm thick strip to simulate the two pawls that pivot on the base plate (again see Fig. 3.15).

The stove chimney

It just goes to show that you should "never knock it before you've tried it". I looked at the proposed task of drilling a 4mm dia. hole down an albeit short length of 6mm dia. dowel to make the angled upper end of the stack, and said, "Fat chance of doing that without splitting everything from here to breakfast time". Wrong! It works if you use progressively increasing sizes of well sharpened drills and drill into the end of an uncut rod for a depth greater than required. When you get to 3mm diameter, coat the outside of the dowel with superglue; it penetrates the outer fibres and inhibits against splitting. The most care is needed when cutting the required length off the rod. Insert a short piece of 4mm dia. dowel into the drilled hole for support and cut the piece off at the correct angle.

The sheet bitt gallows

The important thing to watch here is the overall height; it has to be such as to support the ship's boat horizontally. Having made up the various parts of the structure, leave the two dowel rods immediately below the cross pieces over-length. The boat support proper and its gratings should be made and offered up to the two locating blocks on the forecastle deck. The final length of the two dowels in the gallows unit can now be correctly assessed and everything glued together. The gallows assembly should be dowelled into the deck with brass pins but, at this stage, it is as well not to permanently fix it in place until essentially required for the rigging process.

The guns

The sides of the carriages are laser cut from ply and, as such, do not look right with exposed laminated edges. Fortunately, history is on our side specifying that they were either left in natural wood or painted red. So, having assembled the four main parts of each carriage, out came the red paint. The wedge-shaped piece, or quoin, that was used to elevate and support the barrel, should be left natural. The little brass cap-squares which hold the barrel on to the carriage should be carefully pinned in place and painted matt black.

The kit does not provide blocks for rigging the guns to the inside of the bulwarks or deck, so you are left with what can only be called a symbolic assembly.

A further point for consideration is two stern chasers, again not featured in the kit, but appear on all of the other drawings that I have seen. Two closed ports, one either side of the rudder post below the lower stern ornamentation can easily be added if you so wish.

The channels and lower shroud deadeyes

No problems were encountered fitting the channels and the associated support brackets, but I considered it best not to fit the anchor linings until after the lower deadeyes and links had been set up. It was when I came to fit the deadeyes that I found a bit of a problem. The pre-formed brass wire chainplates provided were not as shown on the drawings and were not capable of being modified to that design, the break in the wire being in entirely the wrong place to give enough length to connect the top end of the link. I had no alternative but to make my own from 38mm lengths of 1mm dia. brass wire. It is also important to recognise that the loop that takes the upper end of the link has to be at ninety degrees to the line of the deadeye in order that the link sits true on the wale. I don't know whether the wrong parts got into my particular kit or whether it was a case of having to make do with the nearest in a standard range of fittings. Either way, over a metre length of brass wire had to be found, there being 32 chainplates to produce for the larger deadeyes. Nothing is provided in the way of pre-formed parts to accommodate the smaller deadeyes that sit on the stools and 0.75mm dia. wire has to be used, although nothing is said anywhere about this either on the drawings or in the instructions.

Locating the position of the bottom of the link on the upper main wale needs to be carefully thought about to get them in line with the shrouds. I set up a dowel as a dummy mast and tied a length of thread where the top of the shrouds would be. Pulling this taut against the edge of the channels gives an indication of the line that the link has to take and its bottom fixing hole can be marked accordingly (Fig. 3.18). When all links have been fixed, the entire link/chainplate assembly below the channel should be painted matt black and the anchor linings fitted. A lot of offering up and fitting is needed to get everything to sit properly in place. Angular edges should be carefully cut so that maximum strength of glued joint is attained.

The lanterns

These comprise a series of turned and etched brass parts which all go together extremely well to produce a very nice set of three lanterns (Fig. 3.19). They are basically cylindrical in shape, something I believe to be questionable, but the final result is certainly better than some of the very artificial cast examples that often appear in kits. Without the tools and skill to produce as good a looking lantern of the correct shape, these will do very nicely thankyou! A strip of clear plastic cut from the fittings packaging, rolled and dropped inside the lantern when assembling, provides a nice glazed effect.

Fig. 3.19 The lanterns.

Fig. 3.18 Note line of links from deadeyes to wale.

Building the Hull – Stage Four

Final assembly

Now is the time to have a dry run at assembling all of the details into place, just to have a final check that everything is OK before opening up the glue. Don't forget to put to one side those items that might make life difficult when doing the rigging later on. You may also decide that the little brass tags with rings attached are better left off at this juncture. Some of them will eventually have blocks tied to them and you could well find that it is easier to assemble block, tag and ring as an integral unit.

An additional feature which provides that little something extra in the way of detail is the helmsman's foot rails. Cut eight lengths of 1mm square strip, 16mm long, and arrange them radially below the end of the tiller, using the centre of the rudder post to swing the required arc (Fig. 3.20).

After everything had been put on board, I had a tidy up on all decks with a damp brush to get any bits of wood dust etc. out of all the nooks and crannies before having a final inspection of the paint and varnish work. Having carried out any touching up necessary, the hull can be put to one side while you are making the ship's boat, masts, yards and bowsprit.

The ship's boat

Here is a nice little project, guaranteed to put your patience to the test. The construction technique involved is a double-planked shell built around a series of frames. The tops of the frames are ultimately removed to leave an open boat ready for putting in a slatted floor and the thwarts. This process is fine when working on larger scale boats, but I would question whether the nature of the materials provided here really lend themselves adequately to the method. Ply frames are not solid enough and the coarseness of grain in the 3 × .05mm strips is not to advantage. Nevertheless, I persevered and although I got a reasonable looking little boat, I think that the quality of the main vessel justified better.

I found that the shell had to be planked entirely with the use of superglue gel. Liquid adhesive disappeared too quickly into the edges of the ply frames and also soaked through the 0.5mm planks with the result that the plank stuck to the fingers rather than the frame!

The first planking, which should not be stuck to any but the first and last frames, was applied longitudinally (Fig. 3.21). Due to the coarse grain of the strips, accurate tapering was difficult and, of course, in the upper areas it was all edge to edge work. With care, the thumbnail makes a good plank nipper to induce some of the more severe curves into the strips before gluing. After this first planking was completed, I covered the entire outer surface with a rubbed-in coat of white PVA adhesive and left it to harden off overnight.

Since the outer surface of the boat had to be painted, I decided that for ease of working, and for added strength, I would apply the second planking at about 45 degrees, again using superglue gel (Fig. 3.22). This worked extremely well and I finished up with a relatively strong shell (Fig. 3.23). I preferred to use some scrap

Fig. 3.20 The helmsman's position.

The Royal Yacht *Caroline* 1749

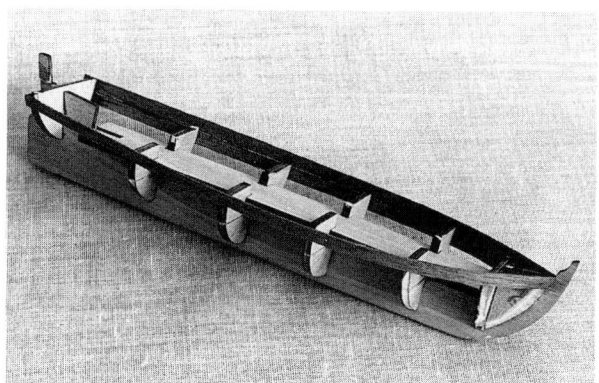

Fig. 3.21 The basic frame for the ship's boat.

ply for the gunwale rails rather than the 3 × 2mm strip suggested in the kit. I did this for two reasons; first the grain structure made the strip difficult to bend and, secondly, cutting from ply enabled both sides to be identical with regard to shape. The first planking of the hull shell, being unsupported at the top, had made it very difficult to attain exactly the same shape on both sides. We are only talking about a maximum of 0.5mm but, of course, at this scale the difference is quite noticeable. The identical ply rails corrected the visible error, the actual error now being translated into 0.25mm variations in rail overhang and not so evident to the eye.

The ribs, slats and thwarts can now be put in place and it only remains to make the oars to complete the project (Fig. 3.24).

Fig. 3.22 Boat planking at 45 degrees.

Fig. 3.23 The finished boat shell.

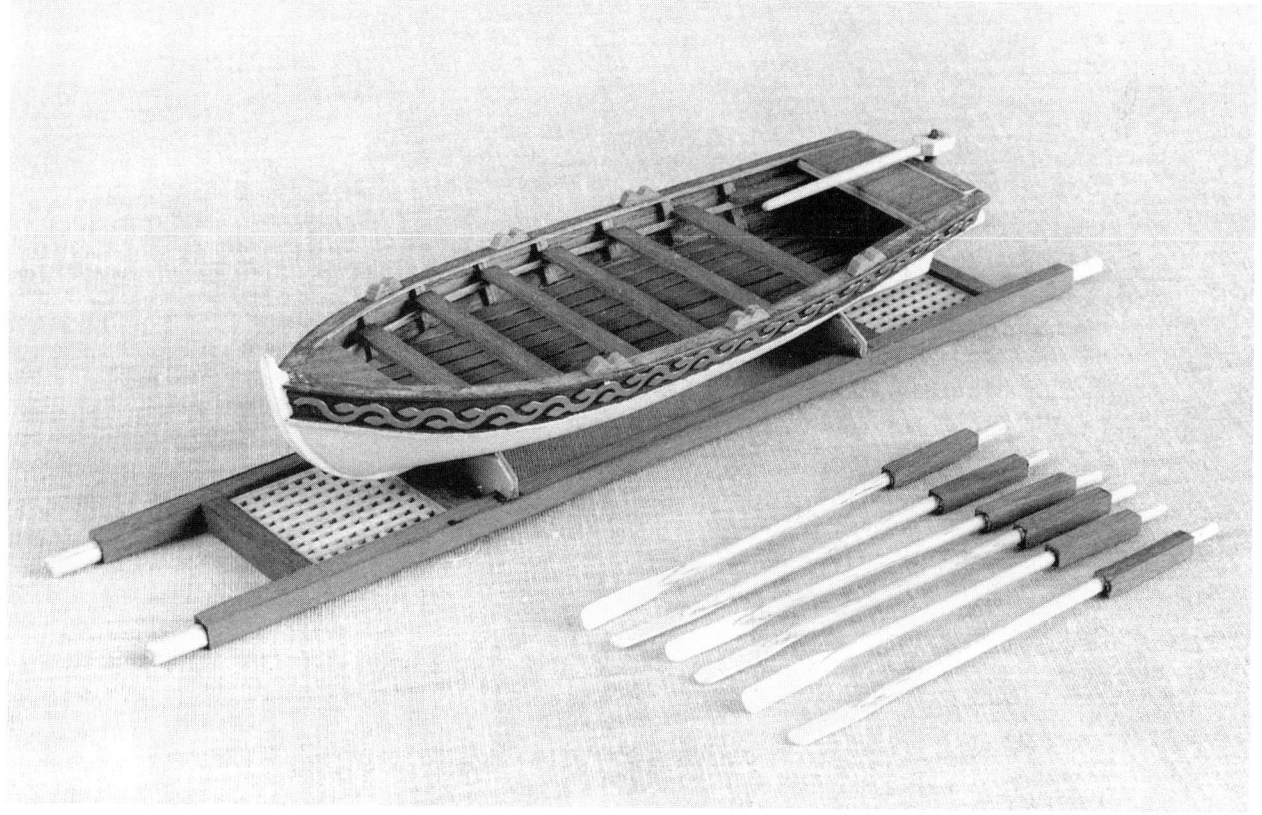

Fig. 3.24 The final boat assembly.

25

The bowsprit (Det. 4)

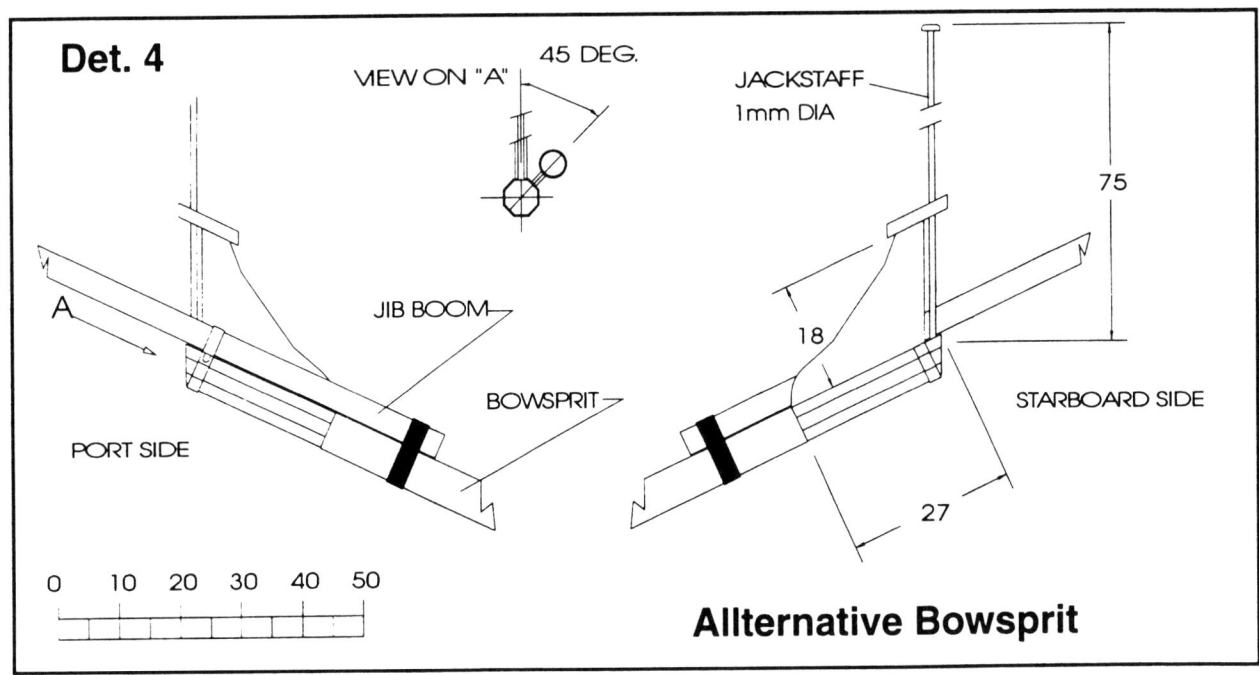

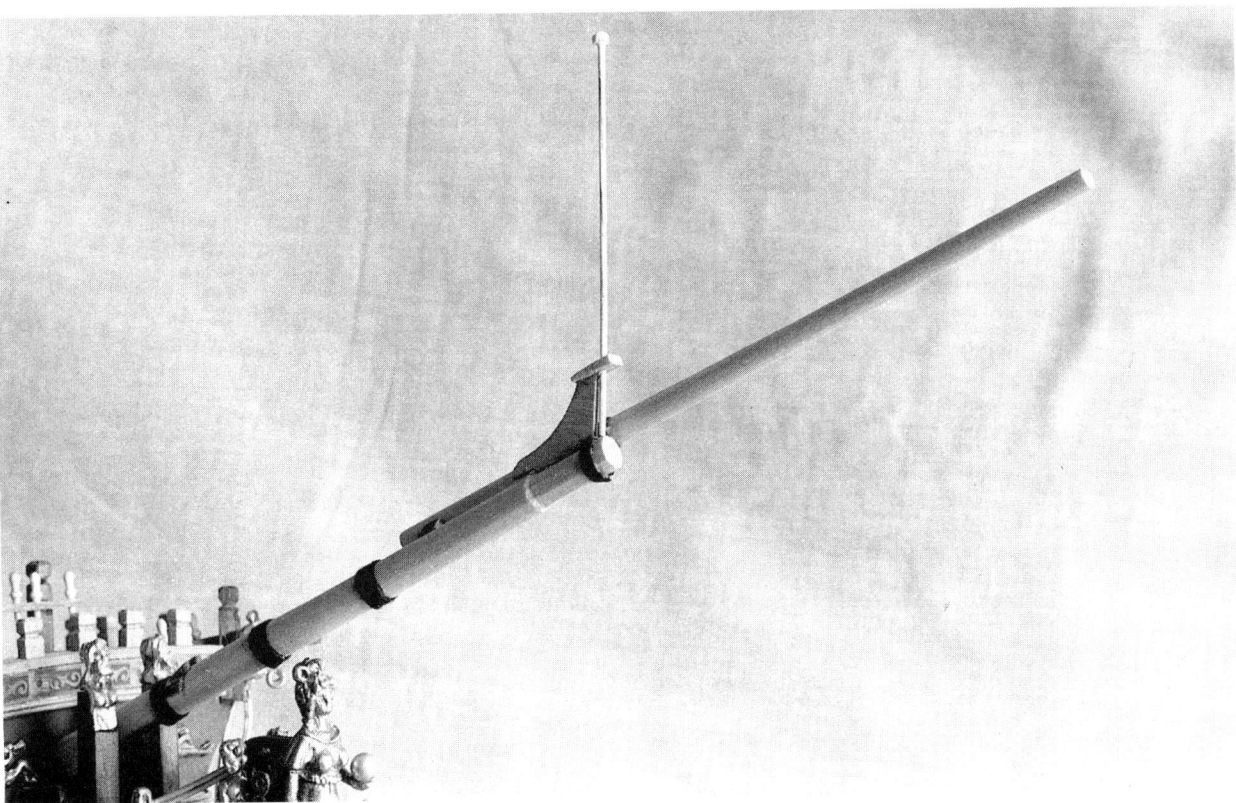

Fig. 3.25 The modified bowsprit.

The instructions for making the bowsprit are minimal and, if you accept the research done by Bellabarba and Osculati that is summarised in the Anatomy of the Ship series, the kit drawings are not accurate. There does not appear to have been a cap on the end of the bowsprit but rather a boom iron for the jib-boom. The end of the bowsprit was octagonal in section on the top face of which was a bracket and cap for a jackstaff (Fig. 3.25).

However, once again there is no problem should you wish to adopt the alternative arrangement, there is adequate material in the kit to do so.

The masts and spars (Det. 5)

Mast Dimensions in mm at 1:47 Scale	
Main Mast (Above deck)	293
Fore Mast (Above deck)	220
Mizzen Mast (Above deck)	207
Main Topsail	217
Fore Topsail	192
Mizzen Topsail	161
Main Topgallant	142
Fore Topgallant	128
Mizzen Topgallant	102

Yard Dimensions in mm at 1:47 Scale	
Main Yard	326
Fore Yard	285
Cross Jack	204
Main Topsail Yard	235
Fore Topsail Yard	205
Mizzen Topsail Yard	153
Main Topgallant Yard	117
Fore Topgallant Yard	102
Mizzen Topgallant Yard	77
Mizzen Yard	271

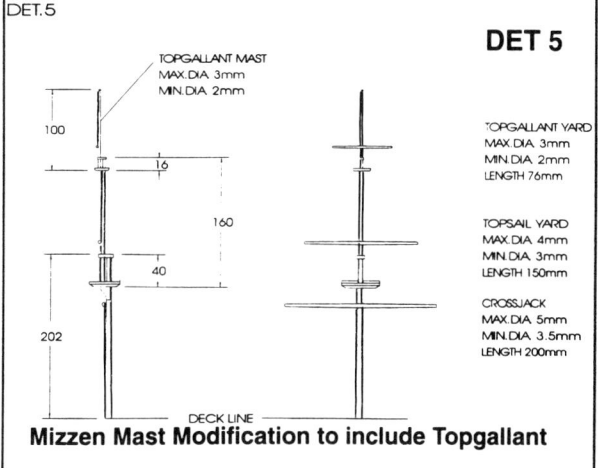

Mizzen Mast Modification to include Topgallant

Please remember that there are no definitive drawings of the masting and rigging of the *Royal Caroline*. The published research on masting was largely based on John Cleverley's painting of the vessel. Cleverley had, in fact, been a shipwright at Deptford and when projected, the proportions of his painting were apparently completely in line with the rules governing masting dimensions for ships of the day. The rigging as shown in the Anatomy book is largely as defined by John Lees in his work *The Masting and Rigging of English Ships of War 1625-1860*.

Bearing all this in mind, it would be unfair to say that the kit is wrong – just different. Again, I decided to follow the book when rigging my model since, not pretending to be an authority on rigging, I have to rely on reference to published works to build up my knowledge. Even so, in some instances there are contradictions between Lees and the Anatomy book and certainly much is left to interpretation.

However, you have to remember that on a model ship, it is not usually practical to put everything in and, like the pictorial artist, the trick is to assess what to leave out. This is all a matter of personal choice of course, and, whatever it is you choose to omit, there will be some clever clogs who once rowed a boat on the Serpentine who will tell you that you've got it wrong! The main aim is to make what you *do put in* reasonably correct.

The most significant change that I made was to add a topgallant mast and yard to the mizzen with the associated additional trestletrees, crosstrees and cap. The majority of the yards were made longer than specified in the kit to bring them basically in line with the 1745 Establishment which, incidently, brought them pretty much the same as the published work on the vessel. The lengths of the masts did not really need to be altered, but should you wish to make the alternative mizzen, I have recorded the dimensions that I used in Detail 5.

The masts

When making the tops, in addition to the holes for the topmast shrouds, remember to drill the holes around the front edge if you choose to rig crowsfeet from the stays (Fig. 3.26). I put 12 on the foremast, 14 on the main and 8 on the mizzenmast. Similarly, on the topmast cross-

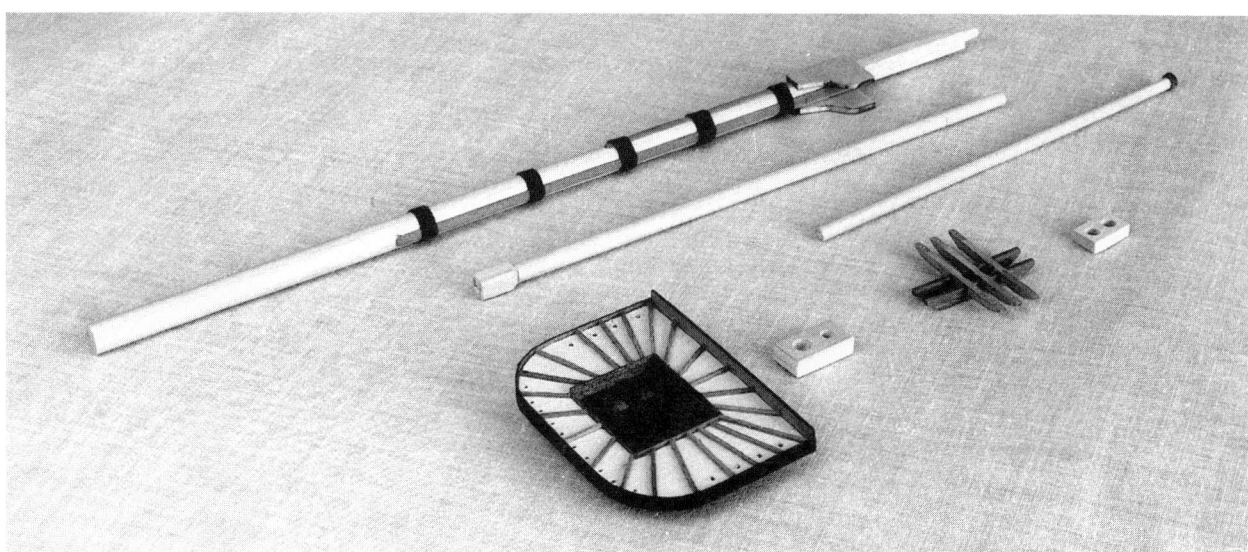

Fig. 3.26 Mast parts. Note holes in the top for the crowsfeet.

trees, holes should be drilled at their ends to take the topgallant shrouds. None of these holes are the easiest to put in once the masts have been assembled. Note that I used four topmast shrouds each side of the fore and mizzenmasts instead of three.

Tapering the masts has to be done by whatever means you find best. I nearly always adopt the quartering and eighthing method with a file, followed by spinning and sanding in an electric drill. It works well enough provided that you take precautions to avoid sand paper snatch, and don't run too fast and burn your fingers.

The caps are made from ply provided in the kit. Drill the holes before cutting them to final size and you should avoid breaking out the outer lamination from the hole to the edge of the cap.

The yards

Whether you work to the kit lengths or adopt the research measurements, all yards should have arm cleats at each end. These are easily made from scrap strip, as are the sling cleats (Fig. 3.27), centrally fixed to the front of the main and fore yards, and the stop cleats (Fig. 3.28), on all other yards except the spritsail yard which has neither. These features are best formed on the yard having secured the correct length of suitable scrap strip with a touch of superglue gel.

Note too, that the ends of the topsail yards should have a hole through them in the vertical plane to take the reef tackle. You won't be rigging this tackle if you are not fitting sails, but the facility should be there nonetheless.

Spinning the yards in an electric drill for sanding gets a bit hairy. The first side is OK because you have a parallel portion of dowel to hold in the chuck, but the second side would have to be held on the tapered first

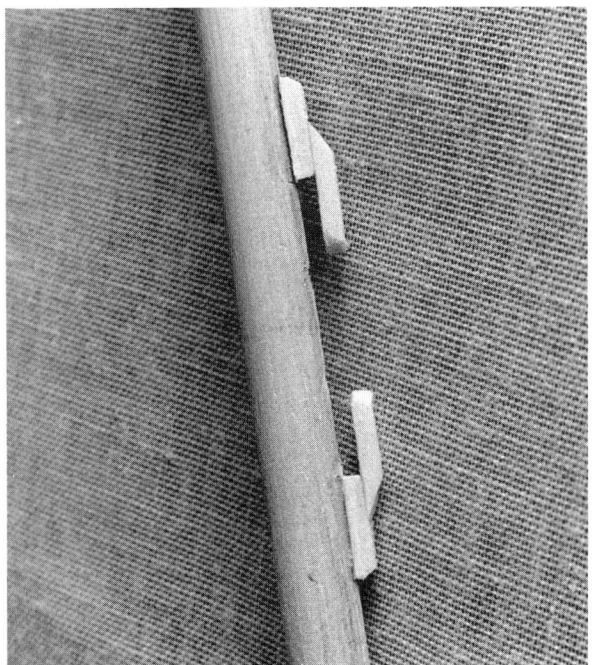

Fig. 3.27 Sling cleats for fore and main yards.

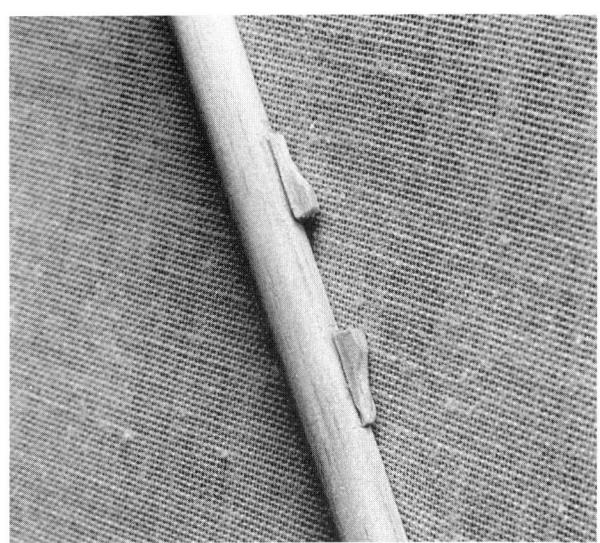

Fig. 3.28 Stop cleats on the topsail and topgallant yards.

side. This, together with the much smaller diameter at the end makes things a mite dangerous, it is back to basics and pure handwork.

The footropes and stirrups should be added next to complete each yard. Thread stiffened with a coating of glue enables you to induce a more natural hang of the footropes between the stirrups. If you consider the use to which the footropes were put, you will appreciate that the end of the stirrup would have to be about 0.75 metres below the yard. At the scale of the model this would be represented by 16mm, somewhat more than is shown on the drawings. Following on from that, it is therefore unlikely that so many stirrups would have been used. In this period, although the footrope was in effect one length, it would almost certainly been lashed to the centre of the yard.

Both, masts and yards should be given a coat of matt varnish before rigging commences.

The standing rigging

The bowsprit. The gammoning is the first rigging to be applied. Each turn should wind from the rear position on the bowsprit to the front of the slot in the stem, giving the appearance of a total twist in the set-up. The whole is then frapped around the middle.

In addition to what is shown on the drawings, a bobstay between the bowsprit and the stem should be rigged (Fig. 3.29). This is pulled up by a lanyard between two deadeyes near the underside of the bowsprit. The two foretack bumkins would also have stays to the stem to counteract the force imposed by the tacks.

Fitting the masts

First of all, I would suggest that you fit the foremast and rig its shrouds and stays before putting up the main mast. Having similarly rigged the main mast the mizzen can then be treated in the same way.

The Royal Yacht *Caroline* 1749

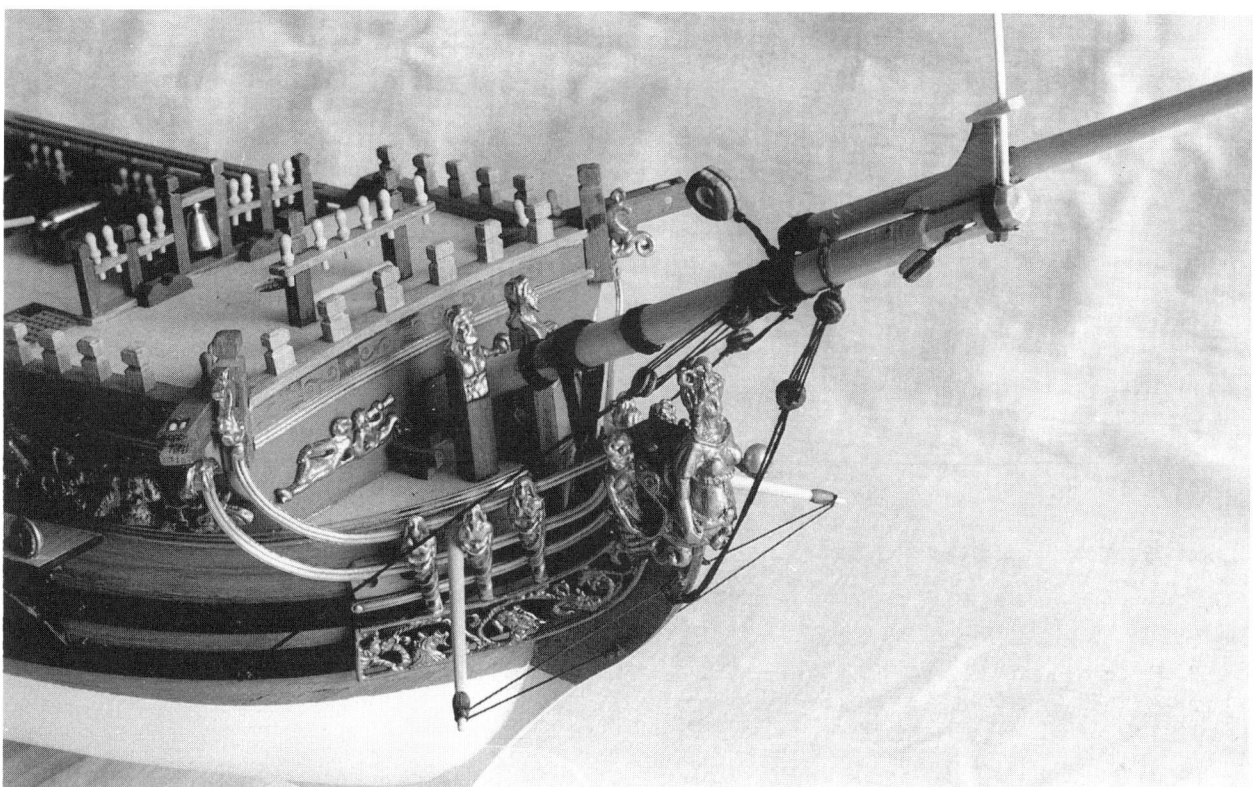

Fig. 3.29 The rigging of the bobstay. Note stays from bumkins to stem.

If you are extremely fortunate, the three masts will all align correctly both from the fore and aft aspect and from the side. More often than not they don't, and corrective measures have to be taken, the simplest method being one akin to that used to secure the full-size masts on ships of the period. First, you need to make a ring with an inside diameter to suit the mast and an outside diameter about 4mm larger. Its top edge should be rounded off. Next, open the upper of the two holes in the deck by about 1mm on diameter. The ring is then slid on to the bottom of the mast and taped up out of the way, then the mast fitted in position. Use pieces of scrap around the mast in the opened out hole in the deck to pack, or wedge, the mast into its correct vertical position looking fore and aft, recognising at the same time any rake that is evident when viewed from the side. The packing pieces should be glued and, when hardened off, trimmed flush with the deck. The ring can now be lowered to cover the tops of the wedges and itself glued in place. This will neatly simulate the tarred canvas apron that was nailed to the mast and roped around the wedges to keep the wet out.

The shrouds

The first forward starboard pair are lashed around the mast above the top followed by the forward port pair, working aft and alternating starboard to port. The deadeyes at the lower ends should be correctly orientated and positioned such, that when pulled up taut with the lanyards, have a space between them and those on the channels of two deadeye diameters. A simple spacing bar with a pair of pins top and bottom for locating in the deadeyes is a useful tool for getting the spacing alike on all shrouds. I make mine with a spacing of two and a half diameters, allowing a half diameter for pulling up the lanyards (Fig. 3.30).

Fig. 3.30 Rigging the shrouds and ratlines. Pin racks are lashed to shrouds just above deck level.

The ratlines

A piece of card wedged between the deck and the underside of the top and behind the shrouds helps get the spacing constant and certainly keeps the eyes better focused. This repetitive task is best done as soon as the shrouds have been set up, and before any further rigging confuses the eye and foils the fingers.

Once the ratlines have been put on, you have the choice of either adding a pin rack just above deck level for belaying running rigging, or using the tag and ring method suggested in the kit.

The forestay

The lower end of the stay should be rigged with two hearts, the bottom one collared around the bowsprit.

The mainstay

Almost certainly the mainstay would not have been a double arrangement as portrayed on the kit drawings, but rigged with two hearts, the lower of which was collared through a hole in the beak just below the bowsprit. According to Lees, the mainstay always passed the foremast on the starboard side and with the lower heart just aft of the forecastle rail (Fig. 3.31).

The mizzen stay

This is rigged to the main mast using a pair of deadeyes, the lower of which is collared around the mast just above the lowest wolding. The upper end of the stay goes to the mizzen top and tension is attained via a lanyard between the two deadeyes at the lower end.

Backstays

These are rigged in a similar fashion to the shrouds using deadeyes and lanyards, but set up on stools aft of the fore and main channels (Fig. 3.32). However, in the case of the main and mizzenmasts, topmast backstays are set up on the same channels as the shrouds. The mizzen topgallant backstay is rigged to a point on the hull just forward of the quarter gallery.

Pin racks

Because of the 'midships Royal Cabin and other design features of the vessel, there are virtually no conventional belaying points available for the running rigging. To overcome this, pin racks were mounted on the insides of the lower shrouds. These provided a belaying point between each shroud and were present on fore, main and mizzenmast shrouds (Fig. 3.33).

Fig. 3.31 The forestay and mainstay.

The Royal Yacht *Caroline* 1749

Fig. 3.32 'Midships view showing foremast backstay set up on stool.

Fig. 3.33 The after deck. Note pin racks lashed to shrouds.

Euphroe blocks and crowsfeet

These are features not illustrated on the plans but almost certainly fitted on the original. The crowsfeet were rigged between the front edge of the top (Fig. 3.34), to a point forward on the stay below via a euphroe block. The purpose of this arrangement was to avoid chafing the roach, or lower edge of the sail above on the front edge of the top. The euphroe block has to be made from 3 × 3mm spare strip and should be drilled with half the number of holes that were previously put around the front edge of the top. A continuous length of thread should be knotted and trimmed at one end and the free end fed up through the first hole to port of centreline in the top. The free end then passes to the euphroe block, through the first (upper) hole in the block and back to the top, now being taken over the front edge and down through the first hole to starboard of centre. The end is then taken up through the second hole to starboard, back to the second hole in the euphroe, returning to the top on the port side. This procedure is continued until the free end passes down through the last vacant hole in the top. The crowsfeet should then be tensioned up, carefully trying not to distort the line of the stay too much. When satisfied with the tension the free end of the thread should be knotted up tight to the underside of the top and trimmed off.

Rigging the yards

I couldn't find anything whatsoever on the drawings that shows how the yards are fixed to their respective masts. Reference again to the Anatomy series book indicated that parrals were used on the fore and main lower yards, the topsail yards and the mizzen yard. The crossjack and spritsail yard were fitted with a truss and, so I suspect, were the topgallant yards. The parrals on the lower yards are shown to be triple row with the remainder being double row. I used a series of threaded small black beads to simulate the requirement and the result was quite effective.

It is helpful to put any blocks in place on the yards before offering them up to the masts and careful reference to the drawings will indicate where they should all be seized. Whether you put all the yards up at one go, just on one mast, or only one at a time before commencing the running rigging is largely a matter of personal choice. The latter procedure is probably the one that keeps maximum access for fingers and tweezers and provides a better chance of keeping the rigging shipshape.

There are no rigging drawings available for naval vessels of the period, riggers were expected to be able to correctly rig a craft by expert knowhow. As I have mentioned earlier, the *Caroline*, with the 'midships cabin, was somewhat different to the norm in that it had a dearth of conventional belaying points. I feel that the rigging as shown on the kit drawings is a little suspect with regard to belaying to the tags on the deck. Having made up the shroud pin racks I used these instead, the actual rigging configuration being basically as drawn.

Rigging the boat

The main difficulty here is to get the correct balance in the rigging system so that the tackle, centrally above the boat, is vertical. The slings to the boat itself, fore and aft, should also adopt a balanced attitude when the central tackle is pulled up. To attain these conditions, the length of the line from the mainmast top has to be just right, and the tackle from the foremast pulled up to suit. Thus all belaying has to be simply tied off at first, so that any necessary adjustments can be made.

Rigging the anchors

Each anchor is shown lashed to the forecastle timberheads with shank painters in two places, with the inner flukes resting on the fore channel (Fig. 3.35). The anchor cable, having been drawn through the hawse hole, then passes through the cut-out at the aft end of the main deck grating to the hold below. This cable was usually too thick to pass round the capstan and was nipped to a more flexible messenger to facilitate stowage.

Finishing off

At each belaying point there should be a coil of rope of the same size used for that particular part of the rigging. Thread soaked in glue and wound round a piece of suitable size dowel will usually provide an adequately shaped coil that will have the right hang to it.

The ensign provided in the kit is of the correct design but, unless you are clever enough to get a realistic shape to it, flying it on the ensign staff at the stern rather spoils the finished model.

All that is left to do now is to locate and remove any

Fig. 3.34 The foremast top and crowsfeet.

Fig. 3.35 Bows view showing anchor rigging.

odd ends of trimmed rigging, dust, shavings and any other undesirable muck that may be lurking among the deck fittings and gun carriages.

Conclusions

I am not surprised to learn that this kit has an excellent sales record. It makes into a very impressive model and, due in no small way to the many perspective drawings, the kit simplifies what would otherwise be a very daunting subject, even for the more experienced.

I am not so sure about the accuracy of the rigging. While it is true that there are no rigging drawings available for research, there are one or two points about the rigging layout depicted in the kit about which I am a little suspicious. The hull details, though, are very good. All historical sources are open to interpretation of course, but I don't think that anyone, apart from the dedicated nitpicker, will be too critical of what Panart has done with the hull. The ornamentation provided is extremely good, but remember that such fittings only complement a well-made model, not convert a hulk into a desirable result.

As I pointed out earlier, as far as the kit contents allowed, I chose to make the model as close as possible to Conway's Anatomy of the Ship publication *The Royal Yacht Caroline*.

This kit is an absolute gem and provides a wealth of exciting and challenging modelmaking.

CHAPTER 4

The French Frigate
La Renommée 1793

Remarkably, there were two frigates named *La Renommée* built in France, both of which were subsequently captured by the English. The earlier, built in Brest in 1744, was captured in 1747 and the later vessel built in 1793, succumbed to the Royal Navy in 1796. In spite of the fact that Euromodel, in its brief historical notes, refer to the date of capture as 1747, I am fairly certain that the drawings depict the 30-gun frigate *La Renommée* built in 1793 and certainly not the 30-gun vessel of 1744. There are several features of the design which strongly support this, significantly the dolphin striker and the principle of mast construction, neither of which were introduced until after the earlier *Renommée* had been broken up in 1771. Unfortunately, I have not been able to find out very much about it apart from the fact that it served as a troop ship from 1800 and finally went to the breakers yard in 1810. Such research as I have so far carried out has not revealed where it started, or ended, its career.

However, we are told that much of the design as kitted has been considerably based on Chapman's *Architectura Navalis Mercatoria*, so we probably have a design typical of the period but based on *Renommée*.

However, it is a very good-looking vessel and the kit builds into an attractive model 830mm long with a height of 690mm.

The Kit

I intended at first to say that this kit was for the experienced modelmaker only but, the more I think about it, the more accurate statement is that it is not for the *absolute beginner*. There is certainly a lot to do if the eighteen sheets of drawings are anything to go by, but that is about quantity rather than degree of skill required. The biggest problem for the inexperienced is undoubtedly the poor instructions and, specifically, no guidance as to the sequence in which things have to be done. In fact the instructions provided, albeit very brief, are misleading and are probably better discarded altogether. To illustrate my point; if, as advised, both decks are fitted prior to planking, there is no way that the guns can be mounted on the lower deck at a later stage. So, a long study of the drawings and the making of copious notes are the order of the day to eliminate such problems of access. This will also do much to sort out some of the minor discrepancies on the otherwise well draughted drawings. Take care too, when referring to the model shown on the box art, it varies in several details from that shown on the drawings.

The materials supplied were of excellent quality although, apart from the obvious planking strips and pre-cut frames, it was quite a task to fathom out for what features other timber was intended.

Castings for the prow and stern decoration were crisp and clean. Other fittings, anchors, gun carriages etc., appeared to come from standard proprietary lists and, as such, some needed quite serious modification to meet the dimensions quoted on the drawings, but more of that later.

Masts come ready tapered but needed quite a bit of work done on them to get everything as it should be on a model of this size and scale.

Strip material was separately boxed and all other bits and pieces were bagged up in clear plastic envelopes. Certainly a very well presented kit and one that comes with pre-cut parts to make a stand for the finished model.

Starting the hull construction

Like many models of this size built from kits, the basic framework comprises a series of frames slotted into a false keel. The edges of the lower deck are also slotted to locate within the frames and it makes sense to use the deck as an assembly jig. It has to be cut longitudinally down the centre in order to fit it in place (Fig. 4.1). Fortunately, the fit of the joints between frames and keel was rather sloppy and a degree of packing was needed, but this did allow the frames to be aligned squarely and to match the slots in the edges of the deck. The depth of joints in the false keel was adjusted so as to ensure that the top of the keel was coincident with the upper edges of the frames that support the lower deck. The frames and the packing were glued in place with the deck

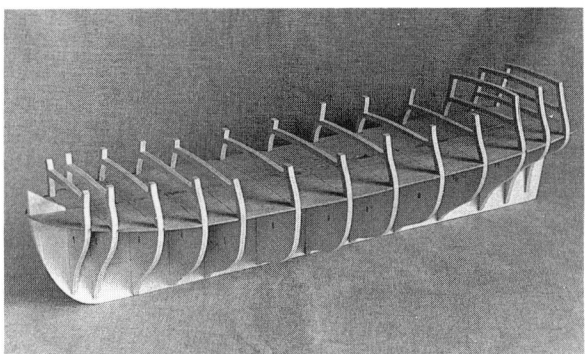

Fig. 4.1 The basic frame assembly. Note lower deck split on centreline.

temporarily pinned in position.

The blocks at bow and stern were then offered up and, using the adjacent frames and keel as guides, marked out for rough shaping (Fig. 4.2). Care was needed on the bow blocks – they had to be overlapped diagonally to get them out of the piece of timber provided. As much of the rough shaping as possible was done before gluing them in place. They were then left for twenty-four hours so that the adhesive could thoroughly harden off.

The deck pieces were then removed, their outer shape checked for accuracy of profile and the mast hole positions confirmed. Remember too, that depending upon what interior detail you wish to include in your model, holes for hatches, companionways, etc. should be cut before final assembly of the two parts of the lower deck.

Having fitted the deck, the inside of the hull above the deck was planked prior to shaping the outside edges of the frames preparatory for the outer planking (again see Fig. 4.2). The bow and stern blocks were then blended with the frames using a planking strip to ensure a smooth run throughout. The first outer skinning was started at the main gun deck level, then worked down towards the keel. Starting at that point helped later on when it came to cutting the gunports. There was a fair amount of tapering to do in order that the planks ran as near as possible to the natural curves of the hull, and some stealers were needed under the stern adjacent to the rudder post position. Make sure that all plank edges are well glued, sprung planks are very difficult to sand smooth to match their neighbours.

At the top, the outer planking was not carried higher than the upper edge of the inner planking. This was to make it more convenient to mark and cut the positions for the gunports. To do this it was necessary to make up one of the larger gun carriage assemblies so that the deck to barrel height could be checked. It was at this point that I found that the carriages provided were far too large to meet the drawing dimensions. At this stage I merely reduced the height and recut the slots for the barrel pivots but, ultimately of course, the width also has to be reduced on all thirty assemblies. Note that the carriage wheels are of two different sizes with the larger at the front. This is most important as the different diameters cater for the deck camber – get it wrong and the level of the barrel as it passes through the sides of the ship will be incorrect.

Having done the planking up to the height previously mentioned, the gunport apertures were then cut. Marking the fourteen positions stem to stern was merely a matter of scaling sizes from the plans. In the other plane, the basic gun carriage assembly was used to establish the height of the barrel from the deck and then cut the first of the gunports. This entailed cutting down the sides with a razor saw, using a scalpel to remove the piece between, gradually lowering the line of the bottom sill until it was in its required position relative to the centre of the gun barrel. The size of the finished ports is 10mm square, thus the width between the saw cuts had to be 14mm to allow for the 2mm thick framing. Obviously, the 14mm would have to be reduced should you decide to use thinner framing material. Having planked only up to the height of the inner bulwark lining meant that the ports could be cut as a U shape rather than a 14mm square hole much easier to control size and squareness (see Fig. 4.3).

I found that it was wise to cut alternate ports and frame them before cutting the intermediate apertures. The framing strengthened the cavity wall structure and avoided the danger of breaking the planking.

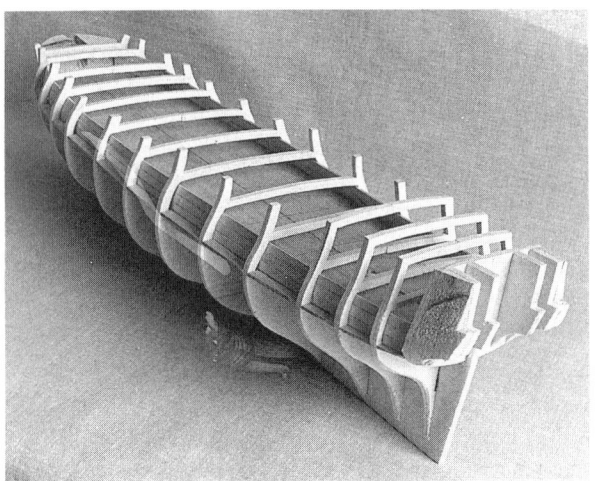

Fig. 4.2 The first of the stern blocks in place. The inside of the hull should also be planked at this stage.

Fig. 4.3 Cutting and lining the gunports.

The gunport sides were lined first, followed by the lower sill (again refer to Fig. 4.3). A 10mm square wooden plug gauge, made specifically for the purpose, permitted the top lining to be fitted accurately. When all the glue was thoroughly dry, the edges of the lining left protruding beyond the surface of the outer hull planking was sanded off flush. Before proceeding further, the gun deck had to be fitted out while everything was still accessible.

Fitting out the gun deck

A fair number of hatches had to be made, most of which were fitted with gratings. The comb jointed pieces provided in the kit were excellent in terms of size, thickness and colour. So often you get pieces produced on different machines that need a lot of sorting and matching – no problems like that here. Real gratings were made up of ledges running across the line of the deck into which were laid battens running fore and aft. So, make sure that your gratings are housed in the hatch coamings the right way round. It might not notice if you get them all wrong, but some right and some wrong really stand out.

With the wealth of detail provided by the drawings, I was surprised to find no information on the ship's stove. There was one sectional detail of the galley on the side elevation of the hull and an indication that there were twin chimneys protruding through the forecastle deck on the plan view, but nothing more. I certainly have no details of a twin stack unit in my library and I supposed that the French, like the English, had stoves with a separate furnace for the officers' food, but took the design a stage further by having one stack for officers and one for other ranks only! With further thought however, I concluded that there was a little draughtsman's licence on the drawing and, in fact, both ovens exhausted into the same stack through the forecastle deck. Certainly, the box art seemed to bear this out. However, it would be remiss of the modelmaker to leave out such an essential feature, even though not too much of it can be seen. Study of the drawings indicated that there was possibly a food preparation area immediately aft of the stove and directly below the belfry, with a window giving a view down the main gun deck towards the stern.

Nine of the gun carriages each side were positioned and fixed in place. These were the ones that could not be got at once the main deck was in place. However, before you fit them, you have to make them. (Fig. 4.4 shows arrangement of deck details.)

The guns and carriages

The larger of the two sizes of carriage provided in the kit needed severe modification to bring them down to the sizes shown on the drawings. They were too high, the wrong shape in the plan view and too long. At least being oversize in all directions allowed me to do something to correct the situation, albeit that there were thirty of them to modify. There was a logical sequence to tackle the problem which provided symmetry in the final result.

First, the height was corrected. This needed to be reduced by 2.5mm by removing the top of each of the sides. In so doing, the locations for the barrel pivots were removed and those, of course, had to be re-cut later on. The height reduction was carried out on all thirty pieces before I proceeded to the next part of the exercise, which was to correct the plan view shape.

The carriages, as supplied, were too wide at 15mm

Fig. 4.4 The gun deck fitted out with hatches, gratings and the soon-to-be inaccessible gun carriages. Note too the galley at the aft end of the forecastle deck line.

and had parallel sides when looking down on top. The modification involved splitting through the floor of the carriage to make left- and right-hand parts. The split edges were trimmed up to reduce the width and to provide a taper such that the width became 11.5mm at the rear and 10mm at the front end. Each half was kept as identical as possible so that the later tidying up of the axle slots on the underside was kept to a minimum. The pieces were glued together and put to one side while the next twenty-nine were dealt with. I found it better to split them one at a time so that if they didn't split straight there was still the right amount of material to play with to achieve the final result. This sequence of steps is shown in Fig. 4.5. I noticed that due to the nature of this modification, the front and rear ends of the carriages were not flat or square to the centreline. In correcting this, the overall length was obviously reduced, nicely taking care of the third original fault.

The axle slots were then trued up and the grooves for the barrel pivots reintroduced into the top edges. Axles were lightly sanded at each end to make sure that the wheels or trucks were not too tight a fit. If they were to be forced on or the hole eased out with a drill, there was an excellent chance that they would break. Be sure to leave some of the axle protruding through the trucks; remember that the trucks were retained on the axles by a cotter pin and, while at this scale you may find the fitting of the pins a little impractical, it would be wrong to cut the axle off too short.

It then only remained to fit the wedge or quoin used for elevating the barrel. Apart from being an essential detail within the total assembly, this small part provides a very convenient support when fixing the barrel (Fig. 4.6).

Eyebolts in the sides and rear end of the assembly prepare the unit for ultimately rigging the gun in place. Because of the access difficulties in the hull construction, the carriages were fixed in position before completing the upper planking. The barrels, with their assembled pivots, were later to be fed through the gunports from the outside and dropped on to the carriages. Thus, if the pivots are fitted at this stage, it is wise to check that their overall length does not exceed the diagonal dimension of the finished lined gunports. The two different sizes of gun are shown assembled in Fig. 4.7.

Fig. 4.6 The carriage assembly showing quoin and barrel in place.

Fig. 4.7 The two sizes of assembled gun carriage ready for rigging in place on deck.

Finishing the first planking

The planking operation was continued upwards to the next deck level as previously described, introducing the smaller gunports and lining them (Fig. 4.8). Finally, the planking was extended to the quarter deck which, of course, could not be put in place until the cabins under the deck had been built up along with hatches and companion ways (Fig. 4.9). You really do have to study the plans in order to ensure that things get done at the right time; failure to do this could well result in much inconvenience later, or worse, the total inability to satisfactorily fit of finish a particular feature.

The wales and second planking

Having carefully marked the position of the main and upper wales, the stem and keel were fitted.

The second, outer layer of planking was then applied, carefully trimming around the gunports to leave a rebate for the lids. I chose to plank the area between the main wale and the upper wale with a lighter shade of timber in order to show off the lines of the vessel to better advantage. The planking procedures were basically the same as for the first planking except that, this time, care had to be taken to attain a snug fit where the forward ends of the planks come to the side faces of the stem. I think you will find, as I did, that it was easier to fit the stern post after the second planking had been completed,

Fig. 4.5 Modifying height and plan view shape of the gun carriages supplied in the kit.

The French Frigate *La Renommée* 1793

Fig. 4.8 The first planking complete up to the line of the quarter deck.

Fig. 4.9 The cabins below the quarter deck in place together with the ship's wheel. The inner lining and smaller gunports framing has also been completed.

when it could be better matched to the thickness of the planks. The keel had been left overlength for final trimming after stern post assembly. The quarter deck was then fitted in place.

With the last of the planking in place, the wales and anchor lining were given an initial coat of paint and the figurehead fixed in position (Fig. 4.10). It seemed to me that this would present a good guide for the forthcoming positioning of head-rails, etc. At the rear end, I now started to fit the foundations for the stern galleries. The inner fascia needed, of course, to be painted before fitting and the gallery deck also had to be planked at this stage (Fig. 4.11). I considered it worth getting all of the diecastings associated with this area gathered together

39

The Period Ship Handbook 2

Fig. 4.10 The second planking, wales and anchor lining fixed and the figurehead in place.

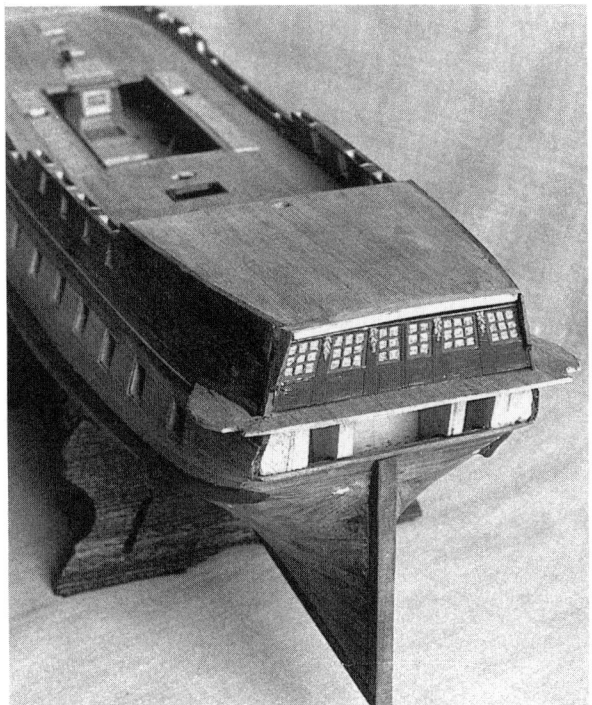

Fig. 4.11 The inner facing and deck of the stern gallery in position.

for use as positional gauges as each additional feature was assembled. The castings were not the same size as the details shown on the drawing and it would have been most awkward to have finished up with the odd half millimetre gap that had to be filled in.

The stern galleries and ornamentation

The basic painting of the castings had to be done before assembly. It all looked rather rough and ready, but the less you have to handle the model in the finishing stages, the better. Besides, too much paint around bare wood is a bit of a risk and a hell of a job to remove if the brush slips! The rear gallery rails were probably the most awkward to fit because the ends had to be shaped to fit between the insides of the large oval shroud casting — all time consuming and fiddly, rather than difficult. Figs. 4.12 to 4.14 show the sequence of assembly.

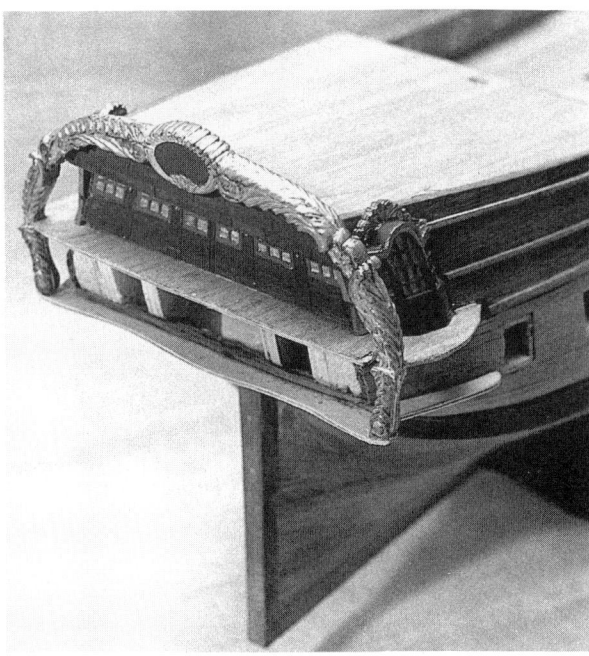

Fig. 4.12 More of the stern construction.

Fig. 4.13 The quarter galleries.

The French Frigate *La Renommée* 1793

Fig. 4.14 The completion of assembly of the stern ornamentation.

Fig. 4.15 The bulwark rails or capping in place together with the upper and lower cheeks.

Fig. 4.16 The headrail assembly. Note the fore starboard channel in place.

The bulwark rails

The top edges of the inner and outer planking were trimmed flat and to the correct contour before fitting the rails. The flat section of the material specified to be used for these rails made bending a difficult and, in my opinion, an unnecessary task. I found it better to laminate two or three strips together to attain the width required to encompass the total curve required. There wasn't a great deal of curve needed but it could not be ignored. The strip was held roughly in position and a pencil run round the top edge of the hull to transfer the actual curve to the underside of the strip. The short vertical rises between the different levels were capped first. Particular attention was given to attain good mitres at the ends of the forecastle rail (Fig. 4.15).

The headrails

These comprised an assembly of several diecast pieces which first had to be identified as either left-handed or right-handed parts. Having done a bit of judicious filing to remove residual flash and attained some reasonably fitting joints, the timbers and rails were put together using a two-part epoxy adhesive. Fortunately the castings were fairly crisp and clean so that the clean up task was not too arduous. A good close-fitting mechanical joint is always to be recommended, even if the adhesive being used does have adequate filling properties.

While the two sub-assemblies were setting, holes were cut through the prow to take the gammoning, also the hole for the bowsprit. The catheads were made, cutting the triple sheave and making the external sheave assembly on the aft face, then fixed in position.

The aforementioned headrails assemblies were then put in place, using the upper cheek, the rear of the figurehead and cathead as datum points for attaining the desired position. Finally, the cathead supports were adjusted for shape and position between the underside of the cathead and the middle headrail. Again, it was helpful to give everything an initial coat of paint while things were still reasonably accessible (Fig. 4.16).

The channels

The channels are detailed and dimensioned on the drawings but, a word of warning. When you have cut the outline shape and correctly matched the rear edge to the curve of the hull, make sure that the actual positions

41

of the gunports are in their correct relationship to the theoretical position of the hole centres of the lower deadeyes and chainplates. Do this *before* drilling the holes!

When considering these positions, do not forget that the chainplates sweep aft to match the line of the shrouds. It must also be remembered that the gunport lids need free space in which to open, and thus should not be impeded by the line of a chainplate.

At this stage, the inner faces of all the gunports were painted red.

The installation of the guns

I again checked that the length of the gun barrel pivots on those guns that had to be assembled from the outside of the hull were not too long to pass through the diagonal opening of the ports. A small blob of epoxy adhesive was applied to the underside of the pivots and the breech end of the barrel inserted through the gunport until the pivots reached the face of the carriage. The barrel was then twisted until the pivots were horizontal, lifted up until clear of the top of the carriage, then pushed back to locate the pivots into their respective grooves. A length of scrap strip material was used to push the top of the barrel down to ensure that everything was firmly in place.

I found that a few dry runs, without adhesive, was advisable so that when it was done for real, adhesive wasn't left in the wrong places. Not that it could be seen, but some had to be left on the pivots to properly fix them!

A similar dry run was done for the other guns on the main deck. These required just a touch of adhesive on the trucks but, again, it doesn't want to be smeared all over the deck. I found that a length of dowel rod, tapered to plug into the end of the barrel, could be passed through the gunport from the outside of the hull and the gun assembly gently pushed on to the end of the rod. Adhesive was carefully applied and the rod withdrawn, thereby guiding and controlling the attitude of the assembly until it was in its correct place. Obviously, those guns on the upper deck were easier to install and needed no special techniques (Fig. 4.17).

The gunport lids

These were made 14mm square to match the size of the gunport recess, with a 10mm backing piece to fit into the port opening proper. A pair of hinges was then fitted on the outer face.

The lids and backing pieces were made up of two or three strips stuck together edge to edge to attain the 14mm width, and when dried, cut off to make the 14mm squares required. A similar procedure was required for the 10mm square backing pieces. The two pieces were then stuck together and painted red on their inner faces. A hole was drilled centrally adjacent to the lower edge to take the port tackle.

The hinges were painted before assembly, then using superglue gel, stuck to the face of the lid such that the spigots protruded beyond the rear edge.

Two holes were drilled in the side of the hull for each lid just above the gunport to take the projecting spigots. Again, superglue gel was used to fix the lids in place and when thoroughly set, the port tackle was installed (Fig. 4.18).

Fig. 4.18 The gunport lids.

Fig. 4.17 The guns on the upper deck. Note also the kevels.

The French Frigate *La Renommée* 1793

Fittings

Prior to making up the many bits and pieces required for fitting out, the stand was made up. The materials provided for this item were excellent and it really was worth spending a little time to get a nice finish on the stand, irrespective of the process chosen, polish or varnish. The nameplate added that final professional touch and you now have a sound cradle in which the model can safely sit (Fig. 4.19). Incidentally, strips of felt stuck along the actual seating edges and the bottom edges prevented marking the finished hull and the top of the unit in which the model may be displayed. The completed model will be no light weight!

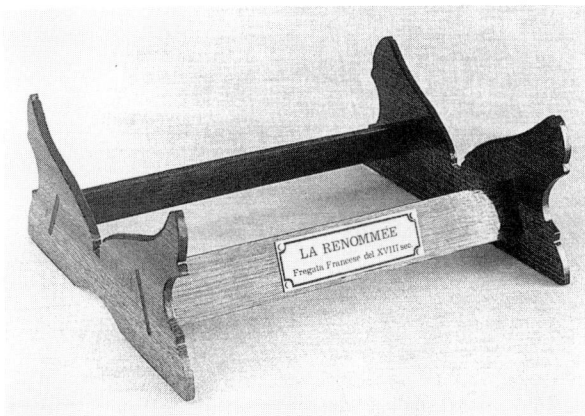

Fig. 4.19 The finished stand.

The pin rails and bitts were all well detailed on the drawings and, apart from suggesting that you should check that the diameter of the holes in the rails are suitable for the size of the belaying pins provided, there is not really much more I can say (Fig. 4.20). Should you decide that the bitts will be deck mounted rather than extend down into the bowels of the vessel as they really should, then do provide a dowel joint into the deck to ensure maximum strength.

Insufficient detail was provided, surprisingly enough, of the rails across the front end of the after deck. They would appear to be integral with the pin rails at the foot of the main mast (Fig. 4.21), but you need to do a bit of extra study further to the drawings provided.

I have already mentioned the problems encountered with the gun carriage assemblies being oversize. Unfortunately, a similar situation existed with the anchors and larger capstan. The castings for the anchor parts were not too bad but the wooden stocks for the larger of the anchors needed a lot of reshaping and those for the smaller units, I replaced altogether. The hoops around the stocks should be simulated strips of card or 0.5 deck planking and painted black or dark grey. Don't forget to fettle off any flash lines from the fluke/shank casting before assembly and make sure that the hole for the anchor ring is clear (Fig. 4.22). Once all parts were put together and the ring was in place, the serving or puddening of the ring was carried out using tan thread 0.5mm diameter.

Fig. 4.20 Foremast bitts and pin rails.

Fig. 4.21 The main mast deck area.

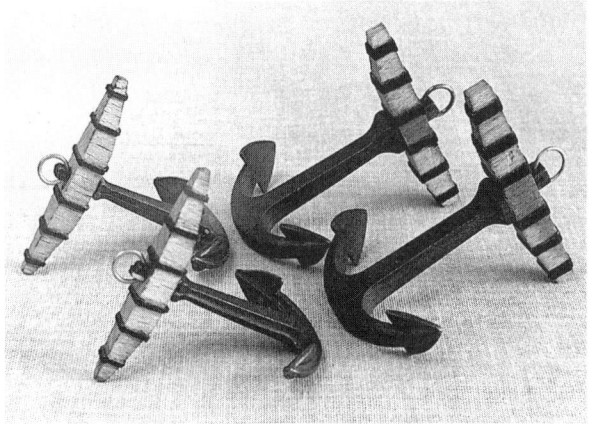

Fig. 4.22 The anchors before puddening the rings.

Fig. 4.23 The modified capstan.

The larger of the two capstans was far too high and had to be reduced drastically. I found the best way was to cut a piece out from the centre spindle, then fit modified whelps to the lower portion. These then provided a nice location for the remaining part of the spindle under the head (Fig. 4.23).

Pre-shaped wooden hull shells were supplied for the two ship's boats. These were ridged to supposedly simulate clinker planking but looked totally wrong. Since boats of either clinker or carvel construction were common, I did not consider it amiss to carve the ridges off. The line of the gunwales were modified to give the graceful curve shown on the drawings and scrap strip used to fit floor slats and thwarts. The large boat (Fig. 4.24) had davits over the stern and the smaller craft had a yoke instead of a tiller at the top of the rudder (Fig. 4.25).

There were a number of kevels to fit at various places around the deck. These were blackened diecast parts and the colouring was filed off before using superglue to fix them in place.

The cleats' positions on deck around the masts (again see Fig. 4.20), needed to be carefully marked out, bearing in mind that there were also a fair number of rings and blocks to be fitted in the same area. It was not

The French Frigate *La Renommée* 1793

Fig. 4.24 The large boat with davits over the stern.

Fig. 4.25 The small boat with tiller yoke.

essential to fit the blocks at this time, but it certainly was advisable to put the rings in place, since it would be much more difficult to get a drill in position once the masts have been stepped. This comment also applies to those rings and blocks across the front end of the forecastle. Again it would be extremely difficult to do once the bowsprit had been put in place.

Finishing and painting

Before proceeding to make up the masts and spars, the hull assembly was finished off. Many of the diecastings were basically painted before assembly of course, but now was the time to get down to detail. Much of the relief work on the ornamentation showed up better by painting in the crevices with a darker gold, followed by what can almost be described as a dry-brush technique with a lighter gold on the raised highlights.

However, don't forget to get rid of all the dust and odd bits of swarf from all those awkward places before opening the paint pots. A saliva dampened paint brush is ideal for picking up most of the less accessible bits.

I chose to coat the decks again with a matt acrylic varnish. This dried quicker than a polyurethane medium and thus did not attract anywhere near so much dust. It was also nice to be able to clean the brushes with water.

The hull below the waterline was coated with white stuff. Now, just how white this was depended largely on the mixture of the month, so to speak. Rosin, oil and brimstone was a fairly common basis but turpentine was sometimes used instead of rosin. Sulphur was reckoned to be a useful additive if the vessel was to be sailed in waters where certain types of marine life were likely to eat their way into the bottom of the hull. All these variations of mix could make subtle changes to the shade of white. Bearing all this in mind and, taking into account the overall appearance of the model itself, I chose to use Barley White vinyl matt emulsion. An inexpensive colour matcher pot from your local DIY store is more than adequate, both in quantity and texture and gives the model a definite sulphurous look.

I painted the main wales, anchor lining, and the ungilded parts of the headrails a very dark brown. Black was probably the more accurate colour but looked far too severe on the model. I have heard something of scale colour for other types of model and I don't doubt there are experts who will put me right, but in this case I reckon that the very dark brown equals scale black!

The inner surfaces of the gunports were just touched in where necessary with matt red paint prior to coating the remaining surfaces of the hull, including the deck fittings, with an acrylic satin varnish. Completion of this interim stage is shown in Fig. 4.26.

Fig. 4.26 The complete basic hull assembly.

The bowsprit

This assembly comprised five main parts; the bowsprit, the jib-boom, the cap, the dolphin striker and flagstaff. Most major works on the subject indicate that dolphin strikers were not introduced until after 1780 and this really was my first clue that the model is of the later *Renommée* rather than the one captured in 1747.

I made the cap first. Of the several cap blanks provided in the kit, not one was suitable. Two holes, one round and one square, had to be introduced through the cap at an angle of 29 degrees, their centres separated by 7mm. When one of the holes has been filed to a square, the end of the bowsprit was fashioned to provide a square spigot to fit and the cap glued in place.

The bees were added each side of the bowsprit immediately abaft the cap, followed by the jib-boom saddle, and the gammoning cleats. You will need to dry assemble the bowsprit to the hull to make sure that you get the cleats in exactly the right position above the holes previously put through the stem to take the gammoning.

The jib-boom was fashioned from plain dowel leaving a stop at its forward end. Immediately behind this, the boom was drilled and slotted through vertically to represent a sheave. A brass pin horizontally across the centre of the slot permits the later rigging to at least look as if it passed around a pulley.

The dolphin striker and flagstaff fitted to the forward and aft side of the cap respectively, noting that while the striker was set centrally below the jib-boom, the flagstaff was offset to starboard.

Various eyebolts were added to complete the assembly and the whole put to one side for later fitting to the hull. Once assembled, it becomes a very prominent feature and a most likely candidate for damage.

The masts

This section describes the construction and assembly of the various items that go to make up the foremast (Fig. 4.27), although the same general description applies to the main and mizzenmasts, albeit that there may not be quite so many bits and pieces in the latter.

The lower mast had cheeks either side and a front fish, all bound together with iron hoops. The length of the cheeks and the fitting of the hoops are, like the dolphin striker, an indication that we really are building a model of the 1793 *Renommée*. Strangely, the box art shows the mast design with rope woldings which would have been correct for the earlier vessel. Nonetheless, I chose to stick with the kit and build as depicted in the drawings.

The mast proper came ready tapered and it was not too difficult to add the cheeks and front fish, but the hoops were another matter. A black page from an old photograph album solved the problem. I cut 1mm wide strips and, using Unibond adhesive, stuck them round the assembly at the appropriate intervals, using a small watchmakers' screwdriver to push the strip tightly into the corners (Fig. 4.28). The hounds were then added ready to take the crosstrees, trestletrees and top.

The tops were well detailed on the drawings, showing the arrangement of the planking and the battens (Fig. 4.29). However, you should look a little further ahead and consult other sheets to establish where you need to

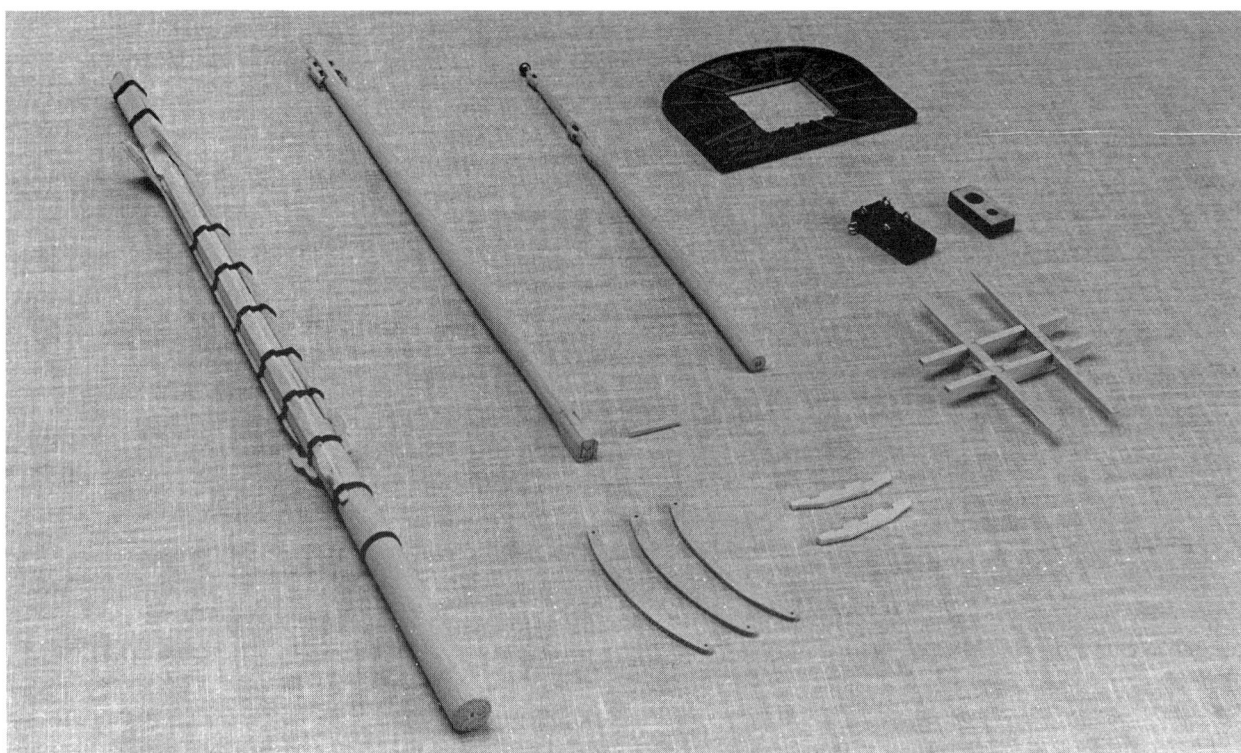

Fig. 4.27 The parts for the foremast ready for assembly.

The French Frigate *La Renommée* 1793

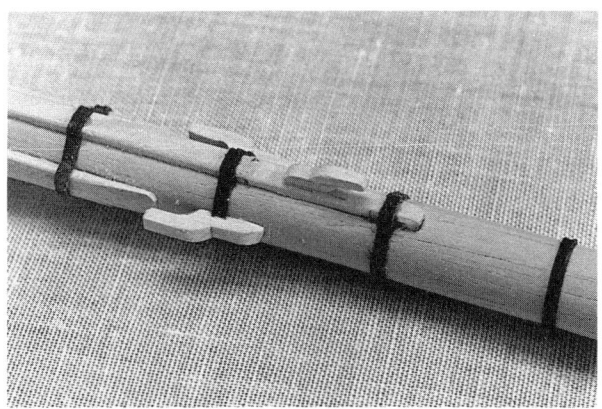

Fig. 4.28 The lower foremast showing the iron banding.

Fig. 4.29 The fore top.

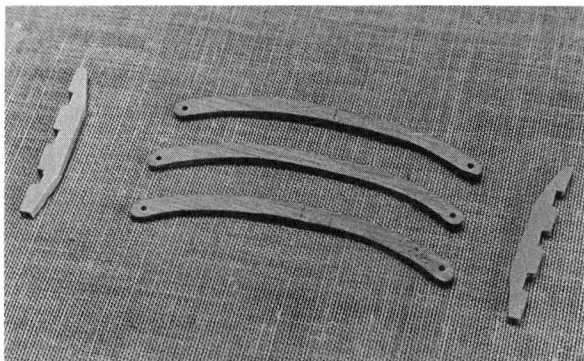

Fig. 4.30 The topmast trestletrees and crosstrees.

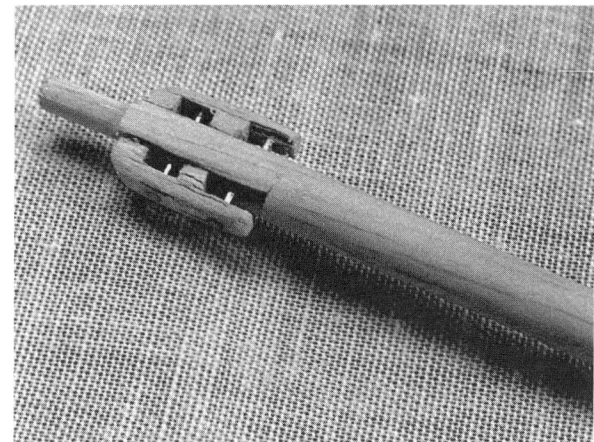

Fig. 4.31 The cheek blocks at the head of the topmast.

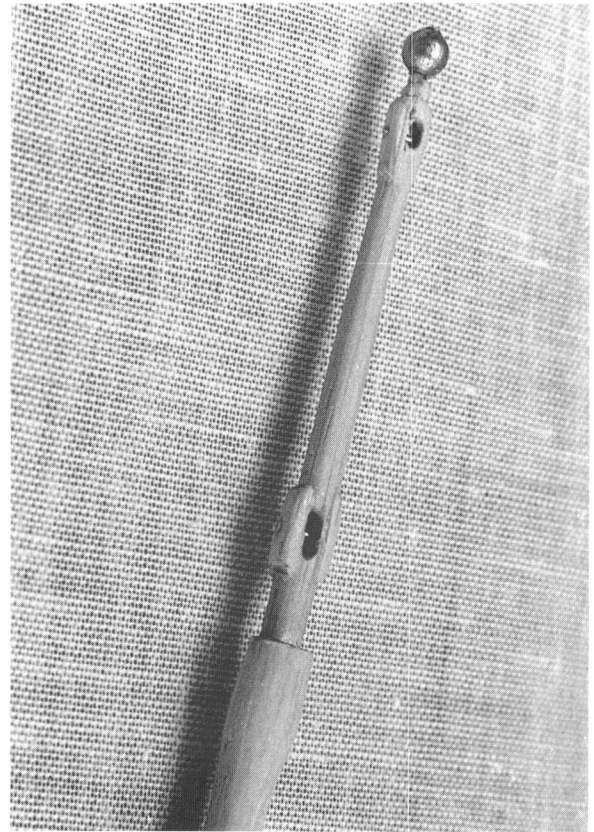

Fig. 4.32 The sheaves through the topgallant mast.

drill holes for the lower deadeyes to the upper shrouds and the position of those holes along the front edge of the top necessary for the crowsfeet.

The topmast trestletrees and crosstrees were jointed together with halving joints. The crosstrees curved aft such that the ends of the forward one were in line with the centre of the topgallant mast. The radii of curvature were indicated on the drawings for both the fore and main mast crosstrees and each piece had to be made separately to get the curves technically correct (Fig. 4.30).

Cheek blocks were mounted each side of the head of the topmast (Fig. 4.31) and sheaves had to be cut fore and aft through the upper portions of the topgallant mast (Fig. 4.32). It is wise to remember to do these at this stage rather than after the masts have been stepped into the hull.

Another feature that must not be forgotten is the fid, the device that stops the upper masts slipping down between the trestletrees! On a point of accuracy, the fid through the heel of the topmast was normally a headed tapered wedge made from timber or iron. For the topgallant mast a fid was often fed in from each side of the heel, with a surrounding iron band to prevent them coming out. This is a minor detail, but one that gives a model that little bit of something extra.

Once the mast assemblies had been completed, they were, together with the bowsprit, stepped into the hull. It is important to recognise that while they should be in line when viewed fore and aft, they do have a slight rake to stern when seen broadside on. It is important to get this right when assembling the masts and not leave things to be pulled into line by the rigging that comes later!

The chainplates

Once the masts had been set into position, the chainplates were assembled and fitted. The kit provides an incorrect design of chainplate proper, and leaves the modeller to use his or her initiative to make up the necessary toe and preventer links from, presumably, the brass wire supplied. I personally felt that a kit in this price range should have done better and included those items ready formed. As it happened, I have a fair size spares box and I took advantage of it, but nonetheless I rate the omission as a bit of a black mark.

One reason for leaving the chainplate assemblies until this time is so that you can use the masts as a means of getting the line of the linkages to match that of the shrouds. A length of thread from the tops allowed the line from the channels down the links to the hull to be correctly angled. The lower link was pinned to the side of the hull (Fig. 4.33), and considerable care was exercised when doing this. I found that a pin pusher was a better tool to use than a hammer; one accidental miss could easily dislodge a gun barrel or put a dent in the square edge of a wale.

The yards

The lower yards were provided ready tapered although considerable work was necessary to bring them to a finished state. First, the centre section should be octagonal rather than round. Unfortunately, it was not good enough to merely file eight flats on to the yard since this resulted in the section becoming undersized. So, having filed the flats, they have to be built up again by adding 0.5mm battens. When the adhesive had set, they were then sanded down at the ends to blend in with the circular section of the original spar.

Secondly, stunsail booms and irons had to be made up and fitted to the ends of the lower yards. At this scale, a fair simulation of iron banding can be achieved by the use of thin strips cut from a spare black page of a photograph album. Sling cleats were fitted to the fore face of the yard such that the stunsail booms adopted a position on the upper fore side of the yard at about 45-degree angle to the centreline.

The footropes and stirrups were something of a fiddly job but careful use of superglue to stiffen and fix the thread did much to lighten to task.

The upper yards had to be tapered from round section dowel rod, achieved quite easily first by rough filing,

Fig. 4.33 The forward chainplate assembly—starboard side and netted side rails.

then finishing off by spinning in the drill chuck.

All yards were put safely to one side until the standing rigging had been completed.

Rails and netting

Before starting on the rigging, the rails around the upper decks were made up, together with those to be fitted to the rear edge of the main and fore top. These are rather vulnerable features and for additional strength, I decided to use 1mm diameter brass wire as stanchions set into the bulwark capping strips and topped off with a wooden handrail. A similar procedure was used for the rails at the two tops.

The drawings showed that all rails, except those on the poop deck, were laced with netting. I pondered on this for a considerable time until, while on a reluctant shopping expedition with my wife, I came across some black tulle in the dress-making department of a large department store. I didn't dare ask for less than half a metre (which cost less than a pound), and got enough to fit out models of the entire English and French fleets at Trafalgar! The size and pattern of the mesh looks very realistic and the material can be stuck to the brass stanchions with either superglue or Unibond adhesive (Fig. 4.34).

The shape required was first drawn out on white paper, which was then pinned to a cutting board. A strip of tulle was then taped down over the pattern using a low tack adhesive tape, 3M 810 Magic tape is ideal, but any will do provided that it stops the mesh from distorting under the action of the knife. A scalpel was used to cut through both the tape and the tulle to produce the pattern previously drawn. The tulle was then stripped off the sticky tape and then glued in place over the brass stanchions.

Preparation for rigging

The draughtsmanship on those sheets of the drawing that show the rigging was generally very good. However, unless you read Italian, there is quite a bit of studying to do in order to fathom out what is a typical, rather than a specific, detail. You will probably find that a reasonable Italian/English dictionary will give you the basic words then, combined with a bit of common sense, the rest will fall into place. Unfortunately, you have to jump around from sheet to sheet to build up the entire picture, particularly when it comes to identifying belaying points.

I considered at some length as to whether or not I would rig sails. One of the factors that led to my decision not to was the fact that there were insufficient blocks provided to do the job properly. Thus you will see that the yards on my model are lowered down to the caps.

It may be that you will want to complete any outstanding woodwork before clearing the bench for rigging. That being the case, you will find that there are three large collars to make, one for the mainstay and one each for the forestay and preventer (Fig. 4.35). In addition to these awkward pieces, you will need three euphroe blocks for rigging the crowsfeet.

These parts all required to be fashioned from some fairly hard, close-grained timber. The collars in particular needed to be carefully drilled and fretted to avoid breakage in manufacture. The euphroe blocks were less difficult, the holes drilled first before shaping.

The cordage provided in the kit was all tan coloured. Depending on how you want your model to appear, you have three options; dye some of it black for the standing rigging, replace some as required from the spares box or

Fig. 4.34 The lower shrouds.

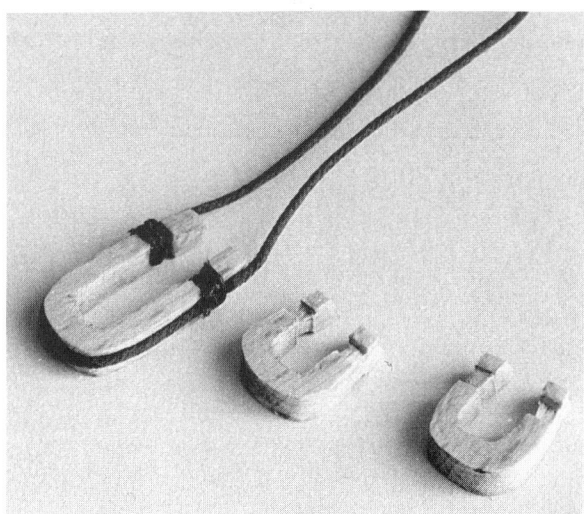

Fig. 4.35 The stay collars.

model shop or rig it all in tan! My stock, accumulated over the years, allowed me to take the second alternative.

Rigging the shrouds and ratlines

Following the correct sequence, fore starboard, fore port, etc. working back in pairs, the lower shrouds to all three masts were put up (Fig. 4.34). The futtock shrouds were then rigged followed by the upper shrouds. I found that it helped to keep everything in line if the lanyards were pulled up in pairs, side to side. Incidentally, you will find it helpful not to rig the backstays at this juncture, they get in the way of tying on the ratlines and many of the other ongoing rigging operations.

The ratlines were, as usual, a bit of a pain. Fortunately, there were not too many on the *Renommée*, but they all had to be tied and which amounts to a lot of knots! One of the problems is that the eye can be drawn to focus on detail behind the shrouds on which you are working. It is the frequent adjusting of focus that tends to put a strain on the eyes. One way of avoiding this is to insert a piece of white card between the shrouds and the mast. It concentrates the eye and you will also find that if working with forceps you don't miss the end of the thread so much!

At this scale, I normally tie the ratlines to each shroud with a simple hitch, sealed with the merest touch of cyano.

Rigging the stays and bowsprit

Purely for reasons of convenience and access, the main preventer stay, then the mainstay were rigged before starting on the bowsprit. These were assembled via a system of collars and hearts at the lower end. The drawings are particularly clear and concise in the finer points of how this should be done.

The sequence of working was again defined by how best to keep things accessible at a later stage. The martingale via the dolphin striker, the bobstays then the bowsprit shrouds get the underside done. Don't forget the two bumkins. These were shown on the rigging drawings but were not detailed or depicted on the main assembly sheet. They angle forward and downward from just below the base of the bowsprit across the top of the main headrail (Fig. 4.36). The outer end is braced back to the prow in order to take the strain imposed by the forecourse tacks. The spritsail yard and its associated rigging completed the main bowsprit, although the footropes were not fitted until after the stay and preventer to the fore topmast has been put in place.

The lower stays to the foremast and mizzenmast were then rigged. The former again used collars and hearts at the lower end (Fig. 4.37), whereas the latter was rigged via just a pair of hearts (Fig. 4.38). These were pulled up fairly taut in order that the addition of later running rigging did not pull the stays out of line.

Before proceeding further, the crowsfeet were set up. The euphroe blocks, together with single blocks were rigged to the stays. Starting at the hole just one side of centre of the relevant top where the end of the crowsfoot is fixed, the line then passed down to the nearest hole in the euphroe block before returning to the hole on the other side of centre in the top. This was threaded over

Fig. 4.36 The bumkins and the anchor rigging. Note the anchor buoy slung for forward shroud.

The French Frigate *La Renommée* 1793

Fig. 4.37 The lower end of the foremast stay and preventer.

Fig. 4.38 The mizzen stay lower end.

the rim of the top to the underside, where it then came up through the next adjacent hole in the top, over the rim and on down to the next available hole in the euphroe block before returning to the other side of the top. This procedure was carried on through until all holes in the top and block had been threaded. There should be half as many holes in the block as there are in the front rim of the top and, having started the process to one side of centre of the top, you should finish at the extreme outer hole in the other side of the top. The crowsfeet were pulled up fairly tightly, but not so much as to distort the stay to which the euphroe block was rigged.

All the remaining upper stays were then rigged, again being careful not to pull up too tight and thus slackening off some of the lower stays.

The belaying points are all indicated in the drawings though not necessarily on the same sheet, you just have to search until you find them. This is not a criticism, a one sheet belaying plan would be a right pig's breakfast and, by and large, the draughtsman concerned hasn't made a bad job of it.

Rigging the yards

Again for the sake of convenience and access, I started on the lower yard of the foremast and worked my way up via the topsail yard to the topgallant yard. It is also imperative at this time to remember that, if you are rigging the sails, the yards will be hoisted high up on their respective masts. If the model is to be unclothed, then the yards will be down on the caps.

The lower yard is hung by jeers, two pairs of triple blocks, and strapped to the mast by truss pendants and falls. Having rigged these, the lifts were then added to

51

stabilise the assembly before moving on to the next yard.

The topsail yard also has jeers but, in this instance, comprise a single block lashed to the centre of the yard and two single blocks slung from mast above the adjacent top. Parrals were fitted to retain the yard to the mast and again the lifts were rigged.

The topgallant yard was more simply rigged with tie, truss and lifts.

Although the brace pendants were conveniently fitted to the ends of the yards at this stage, the rigging of the actual braces was left until much later in the process. The sequence of setting up the yards on the main mast was basically the same.

The mizzenmast was a little different of course, in that it has a fore and aft mizzen yard which should be set up first. It was hung using a jeer block and parral. At its lower end, the mizzen bowlines run through deck-mounted blocks and are belayed on adjacent pin racks. At the top end, a simple crowsfoot system was rigged to the topmast.

The crossjack and topsail yard were set up in the same manner as the upper yards on the foremast.

The braces

Many of the braces run through blocks strapped to the stays or slung below the tops. It was essential to ensure that those fixed to the stays were in the right position or the braces would not have run correctly and conveniently to their respective belaying positions. Thus, before permanently fixing the position of the blocks, the braces were run from start to finish to establish the right line, the position of the blocks adjusted as required, then temporarily belayed at the bottom end. As before, they were not pulled up too tightly so as to distort the line of the stay. The braces on the opposite side were assembled in the same manner and the tension balanced, side to side, before permanently belaying both sides. The only difference between the various braces is the point and method by which they are belayed. These details were clearly advised on the drawings.

Rigging the backstays

Now that the majority of the basic rigging had been completed, the backstays to the fore and main masts could be set up. They were rigged to the two aft-end deadeyes on their respective chainplates, and were pulled up with lanyards in the same way as the shrouds.

Rigging the anchors

Having made the anchors some time ago, a check was made to ensure that they were complete and that the puddening had been applied to the rings. A lot of models are spoilt by omitting this binding and a plain brass ring does tend to stand out. Both forward anchors were suspended from the catheads with catfalls via a triple block, their lower ends being tied up to kevels on the forecastle deck. The two remaining anchors were lashed to the foremast chainplate.

The anchor cables were clinched to the rings and passed forward through the hawse holes. It was worth spending a little time to get the hang of the cables looking right. A good coating of white PVA adhesive prior to rigging helps stiffen the cordage to advantage. An anchor buoy was rigged to the fore anchor and slung from the adjacent shroud. All anchor rigging features are shown in Fig. 4.36.

Finishing off

The only major task then remaining was to make up the coils of rope to either lay on deck or hang on the various belaying pins. They should, of course, look as though they are part of the falls of rigging belayed at those particular points and those that hang on the pins needed particular care in shaping to give that natural hanging look.

A visual tour around the vessel was taken to make sure that there were no untrimmed ends of rigging, or odd ends that had been trimmed and had hidden themselves under a gun carriage or whatever. A light brush over with a large soft paint brush removed the accumulated dust of weeks on the workbench.

Conclusions

I rather liked the look of the completed model, it had bags of detail, a reasonable amount of ornamentation and was not too big. Having said all that, there was much that needed to be done that many modellers purchasing a kit would not expect to do, or maybe not have the facilities to do. The modifications to the gun carriages and the making of the main and forestay collars, for instance, really required facilities that many kit builders might not have. The quality of drawings was excellent, supported with ample strip material, good diecast ornamentation and a host of good quality parts apparently drawn from standard proprietary ranges of ships' fittings. Such fittings can, of course, cause a few problems in terms of scale and style. In fact, I would say that the *Renommée* is halfway between a kit-built and a scratch-built model. I had to work hard, in many instances, to adapt and modify what was provided, but to be fair, I didn't have to discard and replace anything. So, there you are, the choice is yours. You will struggle without some workshop facilities, but with some ingenuity and adaptability, you can produce a fine looking model.

CHAPTER 5

An Armed Pinnace Circa 1803

Ships' boats were variously armed depending on the size, or rate, of the ship that carried them. The armament might be a carronade or a cannon sliding between frames under recoil and mounted in either the bow or stern of the boat. The boats were used for coastal patrol work and escort duties and were usually very manoeuvrable and stable.

The subject chosen by Panart for its kit is a 32ft. pinnace with what appears to be a bow mounted 4-pounder cannon with a pair of 1/2 pounder swivels mounted on the gunwales to stern. At 1/16th scale, this makes up into a museum standard model 24″ (610mm) long. The degree of detail in both the boat construction and the fitting out makes it a worthy challenge to the model boat builder and it is no surprise that a model built from this kit won a bronze medal at the 62nd Model Engineer and Modelling Exhibition at Olympia.

The Kit

The materials were of extremely high quality with all sheet parts laser cut. All strip was straight grained and I didn't find one flawed piece. Dowelling all matched for colour and fittings all came bubble packed. Turned parts are provided in both wood and brass but, nonetheless, there are several parts to be made up from brass strip and heavy gauge wire.

In retrospect, if I have one slightly adverse comment, it would be that there was only just enough of some materials, so be careful how you cut and don't lose any of the smaller fittings.

The multilingual manual was quite adequate, but beware, it is not quite sequential with regard to the order of construction but, if you do things properly and read it all before you start, this is very apparent and not a problem. Make sure that you flick through the entire booklet and not just isolate the English instructions because there are some valuable sketches to be found at the end supporting further English text on the subject of planking. A most helpful parts list is also incorporated within the manual.

Hull construction

The hull is basically a triple-planked shell built around a removable core. Eight individual frames, five of them subsequently to be removed, are slotted into a keel and locked in place by a longitudinal plate of 5mm ply (Fig. 5.1). The stem is reinforced either side and shaped, together with the first two frames, to conform to the natural curvature of the finished hull. It is imperative that this assembly is put together square and true because upon it depends the final shape of the hull shell.

The first planking is of walnut and, of course, the inner surface forms the exposed inside of the boat. The edges of the five central frames and the upper part of the sixth should either be waxed or covered with a strip of Sellotape to make sure that the planks are not glued to them. Each plank should be permanently glued to the end frames and pinned to all the others, but ensuring that edge-to-edge joints are well glued. White PVA adhesive is ideal.

After putting a plank in position, the inside of the hull should be wiped clean to remove any splurge of adhesive that has seeped through to the inner surface. This is not so easy to remove once the glue has set. The drawings and manual provide good guidance as to the sequence of applying the planks and, once the first planking is complete and the adhesive cured, all the pins should be removed and the surface generally tidied up.

Lime strips are used for the second planking and are applied in basically the same pattern as before. However, a contact adhesive may be used for this layer provided that some initial bend is induced into each plank before gluing. The lime strips are 1mm narrower than the walnut planks used for the inner and outer surfaces, thus the edge joints do not coincide and a really strong shell is produced. When completely covered, the outer surface should be thoroughly rubbed down to provided a smooth and even surface upon which to do the third and final planking.

The outer layer is again applied in a similar manner to the second, using a contact adhesive. Additional care is required to cut the fore end of each strip to accurately match the side of the prow and that tapering is done to ensure that every part of the plank sits flat down on the outer surface of the previous planking. I used cabinet-makers' scrapers to provide a good smooth surface to which I applied a couple of coats of sanding sealer to harden everything off. A word of warning – it is wise to avoid cellulose preparations as they may adversely react with some of the contact adhesives resulting in a series of sprung planks!

After a final sanding to the outside, the lock plate and

Fig. 5.1 The core frame around which the hull shell is built.

five frames can be unpinned and removed, leaving the inner surface clear for cleaning up. This is not a five minute job but just how long it takes is largely dependent on how well you have carried out the first planking. The lower portions of five frames are now replaced into the hull shell to help form a support for the floor of the boat (Fig. 5.2). Other supporting members are also put in place together with small areas of decking fore and aft. These, together with the faces of the end frames are planked and finished off with the addition of framed and planked hatches (Figs 5.3 and 5.4).

At this juncture, the stand should be assembled in order to provide support during the ongoing construction. The stand as provided in the kit is very basic and will need some work done on it to make it suitable for permanent display. To that end make the assembly a temporary affair at this stage, capable of being taken apart and enhanced later.

The floor frame should now be fitted then the ribs. With a couple of exceptions, these are equally spaced along the inside of the shell and it is worth making up a spacing gauge to ensure that they are all correctly positioned. With gentle finger pressure, the strip supplied in my kit was flexible enough to take bend without recourse to wetting or heating. The use of cyanoacrylate was an added advantage and, what I originally thought to be a potentially difficult task, in fact proved quite straightforward. Contrary to the sequence indicated in the manual, I would advise that the ribs be positioned before fixing the rail around the top edge of the boat. The top edge of the hull shell and the top of the ribs can both be trimmed and flattened at the same time.

The rails, fabricated from 10 × 3.5mm beech strips, have to be made in segments to take up the curve at the bows. Rather than use the shape as drawn on the plans, I would recommend that you trace the actual shape of the hull on to a piece of cardboard and use this as a cutting and assembly template. In this way the inner and outer overlap of the rail to the hull shell will be even all round. The rail across the top of the transom has a slight curve and this should be induced into the strip before making the mating joints with the side rails (Fig. 5.5).

Fig. 5.3 The after deck and transom planked.

Fig. 5.4 The fore deck planked and hatch fitted in bulkhead.

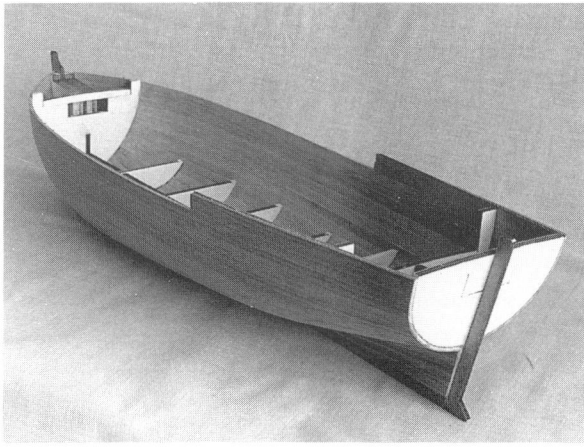

Fig. 5.2 The completed hull shell removed.

Fig. 5.5 Note spacing of ribs and subsequent fitting of rails.

The longitudinal stringers are both glued and pinned in place, the glue forming the main bond with the pins added afterwards (Fig. 5.6). Take care when drilling the holes for the shortened pins that you don't drill through to the outside of the hull. Choose a drill size slightly smaller than the pin diameter and the pins may then be quite readily pushed into place.

I chose to frame and make the floor parts before proceeding further (Fig. 5.7). These comprise a mixture of shuttering and grating, all of which I decided to fix permanently in the bottom of the boat. The 2×2mm bracing strips on top of the shuttering must be positioned in line and correctly spaced to look right, so again it is worth making up some spacers and taking that extra bit of care. The spaces between the ribs, the floor frame and the inside surface of the hull have to be filled with pieces of strip; each of these pieces must be individually fitted with regard to both section and length to attain the ultimate fit.

The support pillars for the two swivel guns must be made and assembled before putting the lateral benches in place and again a fair degree of filing, trimming and offering up is required to get the snug fit and correct attitude (Fig. 5.8).

The rubbing strakes and stabilisers may now be added, the shorter strakes at the stern being a continuation of the main rail. The main strake should be parallel to the main rail and, of course, sit snugly against the stem. Cyano adhesive is most useful getting this strip on, gradually working from stem to stern using a spacer to maintain parallelism. The stabilisers are a bit more difficult, being of greater section and requiring to be bent on width rather than thickness. I sacrificed a little of the width and filed some of the curve into the strip then used cyano to gradually induce the rest as I assembled it to the lower part of the hull. You need to carefully mark out the position on the hull before starting with the superglue, you would almost certainly ruin the planking trying to remove a wrongly placed strip. Having got the stabilisers in place the edge of the keel can be capped and trimmed.

At this stage I decided to paint the lower half of the hull white, with the area between the upper strake and rail around the stern, blue. While the several coats needed are drying, the stern decoration pieces can be made up and gilded. After putting them in place the two holes through the transom can be drilled and the internal reinforcing pieces added (Fig. 5.9).

Work on the inside of the hull is continued by assembling the thwart at the mast position. The block which houses the heel of the mast sits on the floor below and its correct position should be attained by a length of 10mm dowel simulating the mast, passing through the thwart and down into the block. Correctly aligning the dowel for perpendicularity will put the block in its right place. Once the glue has set, the mast partners can be fitted between the underside of the thwart and the top of the block. The thwart reinforcement strips, glued and lashed in place, finish the construction of the tabernacle area and the remaining thwarts can be fitted (again see Fig. 5.8). These are supported from below by turned spindles, mounted on 6mm square sectioned blocks, glued and dowelled together. The blocks should be cut

Fig. 5.6 The longitudinal stringers in place.

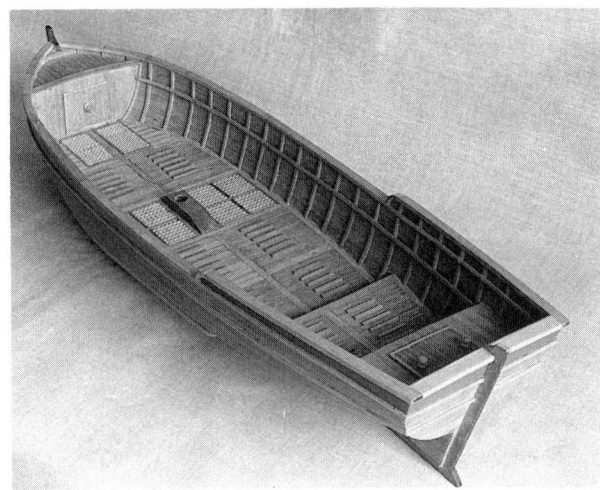

Fig. 5.7 The floor shuttering and gratings.

Fig. 5.8 The benches and thwarts in place. Note the pillars for the swivel guns.

An Armed Pinnace Circa 1803

Fig. 5.9 Stern decoration. Do the gilding before assembly.

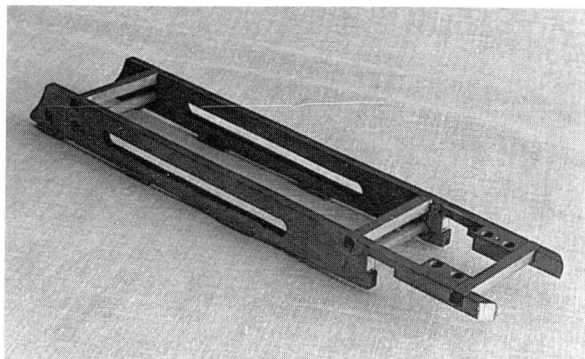

Fig. 5.11 The gun frame.

overlength and trimmed individually after assembly to get the right fit between the underside of the thwart and the floor of the boat.

It only remains now to fit the knees between the thwarts and the inside of the boat and add the fillets at the ends of the longitudinal stringers to complete the main hull construction.

The Gun Carriage and Frame

The drawings provide excellent exploded views of the construction of both carriage and frame and little elaboration is needed. Without doubt, the carriage should be made first and totally completed including any surface finishing, varnishing etc. that you wish to do (Fig. 5.10).

The width between the frame sides is governed by the width of the carriage supports thus the cross members for the frame should be cut accordingly. The frame

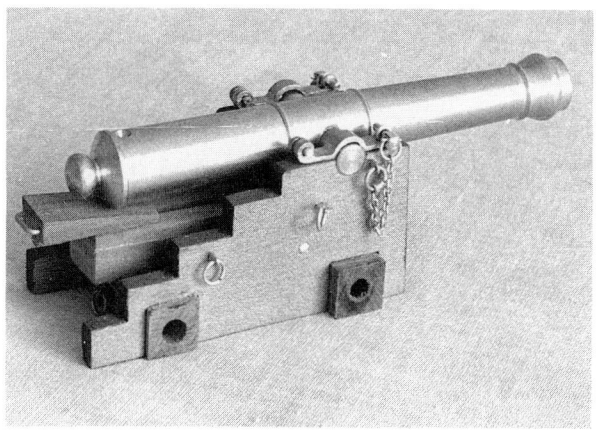

Fig. 5.10 The gun carriage.

assembly rests, at its forward end, on the small prow deck area with the remainder supported by the first three thwarts. Depending on how accurately you have constructed the hull shell, some very minor adjustment to the frame may be required to get the total seating correct. Once you are satisfied with the fit, the frame can be completed to the same standard as the carriage (Fig. 5.11). The two parts can now be brought together and the whole unit assembled into the boat (Fig. 5.12).

The fittings

The rudder and its fitting is relatively straightforward, but the tiller, recommended to be made by bending a 5×3.5mm strip, is more easily fabricated by laminating two or three pieces together, particularly if you do not have any sophisticated bending equipment to induce the severe bends required (Fig. 5.13).

The thole pins and cleats I found easier to make up in the strip then separate them after shaping. This helped guarantee that they all finished up the same shape and size (Fig. 5.14).

The straps for securing the shroud rigging are made up from brass strip. Do your marking out well here, because there is only just enough material provided and you cannot afford any scrap. However, they are not difficult to make once you have determined the actual length needed for each strap.

The mast, spar and sail

The mast is made from 12mm diameter dowel tapered by 2mm on diameter to the top end. The heel has a parallel portion of 10mm diameter to pass through the thwart and into the heel block on the floor of the boat. I did the tapering by filing four, then eight flats on the diameter, then spinning in an electric drill to sand the corners off. Make sure that the dowel runs fairly true in the chuck before turning on the power and that the chuck jaws are reasonably tightened up! The heel end really needs the services of a lathe to turn the 10mm diameter parallel portion but it can be done by careful use of file and callipers, again by producing an octagonal section before reducing to the round. The mast head is made by

The Period Ship Handbook 2

Fig. 5.12 The carriage and frame assembled in the boat.

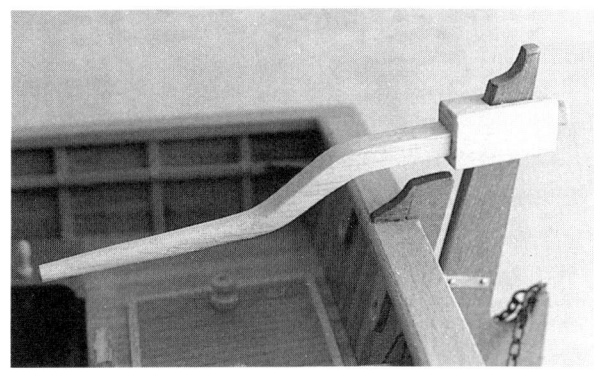

Fig. 5.13 The tiller assembly. Bend it or laminate it.

Fig. 5.14 Cleats and thole pins.

An Armed Pinnace Circa 1803

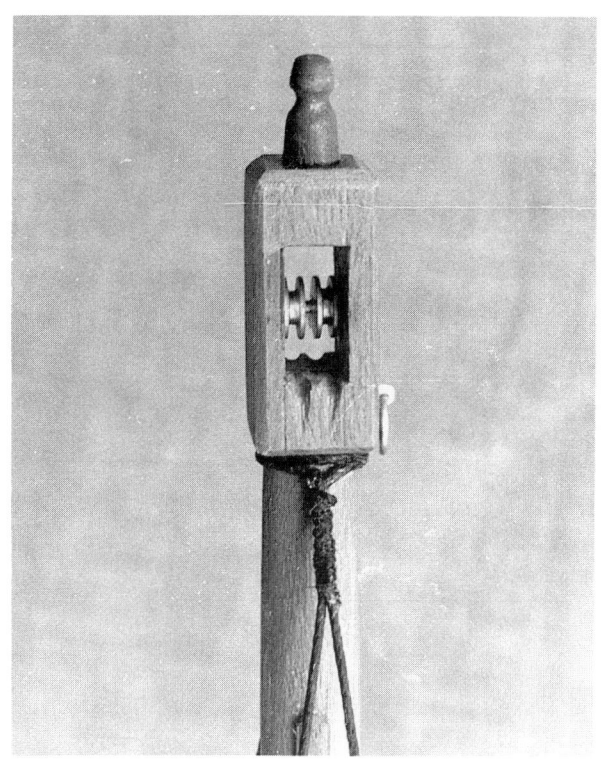

Fig. 5.15 The mast head assembly – an interesting mini-project.

The sail is basically triangular in shape (Fig. 5.16), roached along the foot, sewn with seams 15mm apart and with edges hemmed and piped about concealed boltropes. The boltropes, exposed at the corners, provide loops for attaching to the spar and rigging the sheets to the lower corner of the sail (Fig. 5.17). This provides quite a needleworking project and a sewing machine really is a must. Score ten extra Brownie points if you can find someone experienced to do the sewing for you!

Equipment

Making up the gear for fitting out the boat is quite a project in itself. Significant amongst these bits and pieces are the oars, eight of them in all, each comprising four parts – handle, stock, shaft and blade (Fig. 5.18). The tricky bit is the slotting of the end of the shaft to take the blade; OK if you have a small circular saw bench, otherwise it is a matter of drilling, sawing and filing.

producing a rectangular slot through a block of 12mm square material into which is fitted a pair of brass pulleys. This fits on to a spigot formed on top of the mast proper (Fig. 5.15). Battens and woldings complete the mast assembly.

The composite lateen spar comprises three sections, each tapered and lashed together. A hoisting strap is attached to the upper part of the central section.

Fig. 5.17 The looped boltrope at the sail corners.

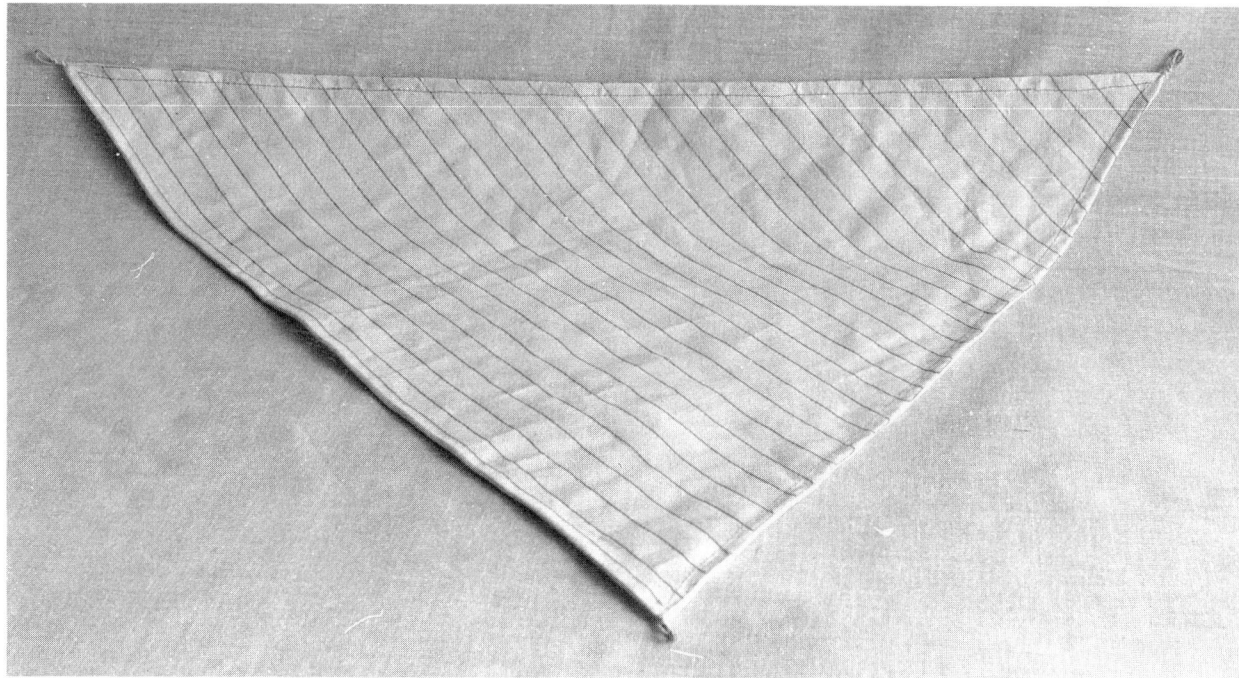

Fig. 5.16 The sail made up with seams, boltrope and piped leeches.

59

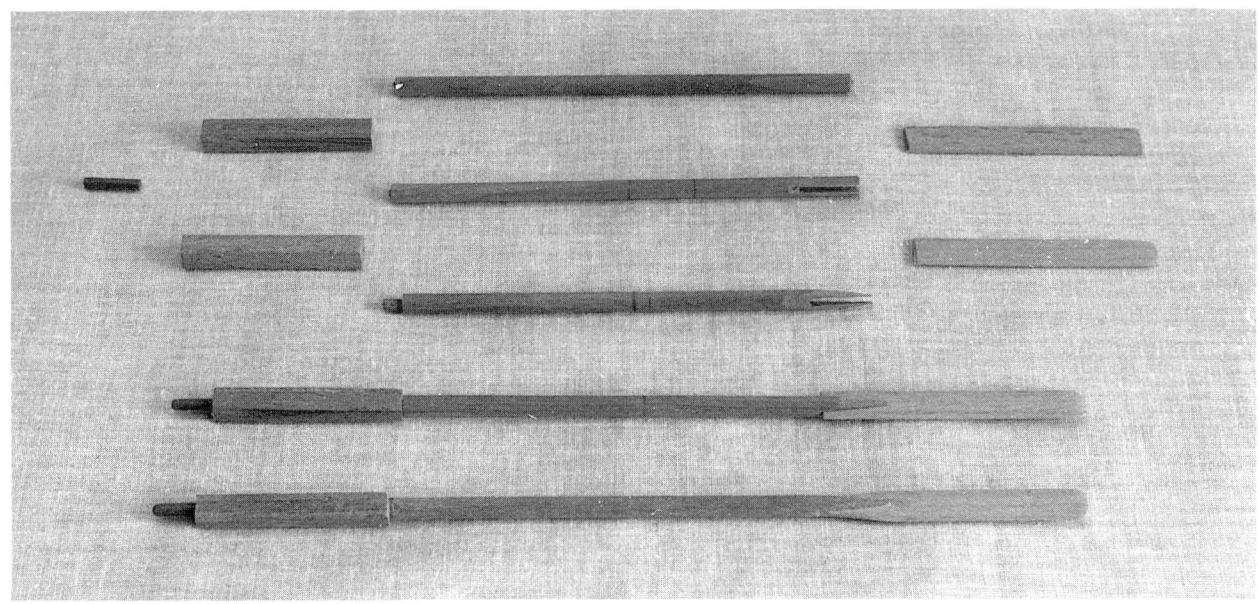

Fig. 5.18 The oars assembly sequence.

There are five wooden staved tubs and water containers, each fabricated by gluing staves around a pair of ply discs, then removing the upper one to leave the lower to form the bottom of the container. Panart suggest that some of the staves are tapered to maintain their perpendicular appearance. I would recommend that all staves are tapered to a lesser degree for an even better effect. The edge of the upper disc has to be inhibited to prevent the staves sticking to it if PVA is used, but if you use superglue with care for sticking the staves to the lower disc and edge to edge themselves, it is not necessary. Before removing the upper disc, I wiped a coating of PVA around the staves, making sure it went into all the joints, then left it to harden off. This strengthened the structure considerably and made the final sanding of the outside a far less hazardous task. Bands of thread are then wound around the vessels and the whole assembly given a coat of matt varnish before removing the top disc (Figs. 5.19 and 5.20). One of the tubs has the disc left in place, upon which is coiled one layer of anchor rope (Fig. 5.21). This simulates a tub full of carefully coiled rope and looks very effective.

Fig. 5.20 The water containers, similar in construction to the tubs.

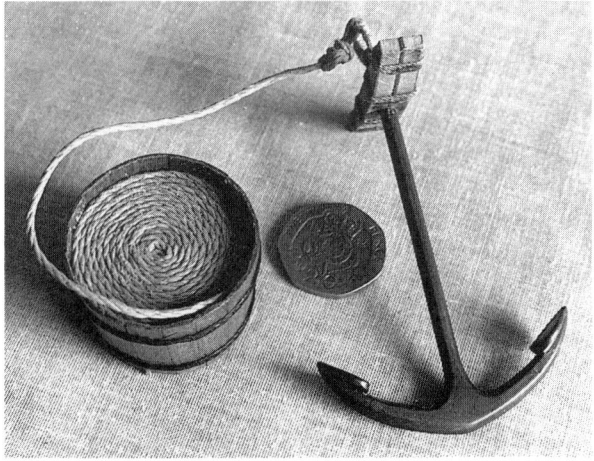

Fig. 5.19 The charge and rag tubs, tapered staves around a pair of discs.

Fig. 5.21 Anchor, cable and tub.

An Armed Pinnace Circa 1803

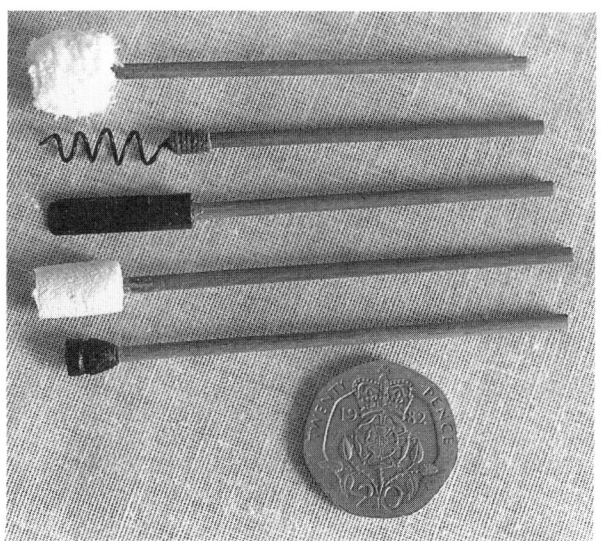

Fig. 5.22 The cannon equipment, another mini-project to test your innovative abilities.

Fig. 5.23 Cannon ball trays.

The cannon accessories make for quite an entertaining project. Swab and scoop construction have been imaginatively thought-out by Panart and the results are very realistic. I have to say that I had my doubts when I started, but was more than pleased with the results (Figs. 5.22 and 5.23).

Rigging

All thread should be pulled through fingers sticky with PVA adhesive in order to lay down those dust catching, microscopic fibres. It also helps to give a more natural look to the set of the rigging.

The rigging process begins with the cannon (Fig. 5.24), and a requirement to form eight hooks from brass wire. In fact, this is a little tricky in that they really do need to be identical in shape and size. So, having established the way to make the first one, it proves to be a good idea to make not only the eight required for rigging the cannon, but a further six for use when rigging the tiller and shrouds. Don't pull up the block and tackle too tightly or you may pull the rather soft brass rings open and lose everything! By the way, before the rigging

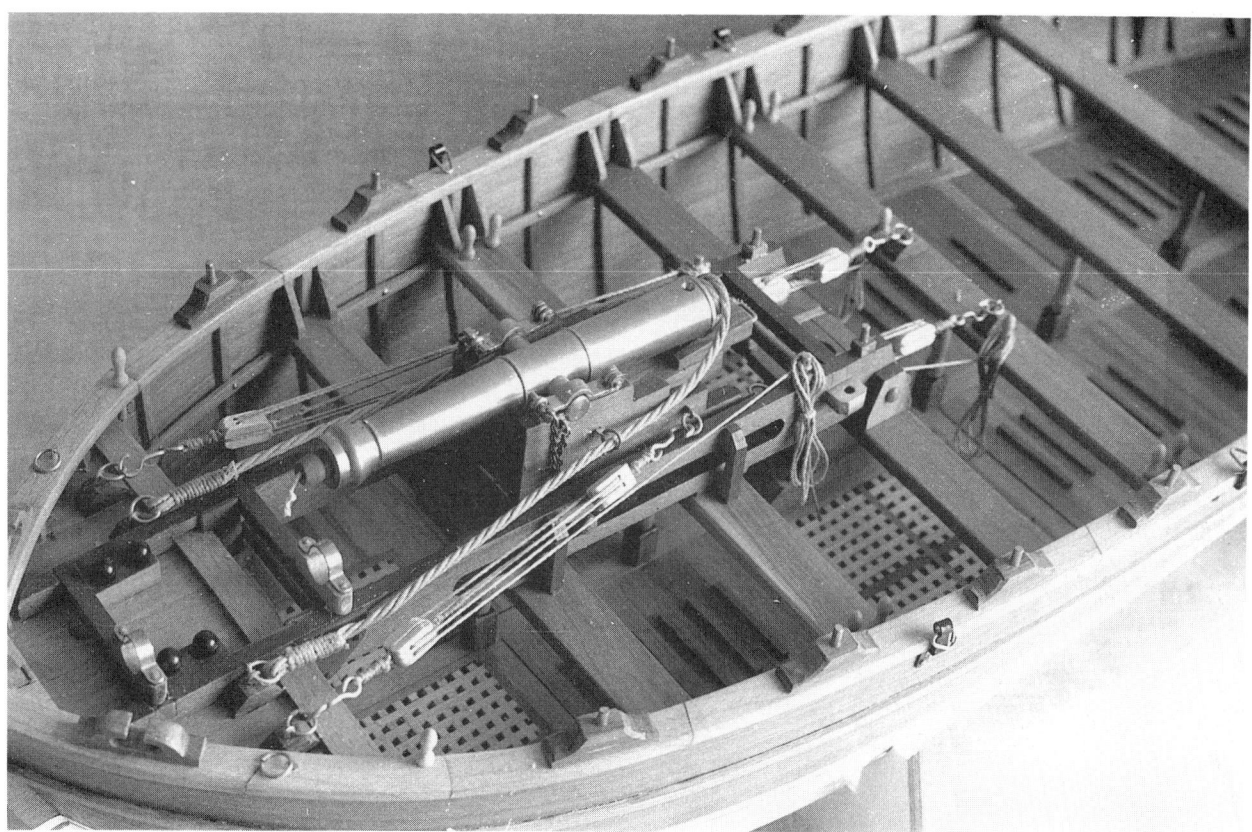

Fig. 5.24 The gun rigging.

process starts, the blocks should all have their holes opened out to take the diameter of thread used.

Having stepped the mast into the tabernacle, the shrouds are next to be rigged. This is a simple block and tackle arrangement tied off at belaying pins in the thwarts (Fig. 5.25). A similar system is employed to rig the tiller (Fig. 5.26).

I would suggest that the sail now be lashed to the lateen spar before rigging the spar to the mast. If you follow the drawing with regard to the spacing of the ties, you will find it relatively easy to get that true furled looked depicted on the box art. Don't forget to leave the ends of the ties hanging. The twin halliard is hitched to the hoisting strap on the spar, passes from starboard to port through the mast head and is belayed at pins on the port side of the thwarts. I would strongly recommend that you do not make permanent belaying until all spar rigging has been completed.

Remember that the small crew had to not only manage the sailing of the craft, but service and fire the cannon and swivels, so efficiency had to be of a fairly high order. Thus, when tying up the sail, the spar would only be lowered sufficiently to accomplish this task then left at a convenient height in order to swiftly revert to sail power when needed. So, position your spar too high and valuable time would be lost resetting the sail; have it too low and it would inconvenience the handling of the artillery.

Tie off the halliards for the right height at the mast, then rig the lines at the upper and lower ends of the spar, temporarily tying them off at the correct belaying points. This allows the correct attitude of the spar to be attained. When this has been done, the two lifts can be rigged from the spar, through the ring on the aft side of the mast head and down to the belaying pins at the starboard ends of the thwarts. Balance the tension in these against the rigging already carried out. Having got everything shipshape, a touch of superglue will make the tying off permanent.

Finishing off

The stand provided in the kit is a very stable and practical assembly, but not very attractive to show off the model. A considerable improvement can be made by simply planking it all over with spare walnut strip and coating it with satin varnish.

What to do with all the gear? The drawings show it distributed throughout the boat in a sensible manner, so perhaps you should be guided by that. If you are going to house the model in a glass case, then everything can be left loose. If, however, the model is going to be exposed to exploring fingers, you may wish to lightly fix it all down. Remember, if it can be moved, it will be moved, often with disastrous results.

And what about that flag at the back? If you can realistically simulate a flag hanging under its own

Fig. 5.25 Setting up and belaying the shrouds.

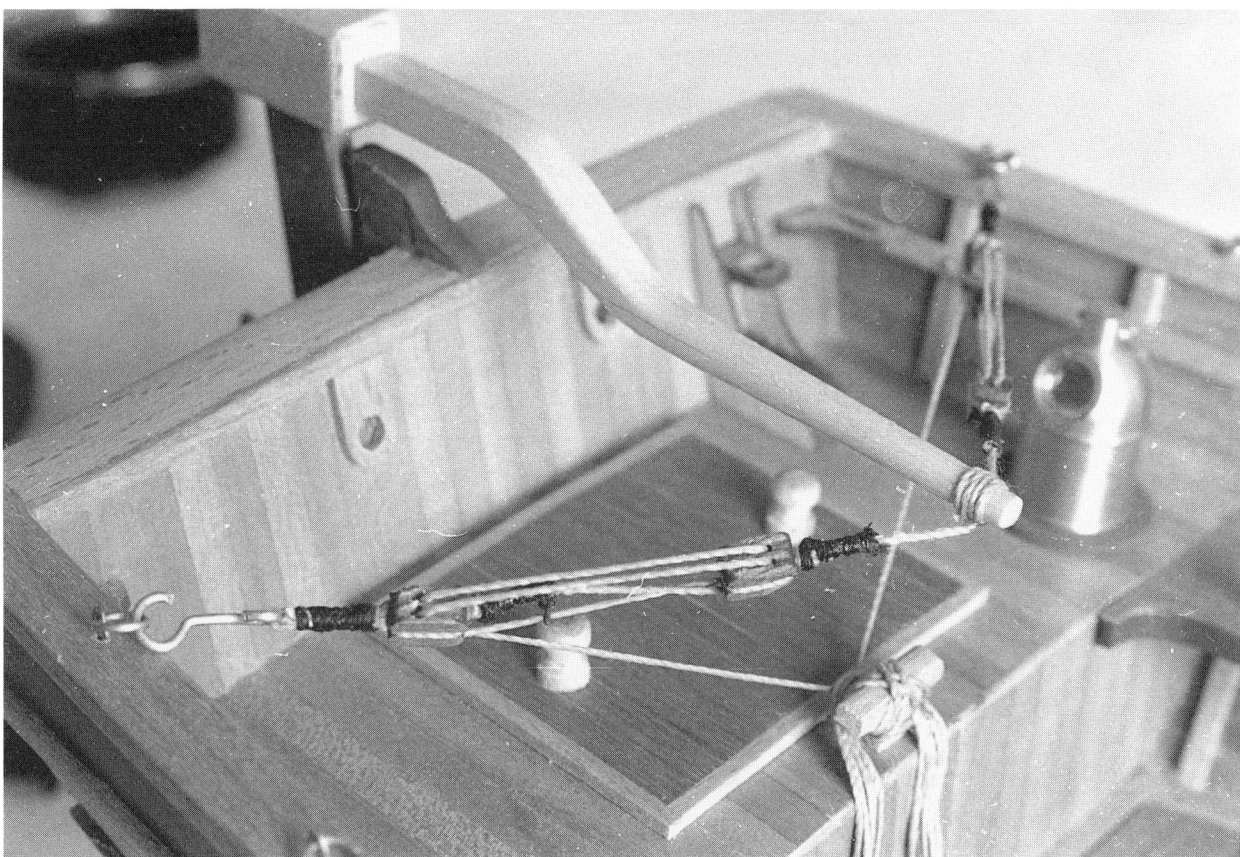

Fig. 5.26 Rigging the tiller.

weight, then fix it to the flagstaff (and write to *Model Boats* with an explanation as to how you do it!), if not, leave it off and don't make a toy out of a scale model!

Conclusions

I cannot remember when I ever enjoyed building a kit so much. Some 200 hours of pleasure for the price of the kit has got to be excellent value for money. No kit is beyond criticism, but I have to confess that any adverse remarks about this one must be considered nitpicking, but I will make them nonetheless. Even the most experienced modelmaker needs some latitude for error, so a little more material, particularly for ribs and gratings would not have been amiss. Apart from that, an excellent kit that builds into an unusual and exhibition quality model. I could quite happily have started all over again.

The Finished Models in Colour

The Royal Yacht *Caroline* **1749.**

The three-masted schooner *Sir Winston Churchill*.

The French frigate *La Renommée* 1793

An armed pinnace circa 1803.

The hermaphrodite brig *Le Hussard* 1848.

A 15th-century Portuguese caravel.

A Portuguese bomb ship *Lancha Bombardeira* 1798.

The clinker built rowing boat *Holly*.

The yacht *Britannia* 1893.

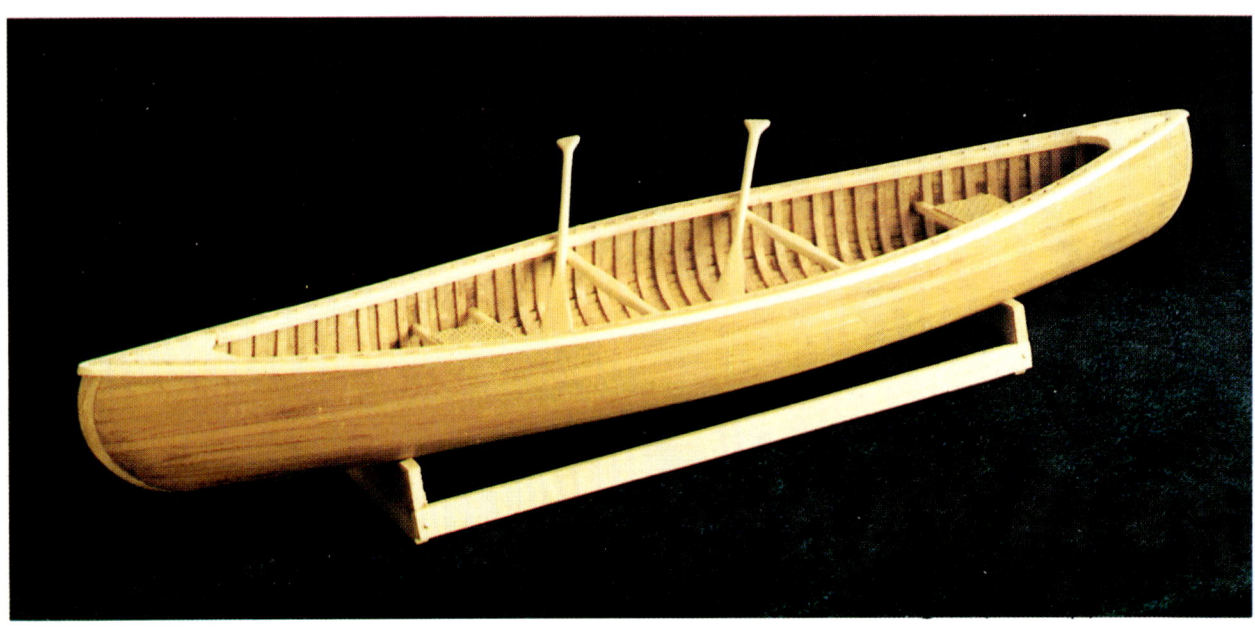

A frontiersman canoe.

CHAPTER 6

A 15th-Century Portuguese Caravel

Artenaval is a relatively new name to UK modelmakers having recently introduced kits for a range of vessels that have some importance in Portuguese maritime history. They provide a welcome change from the usual catalogue listings and, in particular, the Caravel with its long period of evolution from the 13th century is a shape well known to maritime historians worldwide. Each of the models in the range has been built and submitted to Maritime Museum experts for assessment as to technical and historical accuracy.

The kit is for a three-masted, lateen-rigged vessel and builds into a 1:50 scale model that finishes up with a length of 570mm (22.44"). This is a fairly straightforward kit to build, nothing too fiddly, not too much rigging, but a little experience of plank bending and general working in wood would be an asset.

The Kit

A very well presented box of materials includes instructions in English, good quality strip wood and accurately routered frames and false keel in extremely good ply sheets. Everything is numbered for easy identification and can be related directly to the parts list provided and the four sheets of plans. The drawings are clear and well draughted and include section views and a numbered rigging diagram. Sail material is included in the kit and is pre-printed with lines to represent the seams. Individually packed pre-shaped parts for smaller fittings and dowel rods for masts and spars complete the kit.

The tool kit required is basic, a good craft knife being an absolute essential, together with a light hammer and a razor saw. A modelmaker's plane and a low voltage electric drill are also very useful pieces of kit to have, together with some plank bending gear (plank nippers are just the job). You will also need various grades of abrasive paper, white PVA adhesive and I would strongly recommend cyanoacrylate superglue; the bottle rather than the tube is probably more convenient to dispense.

Building the hull

Do read the first page of the assembly instructions **and heed the advice given** by studying the drawings closely and reading through the entire instruction booklet before picking up your tools.

The basic framework of the hull is the conventional false keel into which is slotted nine frames and a hold floor (Fig. 6.1). However, the last three frames to stern support the upper deck and I would recommend that the tops be chamfered to the correct deck angle before gluing them in place. This is particularly advisable with the two frames with the integral deck beams, features that are a bit flimsy to stand up to being worked on after assembly. These same two frames also have cut-outs in their top edges to take deck supports to be fitted later; another feature worth measuring and cutting at this earlier stage of construction.

The edges of all frames have to be chamfered to conform to the curves of the ship so that each plank sits in total contact across those edges. The model is single planked and this operation is started at deck level, working down towards the keel (Fig. 6.2). Each plank needs to have slightly bevelled edges so that it fits snugly against its neighbour. After the first, totally parallel plank is in position each side, subsequent strips need to be tapered at the bow end, reducing the width to about 3mm over a length of about 12cm. Working alternately port to starboard, and having five planks each side, the curve of the hull dictates that planking should then be continued from the keel upwards. Stealers at the stern avoid undue twists and bends. Particular attention should be paid to the bow end of each plank to where it should be chamfered and bevelled to fit correctly against the stem.

The instructions tell you to glue the planks to the frame edges; I strongly recommend that you glue *and* pin. The kit contains all the pins you will need, in fact they are about the best quality pins that I have seen in a kit for a very long time. Remember to drill the holes first or you are liable to split the plank. If you drill the hole sufficiently deep, only about the final 25% of the pin's length needs to be effective. This is usually quite adequate and it makes it easier to remove them before sanding down later on.

The blocks for supporting the masts are now fitted and, when set, drilled out to the appropriate diameter. The instructions now tell you to taper and fit the foremast

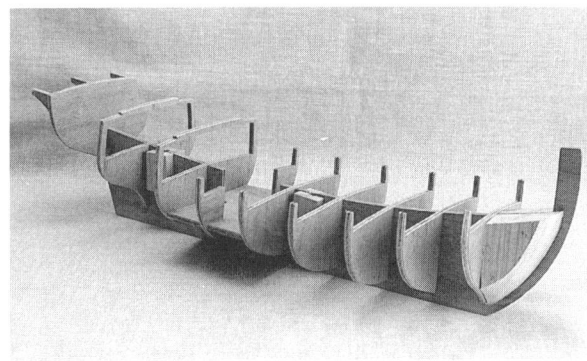

Fig. 6.1 The basic framework. Align last three frames and chamfer tops to take upper deck. Cut recesses in integral beams for deck supports fitted later.

Fig. 6.2 The single planking starts at deck level and works down five planks then proceeds from the keel upwards.

A 15th-Century Portuguese Caravel

and mizzenmast. This seemed to me to be an operation that should come much later in the proceedings, after finishing the main hull construction. However, I made up the masts as instructed in case I had missed something during my earlier reading of the instructions, but I did not glue them in place. See later in this review for notes on mast making.

The next operation is to plank the deck. Do this before finishing the hull side planking above the deck level and you will have more room to sand the deck (Fig. 6.3). The major part of the deck planking comprises 5 × 1.5mm pine strips which have to be pinned and glued directly to the top edges of the frames. These strips, being pine, suffered from a degree of bend and twist and needed some gentle persuasion to fix in place accurately. I found that by using a black marker pen on one edge of each plank, a reasonable representation of caulking was attained when the planks were assembled edge-to-edge and sanded smooth. I soon found that masts got in the way and I removed them for easier working. Plank half the deck first, then cut half the apertures for the hold and the masts. This leaves starting space for cutting the other half after the deck planking has been completed. Note too, that at this stage of the proceedings, the planking can only be done so far towards the sides of the hull due to the frame extensions.

The bulwarks and the remainder of the side planking above the main deck level can now be finished off (Fig. 6.4). This calls for a bit of pre-bending in the bow area. I found that this was quite easily done using the thumb and the two first fingers to apply gentle pressure to the planking strips (Fig. 6.5). Several applications along the strip soon produce the required curve. This is not a procedure that can be applied to all sections and all types of wood, but the strips provided in this kit do lend themselves to the method. Practise a little first on a spare strip remembering that it is all about balancing the degree of pressure with the distance between the two fingers.

The fitting of the planks is edge-to-edge work and needs to be fairly accurately done to keep it in line with its neighbour. Superglue over a length of about 4cm at a time, starting at the stem, worked very well. The planks may be clipped or pinned to the tops of the frames, but not glued, since these parts of the frames have to be removed when the edge-to-edge adhesive has thoroughly cured. The deck planking can then be completed.

The stern panel planking needs a little thought before cutting the strips to length. The side planking overlaps the panel and the strips have to be cut with both angles and bevels at each end to fit snugly inside the side planking (Fig. 6.6). This is not too difficult once you realise what has to be done, but something a newcomer to model boat building might initially overlook.

Fig. 6.4 Decks finished and bulwarks planked. The bow end has a rather severe curve.

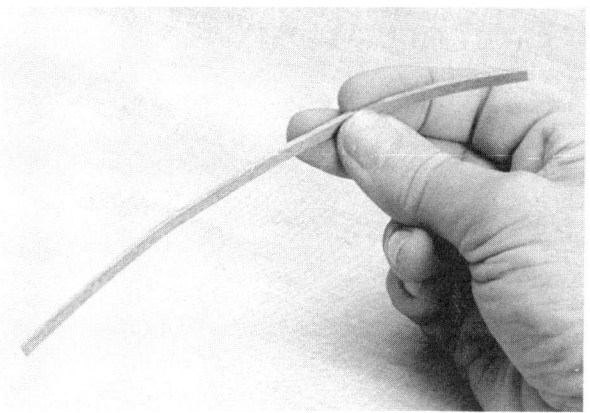

Fig. 6.5 The strips in the kit lend themselves to the thumb and fingers method.

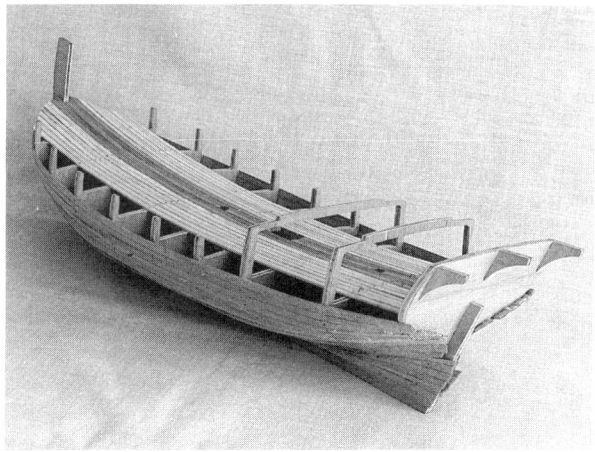

Fig. 6.3 Planking the deck. Note centre planks are darker wood.

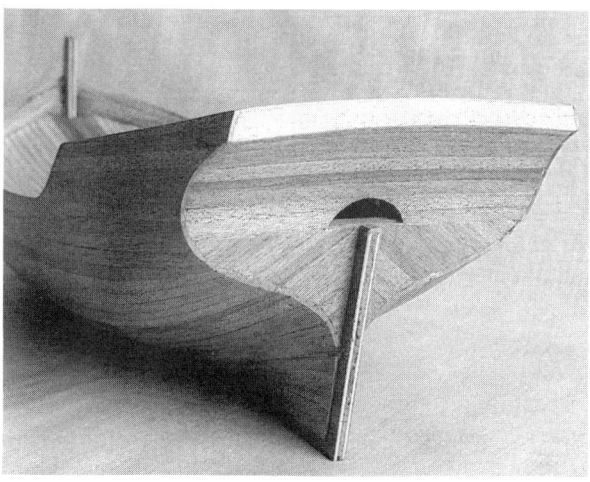

Fig. 6.6 The stern planking sits inside the side planking. The aperture is for later fitting of the tiller.

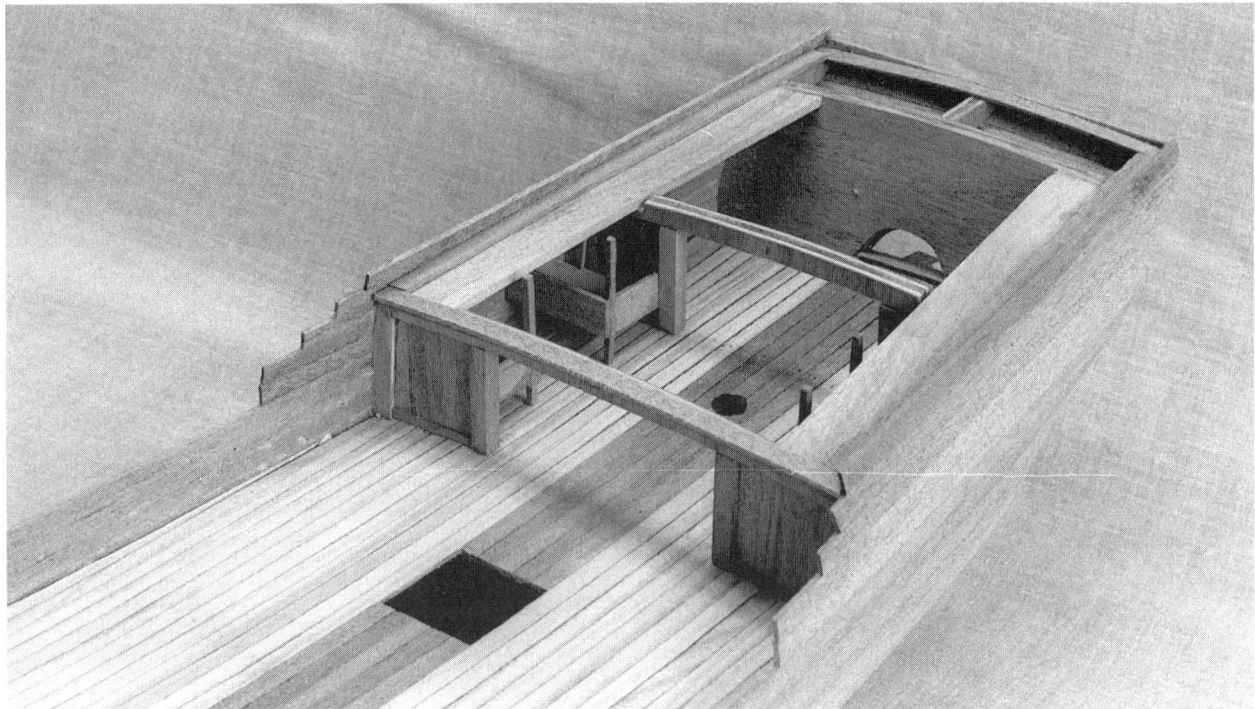

Fig. 6.7 Four berths assembled and fitted prior to planking the upper deck.

The four berths should be made up and fitted in place under the upper deck (Fig. 6.7), and the deck itself then planked. This completes the basic hull construction and the model is now ready for the first rubbing down. **Make sure that you take all of the pins out first!** A cabinet-maker's scraper is an ideal tool to get a basic even surface before using abrasive paper.

A more challenging task is first the trimming and shaping of the top edge of the bulwarks (Fig. 6.8), then the capping to form the gunwales. The latter is done by gluing a strip either side of the top bulwark plank thus making, by lamination, a rail nominally 5.5mm wide. This has to be started at the stem, continued along the sides of the main deck, then swept up through a fairly tight curve to a point at least 16mm above the surface of the afterdeck (Fig. 6.9). Almost certainly you will find it much easier to apply the strips in two parts, making the join just forward of the start of the upswept curve. Thorough soaking in hot water then the careful application of the thumb and two finger method described earlier will form the bend required. Superglue gel is probably the best adhesive to use; applied in relatively short lengths, the alignment of the strips is readily attained. Careful filing and sanding provides a continuous flat top all the way along.

Fitting out

The fittings content of the kit is really a series of packets each containing those pre-cut materials needed to make up the various deck-mounted units (Figs 6.10, 6.11 and 6.12). Hatches, bitts and windlass are all nice little projects in themselves. The two ladders are a bit more

Fig. 6.8 The upper deck in place, edges trimmed to shape and the planking rubbed down.

Fig. 6.9 Gunwale capping and rubbing strakes in place. Note capping protrudes above upper deck to form front of balustrading.

fiddly, the secret being to ensure that all the step pieces are exactly the same length before attempting assembly.

This is also the right time to fit all the rigging hooks to the deck while there is uncluttered access for the drill;

Fig. 6.10 Hatches and ladders with mast partners and barrel.

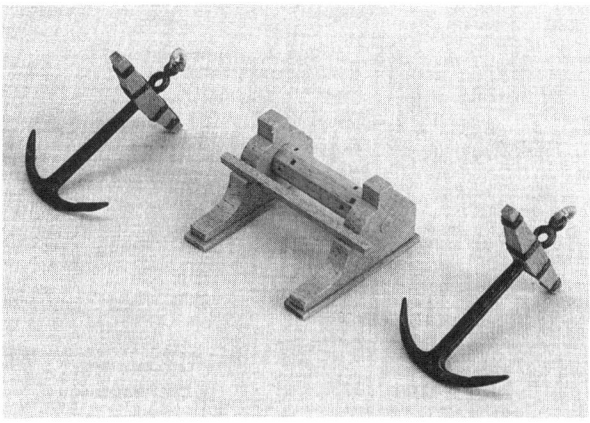

Fig. 6.11 Windlass and anchors. Rope puddening around anchor rings and square holes in windlass barrel add to the quality of the finished model.

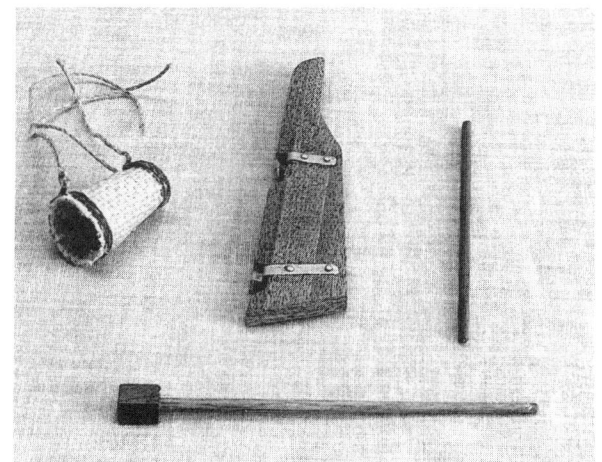

Fig. 6.12 The crow's nest and rudder.

the drawings clearly show where they all go.

The gudgeon part of the rudder hinges should be fitted to the stern post. They have to be cut so as not to extend on to the hull planking.

Finally, the balustrading around the afterdeck has to be built. This is not the formidable task you may at first envisage provided that you are methodical in your approach. Drill a small hole for each of the posts bearing in mind that while they are perpendicular in one plane, in the other they follow the tumblehome of the hull. The tang of a small file pressed into each hole will provide a snug fit for the square sectioned material of the posts which, cut a little overlength, can then be glued in place and left to harden off. The bottom rails can then be fitted parallel to the deck using a couple of spacing pieces made from scrap. The structure is now largely self-supporting and the middle and top rails can follow in sequence. When the adhesive has properly dried out, the tops of the posts can be gently trimmed level with the top rails. It only remains to fit a capping strip all round to finish off the job (Fig. 6.13). The finish to be applied to the hull is largely a matter of personal choice. I chose to use matt acrylic varnish for the decks and a satin finish for the exterior surfaces of the hull. The completed hull is shown in Fig. 6.14.

Before putting the hull to one side, consult the drawings and position as many of the deck-fitted eyebolts as possible. Do this after varnishing to avoid blocking up the apertures.

The stand

A pack of materials is provided to make a stand and a brief sketch outlines the structure on one of the plan

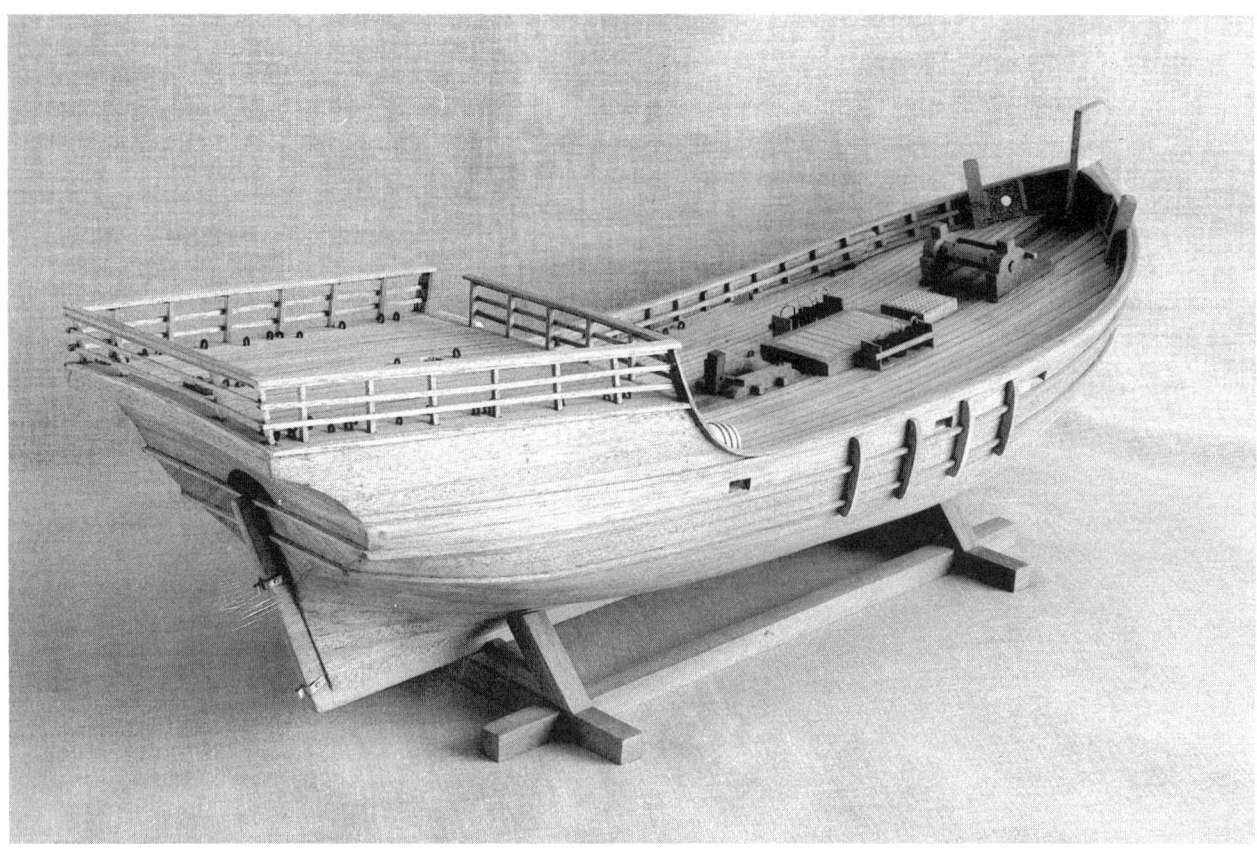

Fig. 6.13 The completed balustrading. Note also the rudder hinges in place on the stern post.

Fig. 6.14 The hull completely fitted out with hawse holes and scuppers cut.

sheets. The assembly is attained largely by cross-halving joints and needs a bit of careful marking out. The actual hull support pieces I set up at 45 degrees but the upper ends have to be shaped by trial and error with the hull sitting squarely in the slots for the keel. Artenaval has given more than a little thought to the stand – it has some character and is in keeping with the period of the model (Fig. 6.15).

A 15th-Century Portuguese Caravel

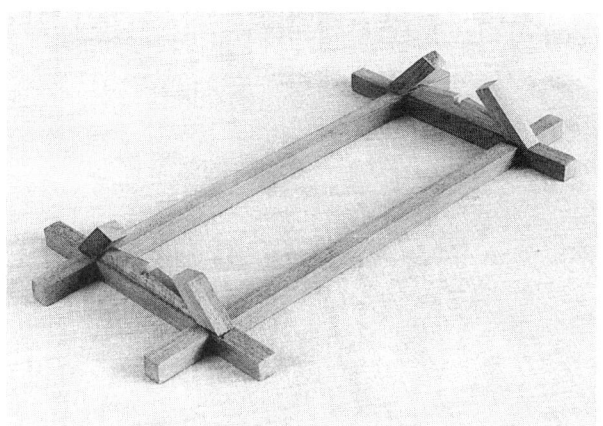

Fig. 6.15 The stand locates the keel and supports the underside of the hull.

The masts and spars

The three masts are simple poles, slightly tapered with a square-sectioned head applied separately (Fig. 6.16). The tapering may be done by filing to first square, then octagonal section, followed by spinning and sanding in an electric drill. Don't forget to finally sand longitudinally with the grain without spinning. The mast heads, having been drilled to simulate the rigging sheaves, should be dowelled and glued to the top of the masts. Each assembly is completed by the addition of cleats, the positions of which can be measured from the drawings. The masts may now be stepped into the hull. Note that the foremast rakes forward by about five degrees.

The tapering of the lateen spars may be done in a similar manner to the masts. However, because they are long and spindly, it is not advisable to spin them in the electric drill, but finish them totally by filing and longitudinal sanding. Each spar is an assembly of two pieces, bound together in four places (also Fig. 6.16).

The sails

The seam lines have been pre-printed on the sail material and each sail should be marked out keeping them in the vertical plane. Allow sufficient material all round to provide a double-folded hem 2mm wide which should be first tacked, then either hand or machine sewn. A boltrope has to be stitched on all edges of the sails.

Rigging

Three sizes of rigging thread are provided and, to make the model look more authentic, the thickest thread, used exclusively for the standing rigging, should be dyed black or very dark brown. The other two sizes should be coloured to a natural or tan shade.

The rigging is quite straightforward, just carefully study the listing of blocks, the names of each line and where it belays and all will be revealed. I found it easier to do the standing rigging first before setting up the spars. This comprises the shrouds and the standing tackle at deck level, no deadeyes, and more to the point, no ratlines! (Fig. 6.17).

The sails should be laced to their respective spars before rigging to the mast. Once again the excellent sketches provided in the kit show the correct lacing and the styles of lashings and knots that should be used. Add blocks where possible before rigging the spars to the masts it saves a lot of hassle later on.

Figs. 6.18 and 6.19 show some of the deck detail before putting up the sails and Fig. 6.20 the hanging and rigging of the rudder.

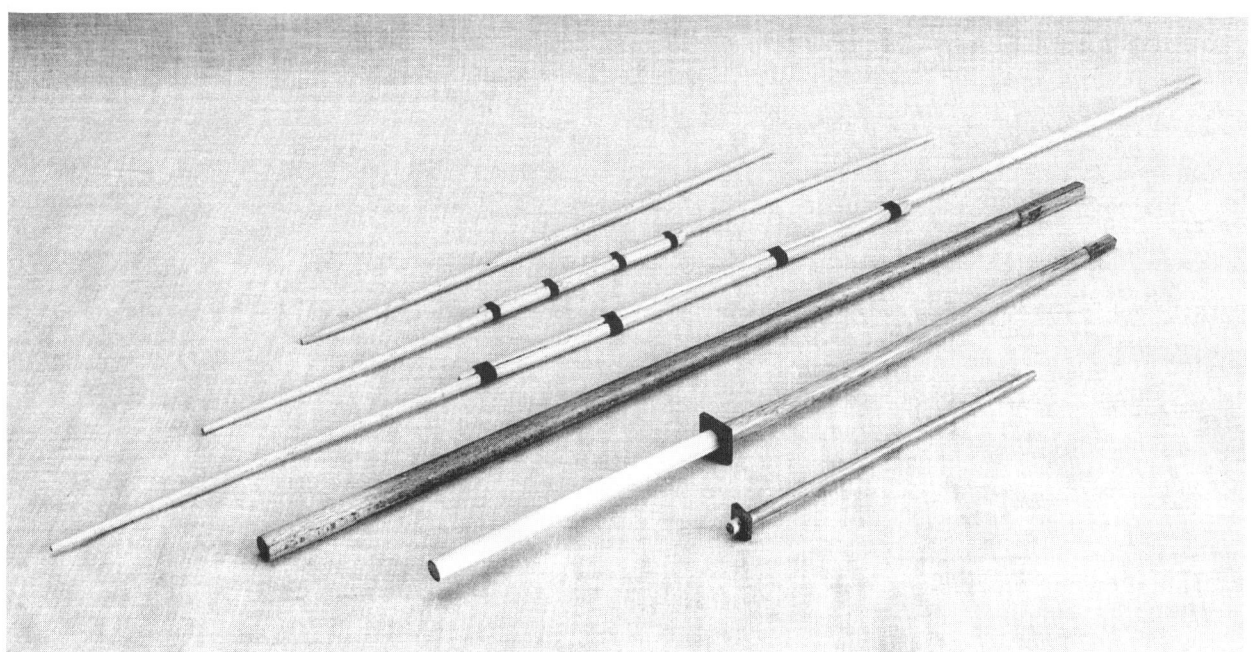

Fig. 6.16 The three masts and lateen spars.

Fig. 6.17 The standing rigging.

Fig. 6.18 The anchors rigged. The two handspikes for the windlass are made from scrap material.

Fig. 6.19 A view 'midships. Note the steps down to the hold and the rope handles on the buckets.

Fig. 6.20 The rudder in place. The tiller passes through the hole in the stern.

The jeers, halliards, vangs etc. can then be set up to position each spar in its correct attitude. Don't tie anything off permanently until you are happy that everything looks right to the drawing. Remember to place a coil of rope at the termination of each line to complete a relatively simple rigging job.

Conclusions

I really was quite impressed with this kit from Artenaval. It is certainly a project that an enthusiastic and dedicated beginner could tackle, but at the same time it also has something to offer the more experienced modeller. You get the definite feeling that the kit has been put together by someone who knows about modelmaking.

A newcomer to model boats often has to work hard to gain the support, or at least the tolerance, of other family members. Dyeing thread in the kitchen is not an activity that is viewed with much enthusiasm, so suitably coloured thread would have been a great asset to the kit.

The drawings were excellent and the English instructions clear and concise. The materials were generally of good standard and everything was quite professionally presented. It made a very pleasant change to make something a bit different and I reckon you get a very good looking craft for about one hundred hours of enjoyable work. It must be considered good value.

CHAPTER 7

The Three-Masted Schooner
Sir Winston Churchill

The *Sir Winston Churchill* was built in Hessle on the River Humber in 1965 for the Sail Training Association. It carries a permanent crew of ten or eleven officers who care for, and train, up to forty young people in the arts of seamanship. A regular participant in the Tall Ships race, her graceful lines are always a pleasure to see. The schooner has a sail area of 817 sq.metres and also carries a 240HP engine.

The Kit

Distributed by Amerang in the United Kingdom, Billing come up to their usual good standard in this kit which produces a 1:75 scale model measuring 635mm long and 515mm high. All sheet parts are well and accurately pressed and virtually no knife work is needed to separate the parts from their respective sheets. There is a wealth of brass parts, two frames of plastic mouldings for deck fittings and etched brass sheets for handrails, portholes, etc. The double-sided drawing sheet is clear in all detail and clearly shows belaying points for the rigging. The multilingual instruction manual is somewhat basic, but adequate. The line drawings contained in it are fine, but I have to say that the manual would have been much improved if the clarity of the photographs had been better. The instructions also need to be a little more detailed if the model is to be built by a less experienced modeller.

Building the hull

As with many Billing kits, the hull is built in two halves which are joined together down the centreline after planking. The central keel is pinned down to a building board and the frames assembled to it in positions clearly marked. Unless you particularly want to sail the finished model and have reason to remove the middle of the frames, my strong recommendation would be that you leave them in place – in fact, ultimately I went so far as to glue them back in position. The reason for this is that the middle pieces give a much stronger frame for the planking operation. I started off as advised in the manual, but broke two frames when applying the fifth and sixth planks. I quickly salvaged the centre pieces from the waste bin! The deck locates on, and is glued to, the tops of the frames which stiffens the whole assembly.

Before commencing the planking operation, the edges of the frames have to be bevelled to follow the curve of the hull so that each plank sits completely across the thickness of each frame. You need to take particular care with those parts of the frames that stand above deck level in order not to break them off.

The top edge of the first plank is fixed at deck level and should be pinned at each frame (Fig. 7.1). When this plank was glued in position, I added the three upper planks to overcome the vulnerability of those ends of frames that protruded above the deck before continuing on down to the bottom of the keel. I found no reason to steam or soak the planks before bending, each followed the previous edge right down to the bottom and only one stealer was found necessary – just about level with the top of the rudder position (Fig. 7.2).

The first sanding of the planks and the first coat of primer is best done before putting the two halves of the hull together. This bringing together is a delicate operation to say the least, but provided that you kept everything flat and square during the frame assembly and planking, the accuracy of the pressed parts leads to a fairly good mating up of the two pieces (Fig. 7.3). Even so, I would recommend that the alignment is based at deck level, with any minor discrepancies around the keel where they are better corrected.

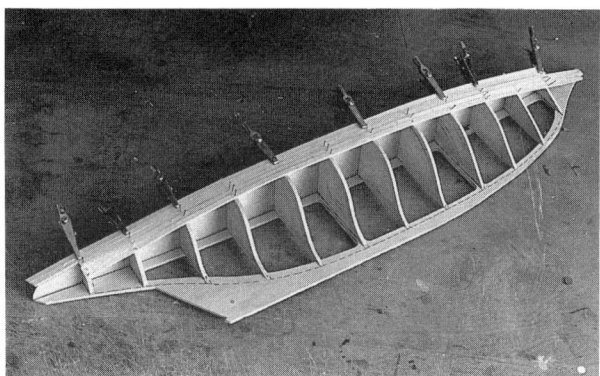

Fig. 7.1 The first four planks on the frame.

Fig. 7.2 The port side planking complete.

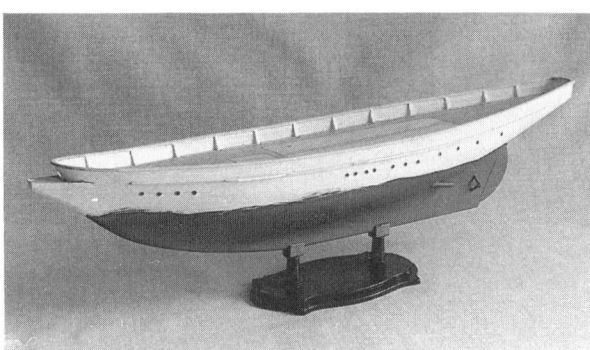

Fig. 7.3 The basic hull, primed and mounted on the stand.

This is the ideal time to make the stand – it will become most useful as the construction proceeds.

The next step is to assemble the gunwales at stern and prow. The shapes from the pressed sheet were not quite right for the best seating, very small deviations in the building process can make quite a difference. I am only talking about 0.5mm but it was worth cutting further parts from scrap material to get the joints absolutely right. Once they have been satisfactorily fitted and the glue set, the edges can be trimmed to shape and the rails fitted – a combination of pressed parts fore and aft and strip material along the sides. Cyanoacrylate is by far the best solution to getting these on, and allows you to

The Three-Masted Schooner *Sir Winston Churchill*

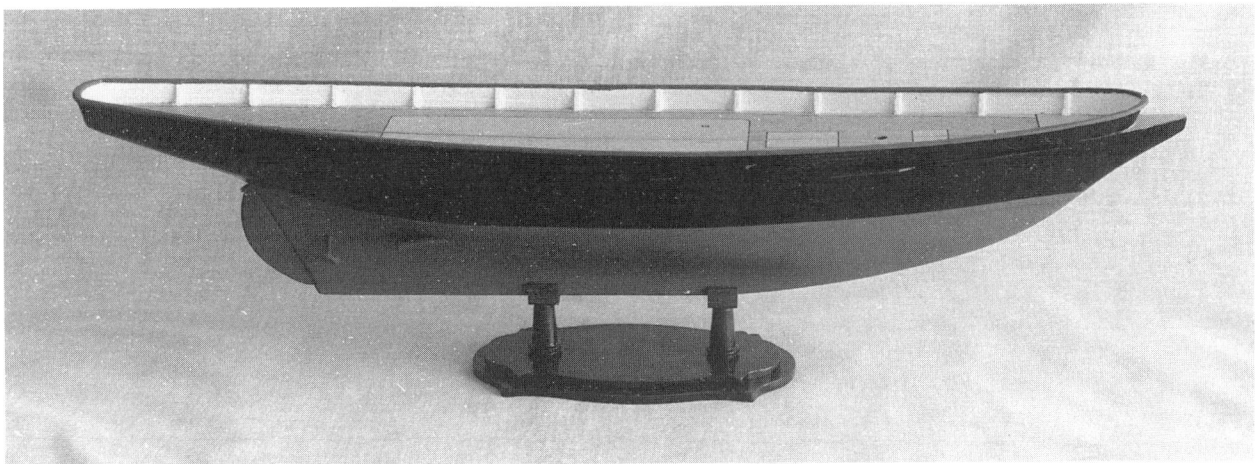

Fig. 7.4 The finished bottom end, decked and railed.

induce the sideways bend into the strip more easily as you work your way round. The protruding part of the frames may now be tapered to match the width of the rails and the channels glued in place.

The final sanding of the hull planking and the drilling and fitting of the port holes in preparation for painting can now be done (Fig. 7.4). I chose to use acrylic paints throughout, mainly due to the convenience of being able to wash the brushes out in water.

The deck fittings

The main cabin, skylight and companionways are fabricated from pre-shaped and pre-cut wooden parts (Fig. 7.5) enhanced with details from the plastic frames supplied in the kit (Fig. 7.6). The winch is a combination of plastic and turned brass pieces. All ventilators are of brass and, as such, need to be painted before assembly. In fact, the majority of the deck fittings need to be

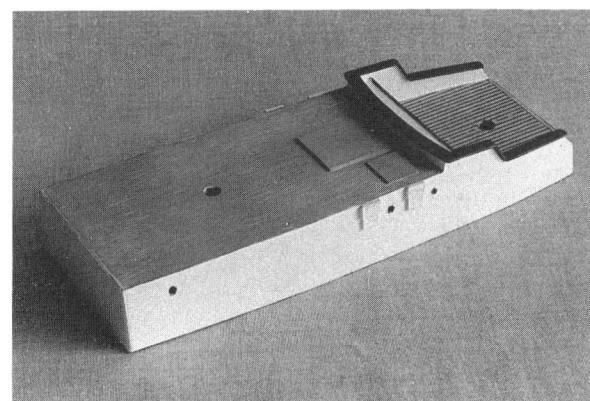

Fig. 7.5 The main cabin shell.

looked at carefully in order to assemble and paint in the right order (Fig. 7.7). Before assembling any of these parts to the deck (Fig. 7.8), it is advisable to fit the bollards, cleats and eyebolts. Particular care should be

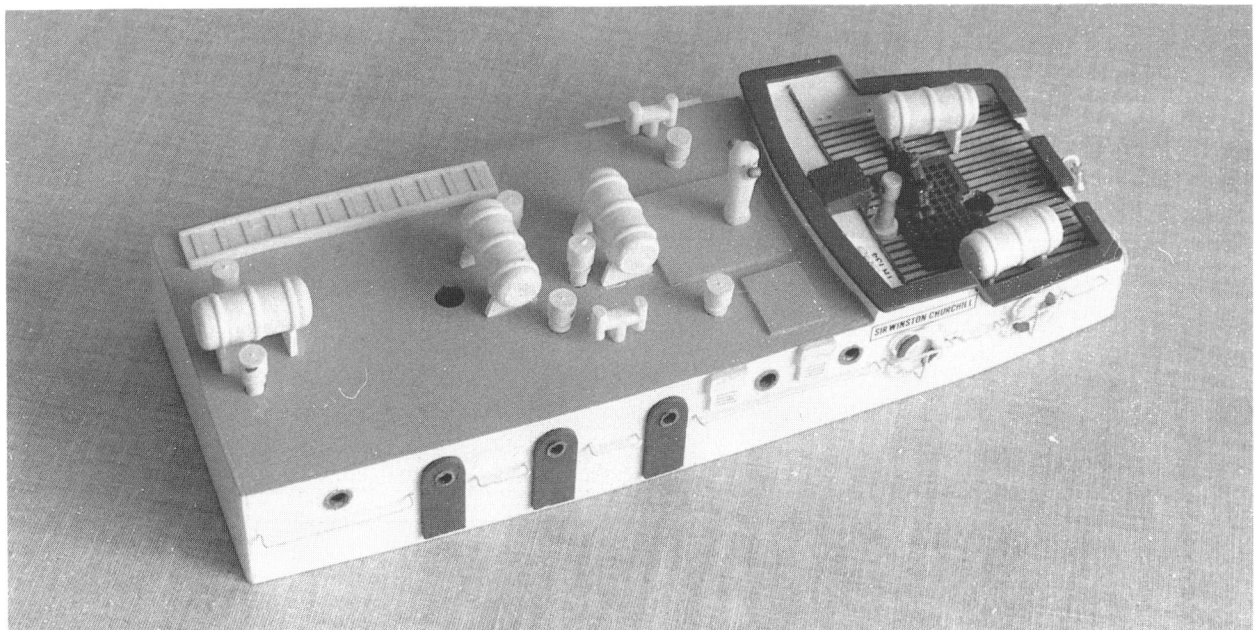

Fig. 7.6 Fittings, rails and doors complete the cabin.

The Period Ship Handbook 2

Fig. 7.7 A made up hatch and some of the fittings.

taken with the latter to ensure that they are firmly fixed in place in order that they can ultimately take the tightening up of the standing rigging (see also Fig. 7.9).

The masts and spars

Although the top third of each of the three masts needs to be slightly tapered, all spars come ready tapered and require little work to be done on them apart from gentle sanding prior to colouring (Fig. 7.10). Masts should be painted aluminium and all other yards and spars, mahogany.

Fig. 7.8 Cabin and fittings assembled to the deck.

Fig. 7.9 Aft of the cabin. Firmly fix all bollards, cleats and eyebolts.

The Three-Masted Schooner *Sir Winston Churchill*

Fig. 7.10 The three masts.

The two yards on the foremast both have footropes which run through fine eyebolts let into the underside of the yards. It is as well to add all rigging blocks at this juncture as it makes life much easier than trying to tie them on as you progress through the rigging process later on (Fig. 7.11). Incidentally, it is absolutely essential to drill out each block before tying on — the holes as supplied are not big enough for the sizes of thread provided.

There are a number of eyebolts to be fitted onto yards, masts and spars. Again, these are items that should be put in place before assembling to the hull. Be sure to consult both sides of the drawing to be certain that you have identified them all. Some are for standing rigging and some are for the attaching of even more blocks. This is also a good time to fit the chainplates and turnbuckles.

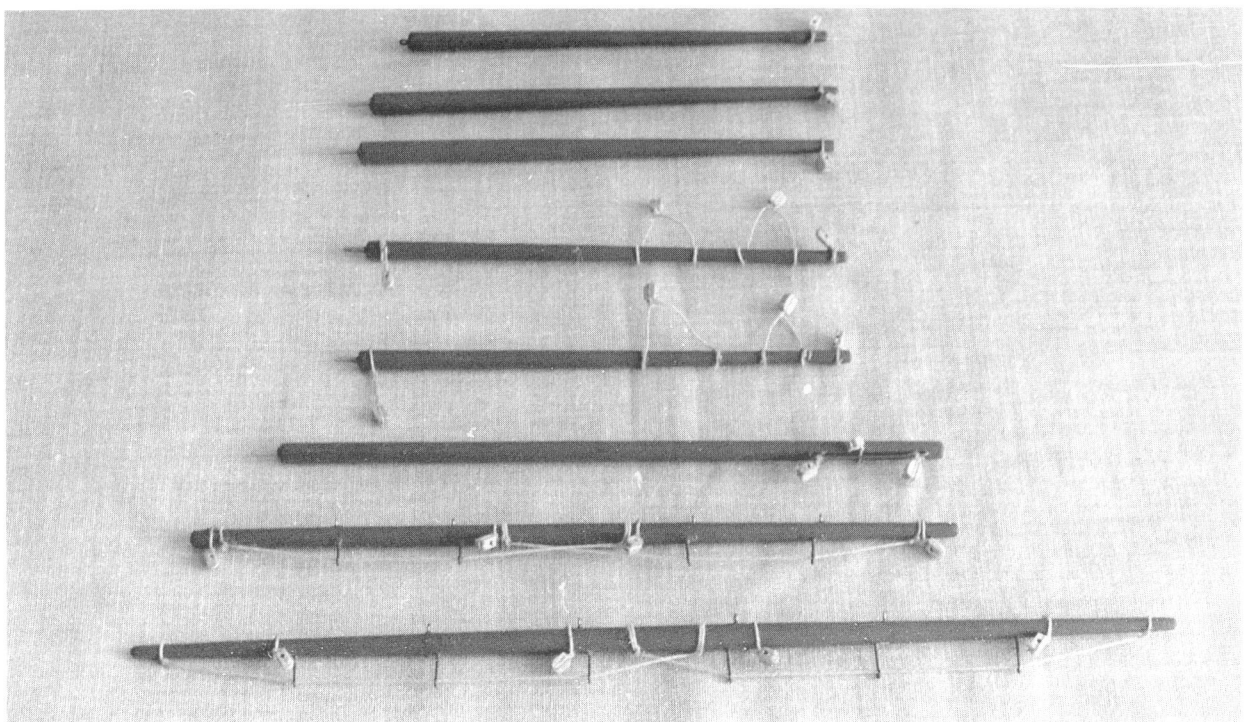

Fig. 7.11 The spars and yards. Note assembled blocks and footropes.

Fig. 7.12 Masts stepped with shrouds and standing rigging.

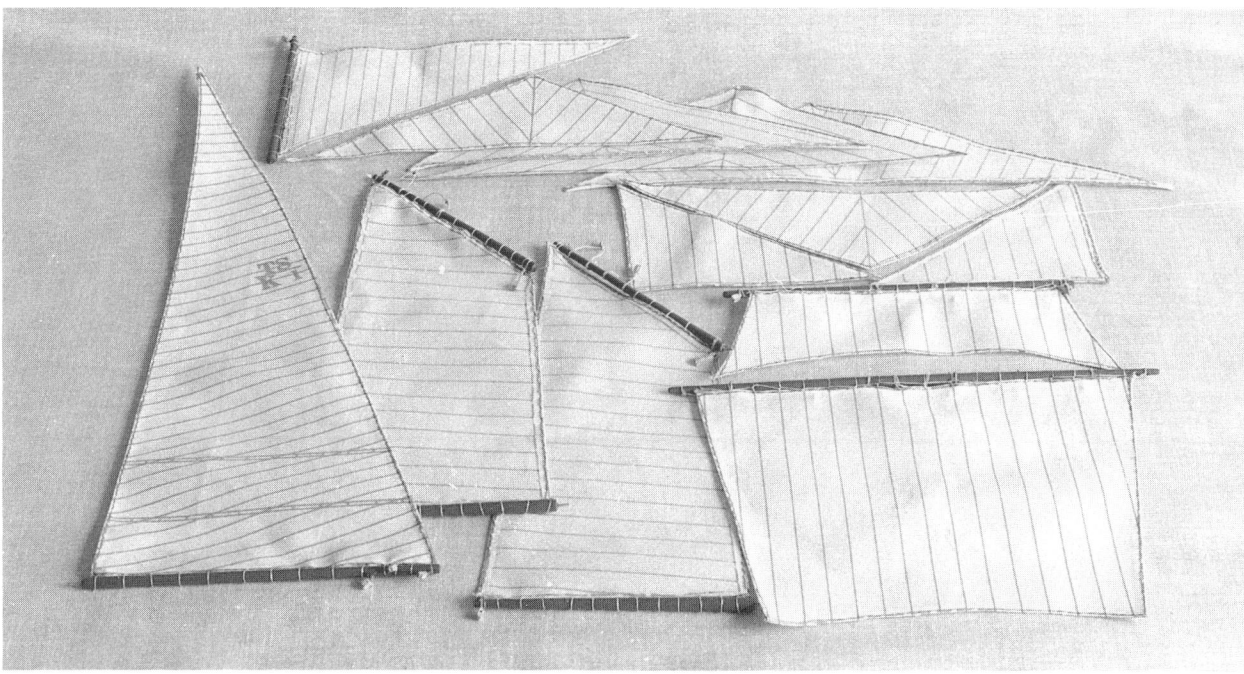

Fig. 7.13 Sails made up and lashed to spars before assembly to masts.

Rigging

The thicker of the two sizes of thread supplied is for the standing rigging and the thinner for running rigging. There is just enough to do the job if you don't go overboard (no pun intended!) with the length allowed for tying and belaying each piece. It helps considerably to stiffen up the thread by pulling it through fingers suitably smeared with PVA adhesive. In addition, a similar application of cyano to the leading end, say 10mm, provides a handy built-in bodkin for threading through blocks.

The belaying diagram and the numbered lines provide an excellent guide through the rigging process and, if you follow the numerical sequence given, you won't go far wrong. The earlier stage is, of course, the standing rigging (Fig. 7.12) and includes the ratlines. Only four flights on this model and each only across three shrouds, so not too much of a headache. Do not be tempted to leave them until later, as things get progressively inaccessible.

It is also wise to make up the sails and lash them to the yards and spars before fixing the woodwork to the masts (Fig. 7.13). Apart from the difficulties of fitting the sails after the spars are in place, there is also the question of getting the angles right and their relative positions on the masts correct. Fitting them as a sub-assembly solves all of these problems. The two square sails on the foremast have buntlines and tacks which may also be attached to advantage before assembly. Similarly, halliards, downhaulers and sheets should be tied to the corners of the triangular sails before hoisting them into place.

The application of the running rigging calls for some pretty intricate work with the forceps, particularly when belaying at the pin rails. Make sure, too, that each line runs straight and true without interfering with those adjacent. This puts a little strain on the eyes as you are working with light tan thread against a similar shade of sail material.

A careful look at the completed model to make sure that you have not left any untrimmed ends is really the final step. Look as well for those odd snippets that may be hiding under the pinrails or the ship's boats, etc. they normally come to light when showing off the model for the first time!

Conclusions

My model was built straight from the box and as instructed in the manual. It made up into an attractive model without any serious difficulty. Apart from a small electric drill, no special tools or equipment were necessary and I would think that most modelmakers would cope quite well. All materials in the kit were of high quality and, apart from being a little let down by the instruction manual photography, I would say that by today's standards, the kit is good value for the money.

CHAPTER 8

A Portuguese Bomb Ship
Lancha Bombardiera 1798

Artenaval have produced this kit for a model of a single masted bomb-vessel used by the Portuguese Navy in the late eighteenth century. The choice of subject comes as a change from the usual listings of sailing warships.

There is some doubt as to the original conception of this type of ship. The use of bomb-ketches at Algiers in 1682 is certainly an early recorded instance of their use. However, it would not be correct to refer to this model as a bomb-ketch. The lateen rig with a square sail on the single mast is not one that I have been able to find among the more common rigging arrangements of the period.

The large mortar in front of the main mast is supplemented by a conventional naval cannon installed in the bow of the vessel. The procedure for using the armament was somewhat crude. Neither the cannon or the mortar had swivelling facilities on this particular vessel, thus the forward rigging would have had to be removed before any engagement, and the line of fire be dependent on the way of the vessel. Such procedures are documented by J. H. Roding in his *Allgemeines Worterbuch der Marine*.

At 1:50 scale, the finished model measures 700mm.

The Kit

The materials provided for building this model are of average quality. The false keel and frames are accurately routered in 5mm ply and need to be separated by fretsawing. The strip materials come straight, although a little on the coarse side. Unusually, blocks and other rigging parts are in metal, finished black, but very crisp and flash free. Sail material, with pre-printed seams is provided together with three different thicknesses of rigging thread, the latter all being in white and in need of dyeing to attain accurate colouring. The four sheets of drawings are extremely well draughted although belaying points for rigging could be better defined. *All* sheets need to be studied in depth in order to properly identify where and how everything goes. This is particularly pertinent to the rigging where one sheet needs to be looked at in conjunction with another when establishing the positions of eyebolts etc. The instructions are multilingual and obviously compiled by an experienced modelmaker.

Building the hull

The hull framework comprises a false keel into which are jointed a series of frames or bulkheads. These are further reinforced by a pair of longitudinal strips which form a honeycomb construction of considerable strength (Fig. 8.1).

To this assembly are added two pairs of bow blocks. It is important to get the blocks the right way round in order to permit the proper bow contours to be attained, so satisfy yourself that all is well before you apply the glue. I found that it was best to glue each pair of blocks together, then carefully mark out the finished shape in three planes. I then roughed off all the surplus timber before permanently fixing them to the basic framework. This made life a lot easier getting down to the final contours around the bows.

The edges of the first few frames, fore and aft, have to be tapered to conform to the lines of the hull and this is best checked with a spare planking strip. It is important that the largest possible seating for the planking across the edge of each frame is attained.

The planking starts at deck level and proceeds downwards towards the keel for five plank widths. The next planking started from the keel and worked upward (Fig. 8.2). When the underside of the fifth plank was reached, planks were laid alternately on the underside of the upper planks and then the upper side of the lower planks until the whole side had been covered. The fore end of each relevant plank should be trimmed to closely fit against the stem post; the rear end should overhang the false keel and last frame for later trimming.

There is quite a severe curve at the bows but, nonetheless, I found that an Amati plank nipper was adequate for the job. The lines of the hull meant that a couple of stealers, fore and aft, were necessary to make life easier.

The pre-shaped stern block was then carefully sized and offered up. A large semi-circular hole to accommodate the swing at the top of the rudder was then marked and cut through the block, noting that the shape was marginally different on the top surface to that on the underside. A series of small holes around the periphery of the semicircle permitted the bulk of the waste material to be pushed out, the final shape being achieved with a half-round file. There is but minimal support for the block on the top edge of the last bulkhead and on the tail of the false keel, so holes drilled to suit, say, five fixing pins are advised to keep the block in place while the glue dries (Fig. 8.3).

The bowsprit was the next feature to be put in place and the deck planked around it, and out from the centre, as far as the false timber heads would allow. It is wise to be careful in the selection of deck planking strips in that I found some variation in thickness and some minimal warping, the former condition not being too easily put to rights once the deck had been laid.

The bulwarks are not so easy to build. This is basically edge-to-edge work and a fair number of mini crocodile clips, or similar devices, are needed to keep the planks in line (Fig. 8.4). The curve at the bows is a steaming

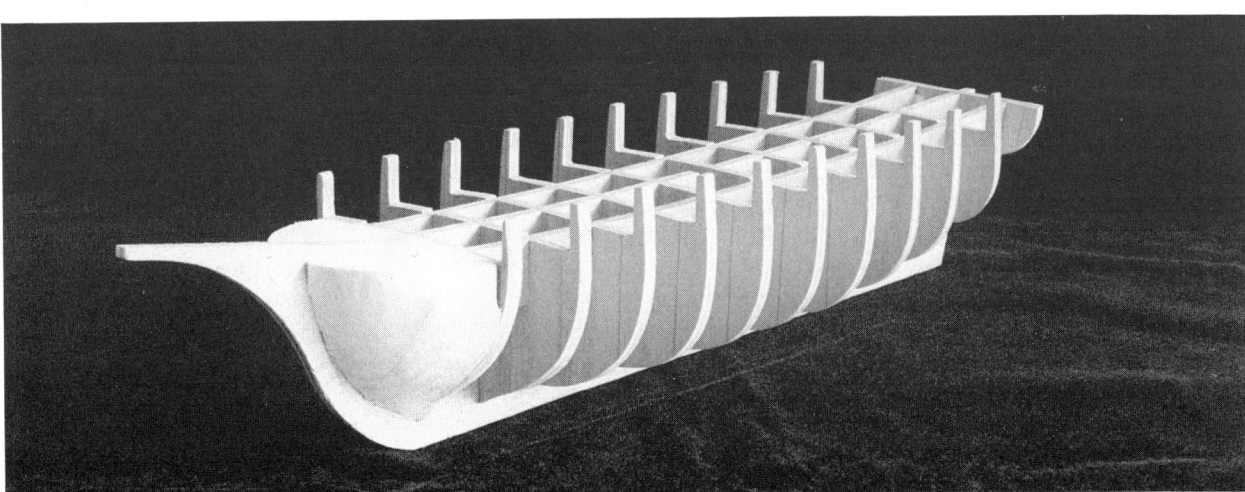

Fig. 8.1 The honeycomb construction provides exceptional strength.

A Portuguese Bomb Ship *Lancha Bombardiera* 1798

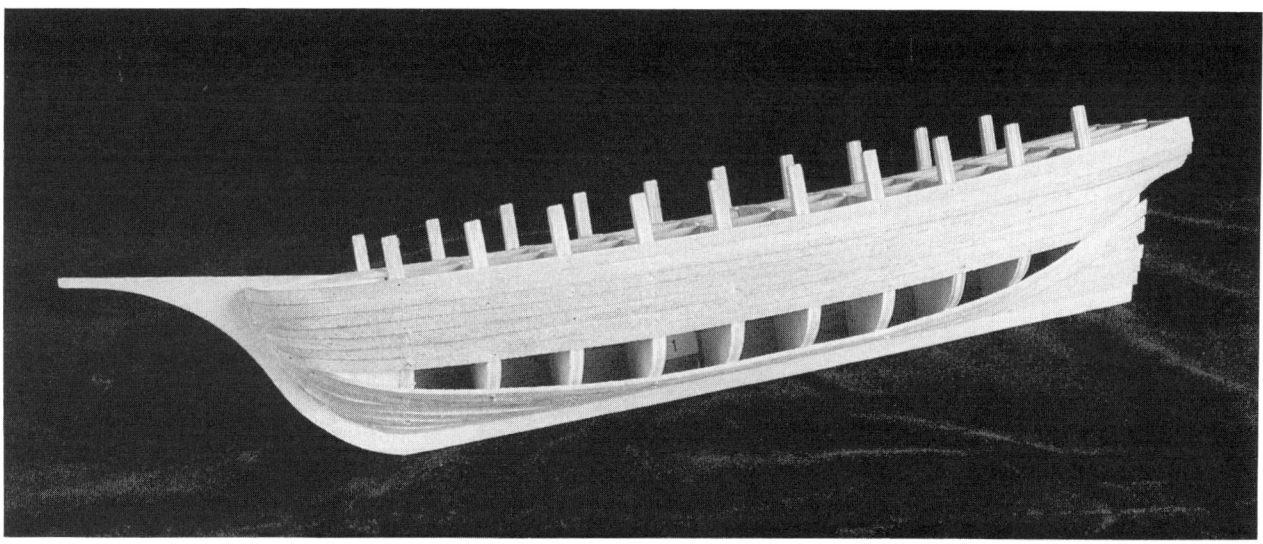

Fig. 8.2 Planking starts at the top for five planks, then from the keel upwards the middle bit is planked alternately from top and bottom.

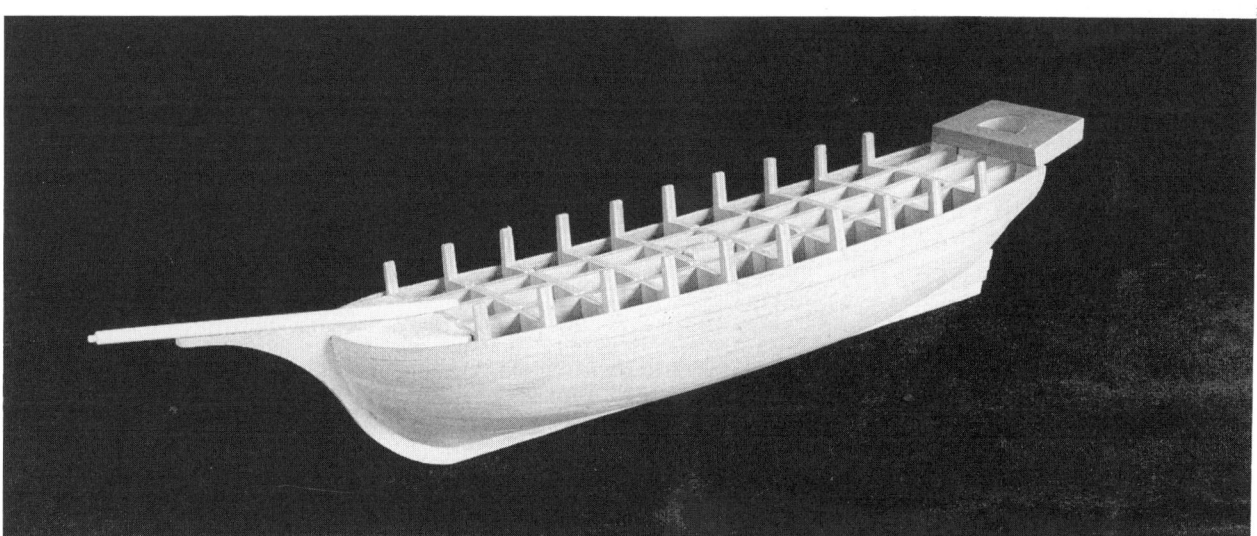

Fig. 8.3 The stern block in place with bowsprit fixed ready for deck planking.

Fig. 8.4 Building the bulwarks.

job, since the plank nipper will leave visible marks on the inside surface. Glue one plank at the time and be sure that the adhesive has fully cured before attempting to set the next plank up. The final longitudinal contour along the top edge of the bulwarks was attained by means of a cardboard template. The false timber heads were then cut off and the deck planking completed.

Attention was then given to the stern. The after side of the last bulkhead has to be planked inside the overhanging main hull planking. The latter is then trimmed off and filed and sanded flush with the stern planking. I missed the implication of this when I first read through the instruction manual, because it would undoubtedly be easier to plank the stern before doing the main planking – another example of how reading the instructions carefully before you start can pay off! The stern panel comprises two pieces; a diecast plate, very flat and crisp, which is mounted on to a wooden back-up piece that has to be filed to exactly the same shape. The two pieces, once assembled together with adhesive are then glued to the stern (Fig. 8.5).

The whole hull surface was then scraped and sanded and given a couple of coats of acrylic matt varnish to seal it.

The cap rails were formed by gluing 2mm square strips along the inner and outer edges of the bulwarks, then sanding the top surfaces to match. The waterways were laid at the junction of deck and bulwarks, and finally the timberheads were simulated with further pieces of 2mm square strip fitted between waterways and the underside of the cap rails (Fig. 8.6). Sections of the cap rail and bulwarks were removable to facilitate the use of oars. Cuts across the rails and on the bulwark sides were made to indicate these positions. The scuppers were also cut at this stage of the proceedings.

The structure at the prow of the ship (Fig. 8.7), so often the cause of great heartache, is fairly straightforward. The only deviation that I made from the instructions was in the sequence of assembly. I found that having fitted the trailboards, the upper wale was best fitted next, before adding the head beams. In order that the curves were kept identical, side to side, I also decided to make a sub-assembly of the head beams and their reinforcing strut, port and starboard. When the adhesive was completely set, they were then trimmed to be absolutely the same size. They were then carefully sprung into place and fixed with a touch of superglue. Cheeks, eking and pin racks were then made up together with the rudder and tiller to complete the basic hull structure.

The stand

I decided that I would again deviate from the instruction manual and build the stand at this stage of the project, on the basis that it would be useful to have somewhere

Fig. 8.5 The primed stern plate and planking.

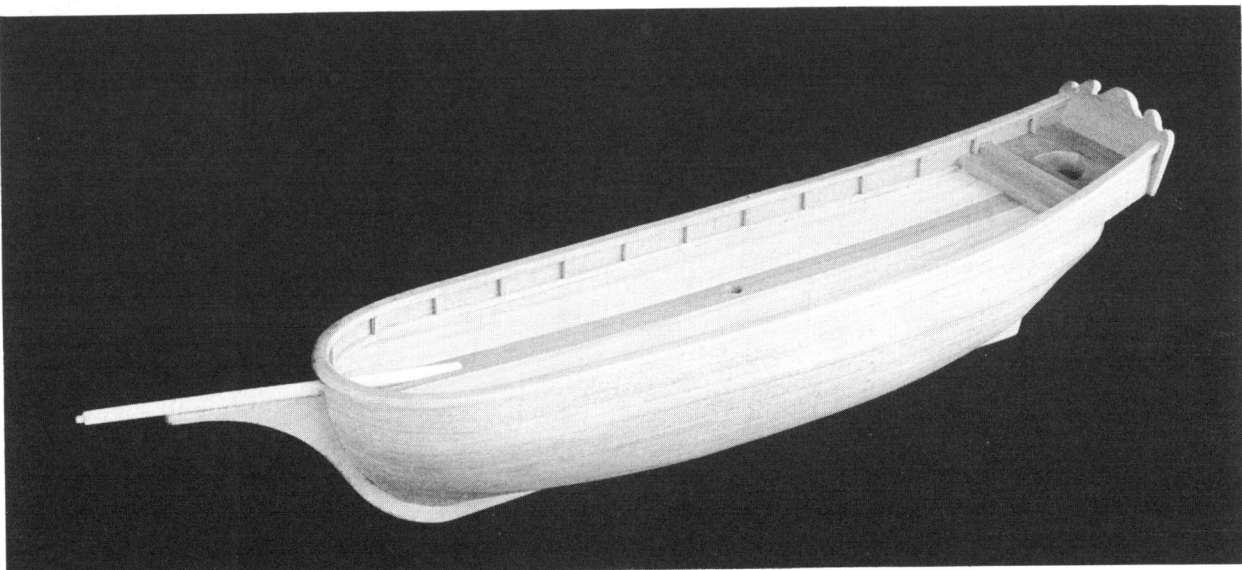

Fig. 8.6 Cap rails and waterways fitted.

A Portuguese Bomb Ship *Lancha Bombardiera* 1798

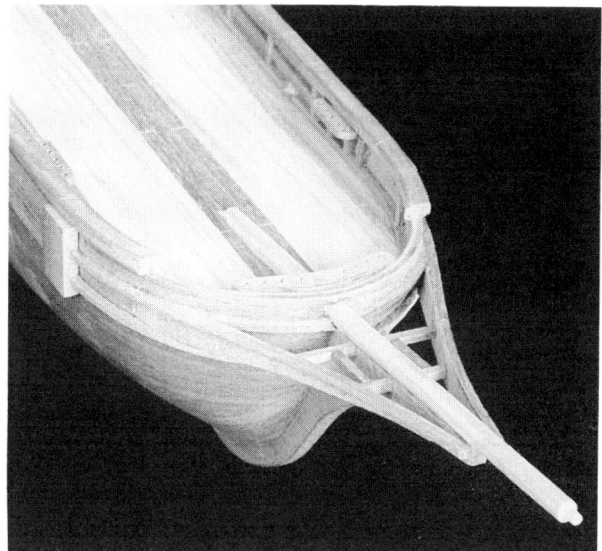

Fig. 8.7 The prow structure, trailboards and head beams.

to rest the model for fitting out.

The stand construction is entirely from 10mm square section material. The base used four cross-halving joints for rigid assembly, careful marking out being the order of the day to get everything square. The bottoms of the four hull support pieces were given a 45-degree seating then, by trial and error, the upper end gradually trimmed and cut to a shape that fitted snug against the underside of the hull.

The design of the stand is entirely functional, looks good, and does not take the eye away from the finished model. Artenaval are to be commended for including the materials for this important item in their kit.

Painting

The stand enables the model to be seated in a true position to permit the marking of the waterline. This runs from the top of the rudder blade, below which the hull should be painted white. I chose to use Barley White vinyl matt emulsion, applying four coats with a good rub down after the first three. In fact, there was not much left on after the first rub down, the initial coat acting mainly as a grain filler.

The areas between the wales and up to the underside of the cap rails was painted matt dark green. All natural wood surfaces were matt varnished. The stern plate was given a couple of coats of matt white all over before adding details in gold, red and blue as instructed. The finer details were picked out with an almost dry brush so that paint did not fill in the crevices. All paints and varnish used were acrylic, lending themselves to easier brush cleaning (Fig. 8.8).

Fitting out

There are a number of items that comprise deck and other fittings, each being a mini-project in itself (Fig. 8.9). For the most part, the instructions and drawings give adequate guidance to the construction of each part and little further comment is required.

However, a couple of problems did arise. First, assuming that the brass wire chainplates link directly to the rings integral with the deadeyes, then the wire provided is too large in diameter. Do not attempt to open out the inside diameter of the ring, because almost certainly it will break up. The solution is to use a smaller gauge of wire.

Fig. 8.8 The painted hull resting on the stand (included in the kit).

The Period Ship Handbook 2

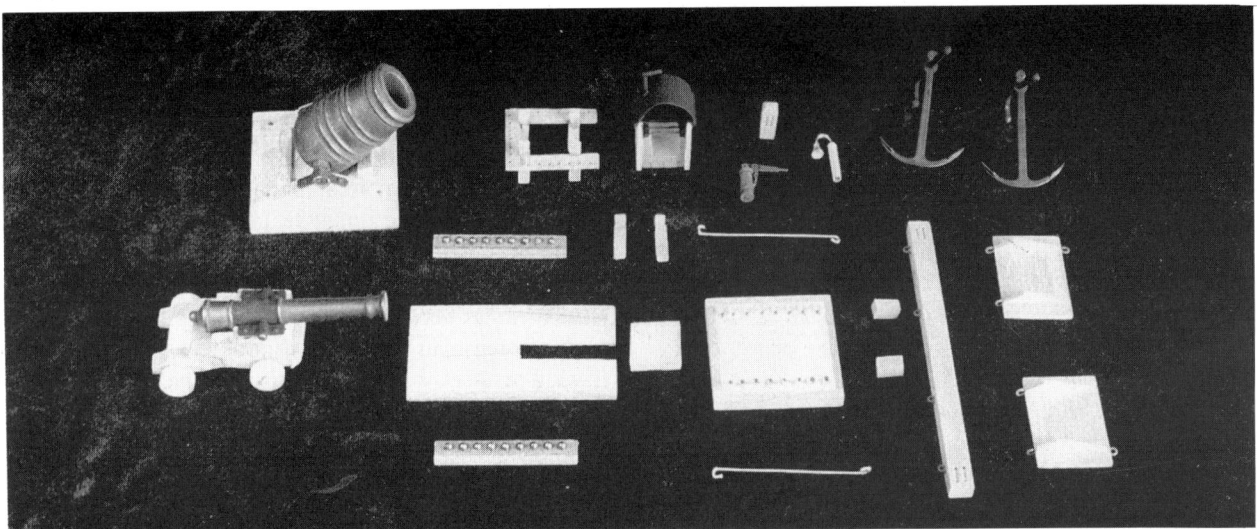

Fig 8.9 The made up fittings

Secondly, when making up the parts for the bombard, the instructions referred to the perspectives plan. Unfortunately, that drawing shows no detail of the bombard, so all information regarding this item had to be gleaned from the conventional plan view, which was very basic in detail. As a result, I never did find out what the four brass strips in the pack containing the bombard parts were for.

The naval cannon was, in contrast, very well depicted both on the main drawings and in perspective. This resulted in a very good looking piece of equipment, several of the individual parts being pre-shaped to supplement an extremely well-formed metal barrel authentically blackened.

The two racks of cannon balls are simple enough in their construction, two wooden strips with a series of nine holes to house the balls. However, a word of warning, to get nine holes in a dead straight line is something not to be taken lightly. One hole out of true stands out like a sore thumb. I used a pointed scriber to centre punch each hole position, using a steel rule to guide the position of the point. Then I chose to drill the holes with a 2mm dia. drill rather than 3mm as suggested in the instructions. This permits a certain amount of adjustment if necessary if one hole is slightly out of alignment. The best check is to lay a ball on each hole and eyeball down the line.

The cannon protection shields, the cathead beam, galley and pump all went together without difficulty.

The ship's bell required drilling to permit fixing. I made several attempts to drill across the lug at the top of the bell but the problems of holding soon led me to

Fig. 8.10 The hull fitted out.

drilling, more successfully, down through the centre instead. A spot of saliva, to lubricate the drill, helps to get through the fairly hard and abrasive diecasting and avoids taking the edge off the drill. All parts are shown assembled to the hull in Fig. 8.10.

The masts and spars

The dowel material provided for making these items was in pine or similar softwood. It was unfortunate that the grain in a couple of the pieces was such that when carrying out the tapering operations, a distinct bend was induced. These pieces had to be replaced from my scrap box.

The construction of the jib and its relevant caps was straightforward, although drilling the caps to fit bowsprit and jib needs sharp drills and careful marking out to avoid splitting the wood.

Again, the mast and topmast presented no problems, just remember not to assemble the truck to the topmast before making up and assembling the crosstrees, trestletrees and cap. A dry run with the fit of these latter parts was carried out to ensure correct alignments and squareness.

The very pale appearance of the timber needed darkening up a bit before painting the areas indicated with white acrylic.

Before stepping the mast and attaching the jib to the bowsprit, the rigging drawings were studied to identify the positions of eyes for subsequent rigging. The drilling associated with these eyes is definitely better done off the boat, so the drawings were studied well to ensure none got overlooked. Don't miss the cleat on the port side of the bitt just aft of the mast! There are also blocks to be attached to the main yard and lateen spar.

The sails and rigging

The first job that needed to be done was to colour the rigging thread. The thread for the standing rigging should be dyed either black or dark brown, the remainder for the running rigging should be tan coloured. You could, at a pinch, leave it as supplied, but it is a bit on the white side.

All thread, having been cut to the length required for the particular part of the rigging concerned, should then be pulled through fingers sparingly coated with white PVA adhesive. This helps not only to stiffen it and allow it to hang realistically, but also smooths down all those little fibrous hairs that catch the dust.

The cannon tackle was set up first while there was still reasonable access to the surrounding deck area. This was followed by the bowsprit and jib-boom rigging (Fig. 8.11), and then the shrouds and backstays (Fig. 8.12).

I am personally not a great lover of sails on static models but, in this case, the model certainly seems to look better with them rigged. The sail material comes with the seams already marked, thus saving quite a bit of work on the sewing machine. The finished outline was marked on the material, ensuring that the seams ran in the right direction. Each sail was then cut out, leaving about 15mm all round the outside for folding and hemming. The material was then dampened and a crease ironed exactly along the finished outline, using an iron heated to the silk or one dot setting. A further crease about 2.5mm outside the first was then introduced and

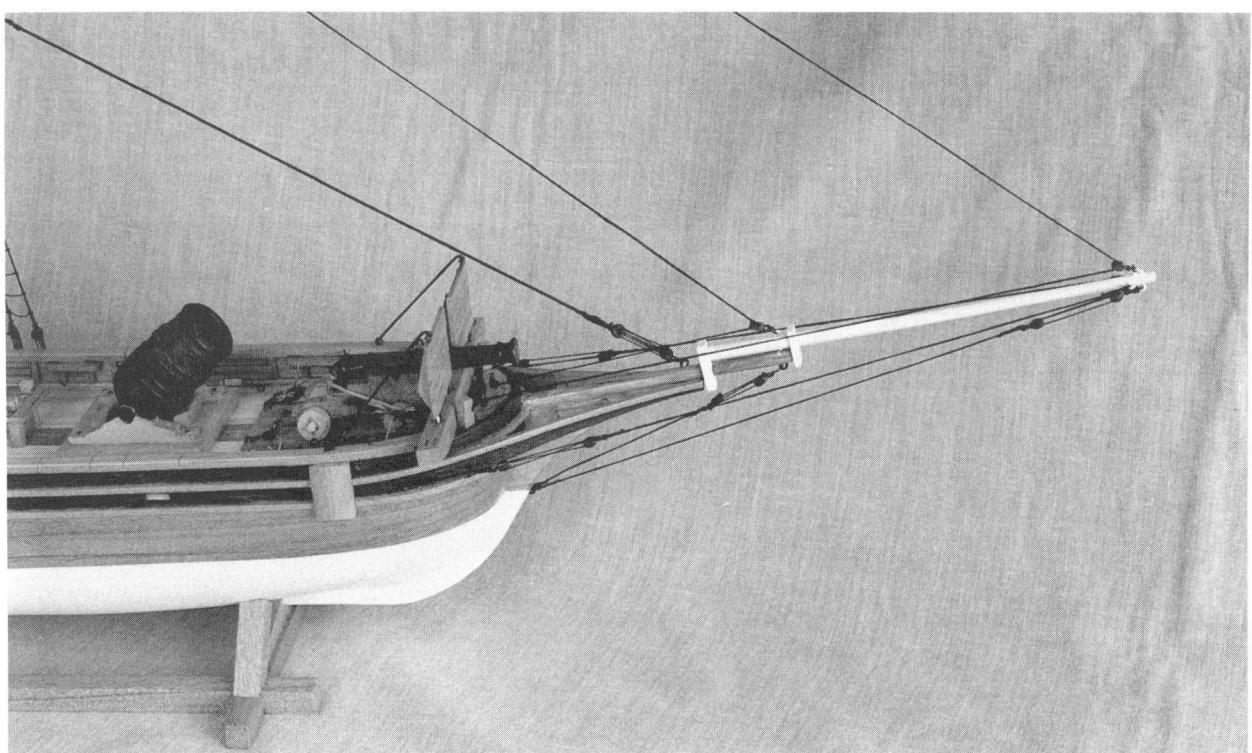

Fig. 8.11 The bowsprit and jib-boom fitting.

The Period Ship Handbook 2

Fig. 8.12 The standing rigging, shrouds and backstays.

Fig. 8.13 The flag flown at the stern. Note also the seams and reef points on the lateen sail.

the residual waste then cut off about 2.5mm outside that. The two creases were then turned in and pressed flat with the iron. According to your prowess with the sewing machine, the hem so formed can then be machined or hand stitched all round. This particular material, when dampened, took the creases very well and seemed to give a better result than that given by conventional tacking stitches. The boltropes were then stitched along the edges of each sail.

The made up sails were then attached to the main yard and lateen spar before rigging these items to the main mast. Again, it was found easier to tie on any blocks necessary on the bench, rather than after assembly to the model.

You have to look very carefully at the drawings to determine the various belaying points, but even so, I found that some were not clearly defined.

The oars

I was not very happy with the oars at all. There were no dimensions given, and just one perspective sketch showing the method of construction. Having made all ten of them, there is no indication as to how, or where, they are stowed on board. For the purposes of showing the deck layout and general fitting out, I have not included them in the accompanying photographs.

Finishing off

Rope coils on deck and hanging from the appropriate belaying points completed the main construction of the model.

Flags are usually a bit of a pain to get hanging right. In this case, I managed a reasonable shape, with a judicious touch of superglue in the right place to hold everything just so and, contrary to my usual practice, I decided to fly it at the stern as shown on the drawings (Fig. 8.13).

You need to leave the model on show for a few days to discover the odd end of untrimmed rigging, or the minute shaving lurking under the mortar. In my case I soon realised that I hadn't rigged the rudder chains!

Conclusions

The overall kit design is very good, providing an extremely strong hull construction. Material quality was average and the information contained on the drawings and in the instructions sometimes a little imprecise. Nevertheless, with care and perseverence, you can produce a very nice model. It is an unusual subject and one that comes as a pleasant departure from the more conventional kit listings.

The whole design has obviously been well researched and the kit put together by someone with a good knowledge of modelmaking techniques. I particularly liked the metal rigging blocks; they were cleanly cast and added a little bit of weight to the rigging which, in turn, helped to attain tautness without too much tension.

Not a kit for the inexperienced, but one that will provide a fair number of hours work for a dedicated and enquiring modelmaker.

CHAPTER 9

The Clinker Built Rowing Boat
Holly

Holly is a clinker built rowing boat of the type seen frequently around the east coast of Ireland since the early 1900s. The original *Holly* was built in 1961 by Joe Redmond Senior and is typical of the design that was imported from Scotland to Greystones, Co. Wicklow at the turn of the century.

The kit for the *Holly*, produced in Ireland by Kish Model Boats, uses the same basic constructional procedures as adopted for the original. It will thus be appreciated that this project does not conform to the usual run-of-the-mill model boat kit format, but is more an extended exercise in miniature carpentry. As such, it is a refreshing change to work to somewhat different rules and disciplines and, right from the time the box was opened, I experienced an eagerness to get started.

The model, at 1:8 scale, measures some 27″ long when finished.

The Kit

The exceptional quality of the timbers supplied was supported by five sheets of working drawings, plus a further drawing for oar construction. A supplementary sheet of eight photographs ensures that, somewhere or other, all stages of building are illustrated.

A plywood base, onto which is built a framed jig for the authentic method of construction, comes with the kit. However, don't expect to find any pre-cut parts. Everything is clearly marked out, but you have to get out the trusty fret saw and coping saw to cut out the ply parts. The actual boat is constructed from Brazilian mahogany and white or red oak.

As I have said, all of the materials are of exceptional quality and this gives an added incentive to give the care and attention that the kit needs to attain the best possible result.

Tools

A fine tenon saw, fret saw, coping saw, paring chisels, screwdriver, light hammer and a modelmaker's plane are essential tools, together with means of producing holes up to 0.50″ diameter. A couple of small G-clamps will also prove useful.

Three different adhesives are recommended; impact, epoxy resin and wood glue and, of course, the usual assortment of abrasive papers will be required.

It is an absolute essential that tools be kept sharp at all times, firstly to do justice to the fine timbers used and secondly, but no less importantly, for safety reasons. Accidents are far more likely with blunt tools.

Building the jig

Before doing anything, I would most strongly recommend that you read through all of the instructions, in sequence, for the entire boat construction, then read them again! I found several points that became clearer during a second reading and, certainly, an insight as to what is to come later helps to better understand the requirements of the earlier stages of building.

Part of the first drawing is taped to the baseboard provided and eight frame guides are pinned square and central across the boat centreline in the positions indicated (Fig. 9.1). I would suggest that the second of each pair of guides is positioned relative to the first, using a piece of the ply from which the frames are cut as a spacer. This will ensure the best snug fit when assembling the frames. Squareness and positional accuracy at this stage will ensure a 'right boat' as construction proceeds.

The transom location and clamp is added to the baseboard in a similar manner, leaving a dovetail clamping strip to be fixed later.

The stem-post clamp requires good accuracy, it being particularly important to get the angles correct (Fig. 9.2). Its relative position to the transom location on the baseboard is important, as this controls the proper holding of the keel assembly during the planking operation.

The keel assembly

The keel is the central and key feature in the construction of the boat and the utmost care should be taken to ensure that it is straight and accurately made with respect to relative stem and transom angles. The distance between these two features on the keel proper is also of paramount importance. The keel is of a laminated construction and care should be exercised to make sure that parts don't move from true position when being clamped up. Thus, it is wise to check constantly that what is drawn and what has been made is consistently accurate.

The angular edges of the transom proper are most important since it is to these surfaces that the stern end

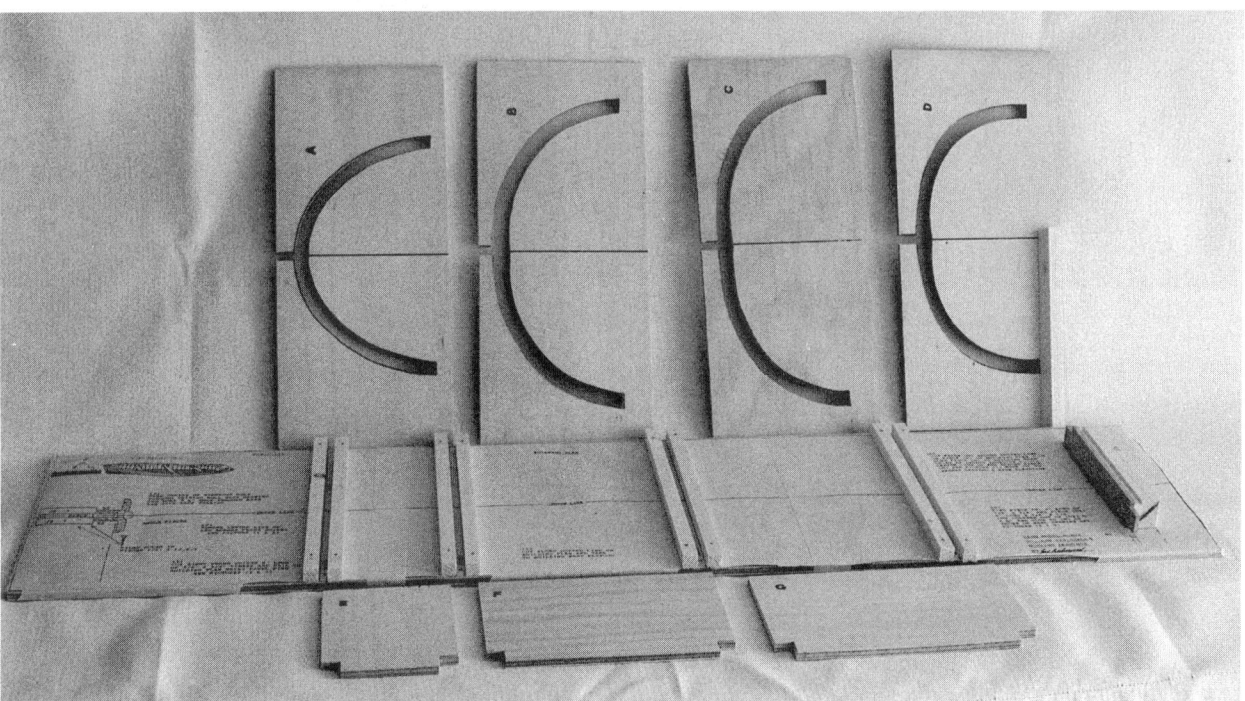

Fig. 9.1 Baseboard locators with frames and spacers ready for assembly. Note transom clamp at right hand end of the baseboard.

The Clinker Built Rowing Boat *Holly*

Fig. 9.2 Stem post locator and clamp.

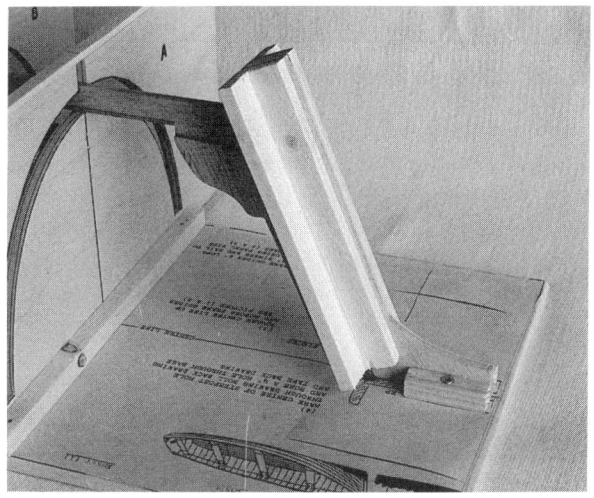

Fig. 9.4 The stem post clamp assembled on baseboard holding the built-up keel in place.

Fig. 9.5 The transom clamp assembly. Note angular edges of transom to permit widest possible seating for planks.

of the planks are fixed. Therefore, getting the angles right provides the widest possible surface on which the planks can seat (Fig. 9.5).

At this point, I would emphasise the necessity to adhere strictly to the sequence of numbered instructions on the drawings right throughout the construction, albeit that you have to jump about from one drawing sheet to another to follow the correct procedure.

The four jig frames have to be fret-sawn (Fig. 9.1) and adherance to the inner form line is necessary to get the line of the forthcoming planking correct. The outer form line restricts the action of tapered wedges and is less important.

When completed, the frames can be assembled to the guides on centreline and the frame spacers fitted and glued (Fig. 9.3). Again, squareness is the order of the day to keep everything shipshape.

The keel is now assembled through the slots in the top of the frames and located and clamped into the stem and transom clamp assemblies, ready for planking to begin (Figs. 9.4 and 9.5).

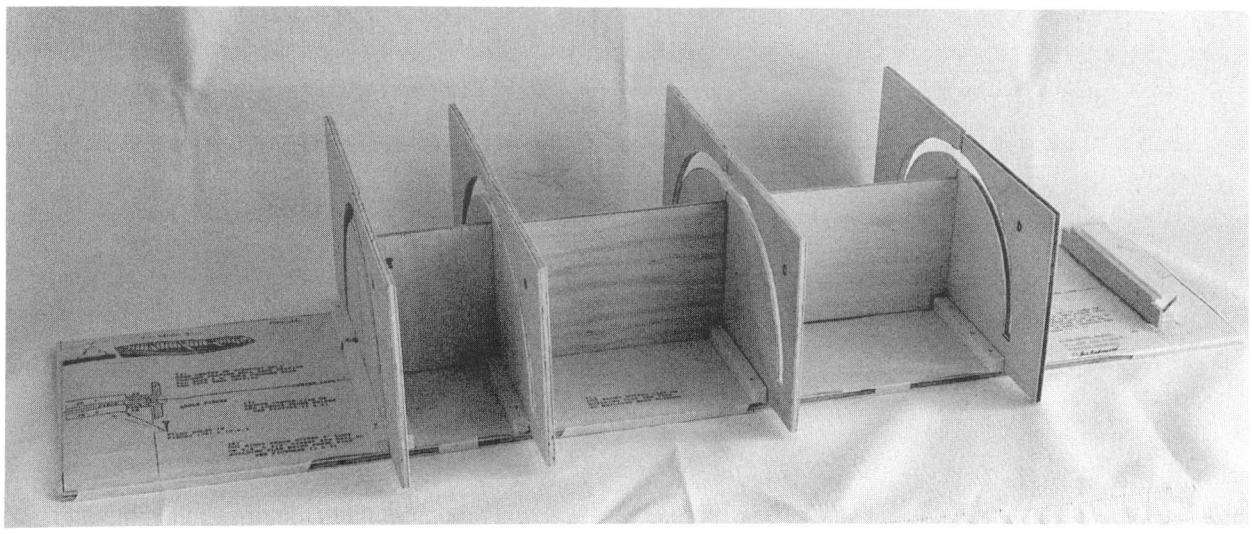

Fig. 9.3 Frame and spacer assembly.

Planking

Each plank is ready spiled and marked out on beautiful timber. Do be careful how you cut each plank, mark and prepare the chamfers at bow and stern, it would be a pity to spoil such lovely wood. It is wise to cut each plank and fix it before moving on to the next. This is strongly advised in the instructions and it is advice that should be well heeded. Treat each plank as a separate project, noting that some chamfers are on one side and some are on the other. Constant reference to the drawings will help ensure that you pare them on the correct face.

There are some rather involved instructions as to lashing the stern end of each plank in position across the edge of the transom. This system certainly does work, but I found it easier and entirely effective to use a large-headed drawing pin pushed into the edge of the transom close to the upper side of the plank being fixed. It is essential, as mentioned earlier, that the fullest possible contact area between the inside of the plank and the transom edge is achieved (Fig. 9.6).

At the front end, the angle on the end of the plank should accurately fit against the stem and a little correction to the plank may be found necessary as the result of the dry run required for each plank assembly. Once an accurate fit has been attained, the glued joint should be clamped up until dry (Fig. 9.7). A small G-clamp with a compensating anvil is ideal, but even so, a pair of wedges to bring the clamping faces more or less parallel helps. I used white PVA adhesive throughout the planking process, allowing each pair of planks, one port and one starboard, to dry out overnight. This process was repeated until all planks had been put in place (Fig.

Fig. 9.6 Early planking at transom. The large-headed pins are an alternative to the thread tie method recommended in the kit.

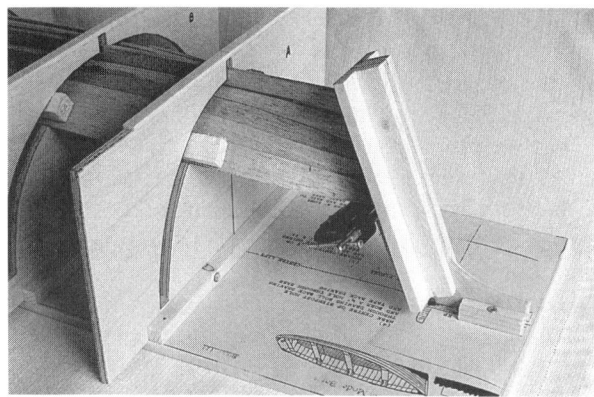

Fig. 9.7 Early planking at the stem post. Wedges secure planks in frames.

Fig. 9.8 The planking completed.

9.8). Care should be taken when applying the glue not to get any seepage on the inside of the boat and to wipe off any surplus from the outside surface.

Before removing the shell from the building jig (Fig. 9.9), remember to mark the position of the waterline. This is an operation easily missed since the instructions do not mention it. However, details as to how to get the right position are given on the small sheet that gives the oar dimensions.

A pair of stealers, fore and aft between the lower edge of the first plank and the keel, now have to be fitted and glued in place.

The gunwales

A reinforcing strip is glued to the inside edge of the top plank each side to form the gunwale. A couple of dry runs will help to get the length and fit just right. Making a snug joint at the prow and trimming at the stern for length makes this relatively straightforward. A series of small crocodile clips or clothes pegs are ideal for holding the strips in place while the glue sets.

The capping strips are a bit more fiddly. Five lengths of wood are provided per side for this feature and you are well advised to mitre the joints at the ends of each piece. In addition, I found that the first two lengths from the stem are better made into two pieces to accommodate the curve around the top of the boat. I chose to glue all of the strips in place and do the shaping *in situ* after the glue had set. The inside edges were trimmed first, making them flush with the inside of the gunwale. Then using this edge as a guide for the thumb, I pencilled a line parallel to it such as to make 1/16" overlap outside the top plank. The residue was planed off and finally sanded to size. The finished gunwales can be seen in Fig. 9.10.

Fitting out

The ribs are next to be fitted and this called for steaming the strips in order to attain the curves around the inside of the hull. Don't be tempted to get away without steaming. Some may turn out alright, but the majority definitely benefit from a bit of softening up. I found that the end five ribs at the fore end were better dealt with in two halves, being cut on the centreline of the keel.

The determination of overall length of each rib is of paramount importance. The fit under the gunwale each side controls the closeness of each rib to the inside of the planking, the planks being required to fit tight against the landing of each plank. The seating of the ribs under the gunwales and the position of the port riser can also be seen in Fig. 9.10.

The risers fit at a constant distance down from the gunwale capping and must be firmly glued to the ribs in order to adequately support the seats. Although I made the seats at this stage as instructed, I refrained from permanently fitting them until after the floor had been

Fig. 9.9 The shell as removed from the building jig.

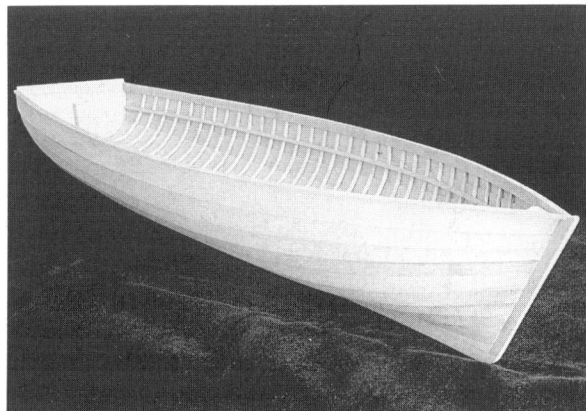

Fig. 9.10 The boat carcase fitted out with ribs and risers.

made and assembled.

The rowlock chockblocks were simple to make and fit, although no detail is given as to the fitting of the oarlock receiver plates. I assumed that the small lengths of brass tube provided passed through the receiver plates and on down into the chockblocks.

The floor comprises a series of boards mounted on bearers that sit on the inside bottom of the boat. To get the correct seating of the floor within the boat, the four central boards were temporarily mounted on the bearers which had been left overlength. The bearers were then carefully chamfered on their ends to match the bottom of the boat and get the floor level and stable (Fig. 9.11). This is another of those trial and error jobs which take a little time. When satisfied with the fit, the remaining outer floorboards can be shaped and put in place (Fig. 9.12). A cardboard template undoubtedly helped to get the correct shape which was then transferred to the wood. The floor is shown to be in two pieces, a separation cut being made beneath the line of seat no. 2. A cover slip is made to cover this join with false cover slips below seats nos 1 and 3. The stringers should then be glued in place around the outside of the outer floor boards, thus permitting the floor to be removed. The stringers are fitted in a similar manner to the risers and

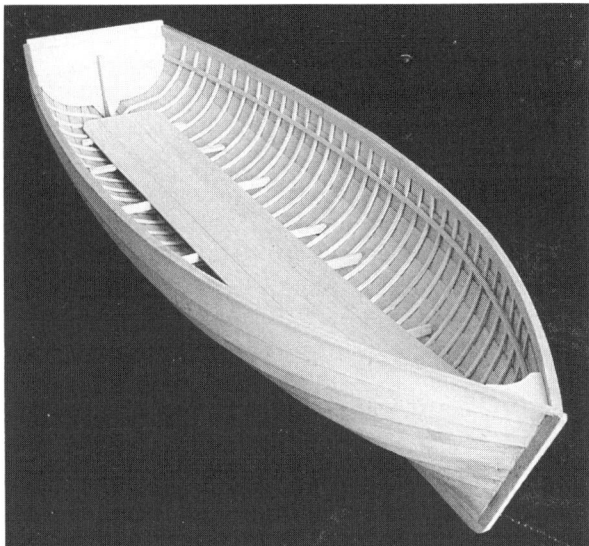

Fig. 9.11 The central floorboards and bearers temporarily fixed in place.

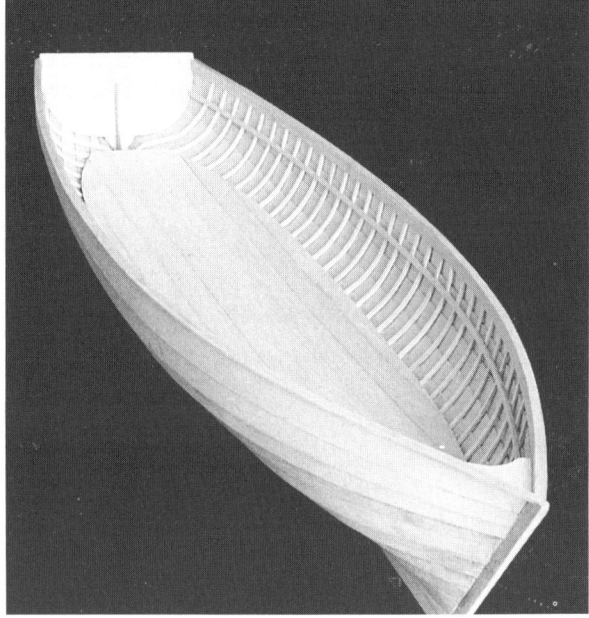

Fig. 9.12 The final floor shape.

braces made from scrap should be strategically placed to keep them in place just clear of the outer edge of the floor.

The seats, or thwarts, were then fixed in place and work started on the knees. Be careful about the back edges of the knees. As advised on the drawings, they will almost certainly not finish up as marked out on the oak strip supplied. It should also be remembered that each of the twelve knees is different, the only helpful similarity being between opposites, port to starboard, where the only difference is the angular back edge that matches the curve of the boat fore and aft. Prepare the bottom edges first, then, by trial and error, attain the correct fit of the back edge against the inside of the boat and gunwale. Knees should not fit against ribs. When you are finally satisfied with this fit, the top edge may be shaped. I found it easiest to make the knees in pairs, 1 and 2, 3 and 4, etc. Bearing in mind that the knees have to be made so that their ends are level at the ends of each seat, the lengths of 3 and 4 should be marked from the lengths of 1 and 2 before shaping the tops of the former pair (Fig. 9.13).

The oars

Oars are usually a bit of a pain to make. In this instance, if you carefully follow the drawing and instructions

Fig. 9.13 The knees at each end of the thwarts. The length should be the same on each thwart.

Fig. 9.14 The oars are quite easy to make if you follow the recommended procedure.

given in the kit you will get a nice pair of oars with very little hassle (Fig. 9.14). The work does need patience and it is particularly important to keep everything balanced either side of the centreline. Thus careful marking out and constant checking for shape and size must be of paramount concern for ultimate success.

I asked Joe Redmond, of Kish Models, why there were only two oars but four oarlock positions. He said that the boat would normally be rowed with two oars, but the rowing position(s) would depend on what gear was being carried or how many people were in the boat.

Finishing

I chose to paint the hull basically white with blue trim. The white used was from a Dulux colour tester for Cornflower White in vinyl matt emulsion. The blue was Humbrol Acrylic matt 5025. The uncoloured parts were varnished with acrylic satin varnish.

The only additional items to those provided in the kit were a pair of oarlocks made from pieces of brass strip and wire soldered together (Fig. 9.15).

Conclusions

A great change from the usual run-of-the-mill boat kit; fantastic quality materials to work with and a worthwhile challenge to boot. This is model boat building in the truest sense and, if you have a feel for working in beautiful wood, this is the one for you. However, I have to say that the kit is not really one for the beginner.

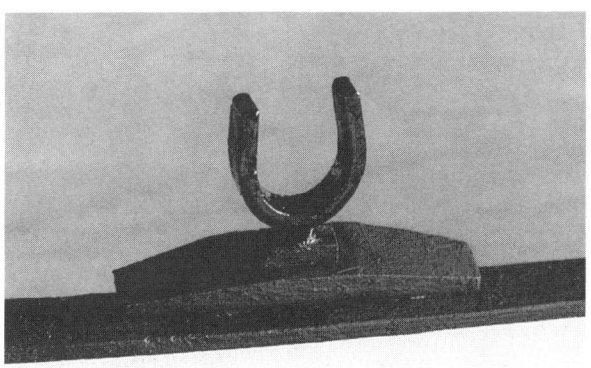

Fig. 9.15 The rowlocks were made from brass strip and wire soldered together.

Any niggles? Just a couple of minor ones. I liked the inclusion of instructions on the drawings, but in retrospect I felt that the positioning of some of the instructions would be more helpful if placed in a more logical sequence. I also thought that the details for determining the waterline would have been better included on the working drawings, rather than on that for the oars, particularly as the marking of the waterline should be done before removing the boat from the building jig. However, this is nitpicking, all the information is there to be used, just study all sheets thoroughly and familiarise yourself with the total construction before cutting into the timber.

This is an unusual kit, constructed in an unusual manner, but one I would thoroughly recommend to those modelmakers who have an urge to perform some real craftsmanship.

CHAPTER 10

The Hermaphrodite Brig
Le Hussard 1848

Le Hussard is described by Artesania Latina as an hermaphrodite brig of the French Navy. It had four square sails on the foremast, a fore-and-aft mainsail, a gaff rigged main topsail and no main yard. There are several learned works that define the hermaphrodite brig, all with subtle variations on the same theme, and this vessel was yet another of them.

The main armament comprised two swivel-mounted cannon, one mounted aft and the other forward. These were supplemented by a pair of carriage-mounted guns, one each side just forward of amidships.

The Kit

The presentation of this kit is certainly different. The inside of the box is printed with identifying layouts of all the sheet parts, while the inside of the lid and the underside of the box features a series of colour pictures showing the construction of the hull and location of the deck fittings. A multilingual instruction manual, albeit a little on the sparse side, supports three sheets of excellent drawings, two of them double sided. The rigging details are particularly well shown and the drawings include a comprehensive parts list. However, don't look for construction techniques, you are left pretty much to you own devices, although there is nothing too difficult to contend with.

Material quality is very good, the sheet parts having about the finest pre-cutting seen to date. Strip material and dowelling are listed in four languages, alongside a colour guide, to accurately identify each of the fifteen sections provided in the kit.

Two clear plastic boxes, with lids, each with ten compartments house the various fittings. Sail material is also provided.

The kit builds into a 1:50 scale model, 735mm long, 550mm high with a beam of 140mm. However, this is yet another kit that does not include the design or materials for a stand.

The basic hull structure

The hull is in the conventional kit style of a false keel and nine bulkheads, onto which reinforcements at bow are added (Fig. 10.1). The three ply decks were then planked and placed in position and glued onto the basic structure (Fig. 10.2).

The mukali strips used for the deck planking are very light in colour and you may, as I did, want to add some caulking effect just to show up the individual planks. I chose to clamp eight strips tightly together, face to face, then run down one side of exposed edges with a felt-tipped black marker pen. I repeated this four times to give thirty-two strips, which are enough for the whole planking job, plus a couple of spare. These were then glued to the ply decks, clean edge to black edge to give the effect required.

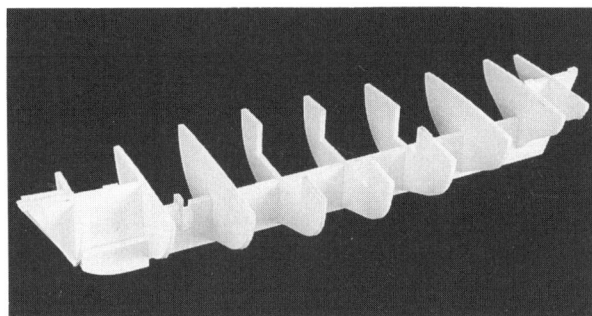

Fig. 10.1 The basic structure.

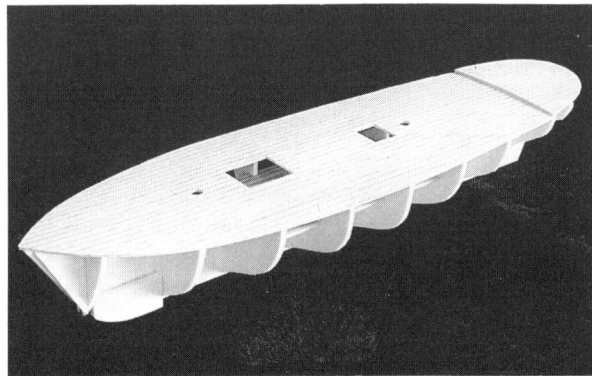

Fig. 10.2 Decks planked and positioned.

One word of warning, don't use a *new* marker pen – the fluid will be a little too runny, and may run down through the grain of the wood. An old, drier pen is best. If you want to use a new one, mark a piece of cloth first and use that to apply the ink to the wood.

The edges of the bulkheads were then chamfered to conform to the true lines of the hull and, at the same time, shaping the reinforcement blocks at stem and stern.

The first planking

Planking the hull was fairly straightforward. Bearing in mind that this first layer had to be later covered with a second, thinner layer, I felt it more important to attain a sound surface rather than worry overduly about the appearance. Thus, as far as possible, I let the planks run naturally without trying to induce to much sidewards bending and twisting. Many of the planks needed to be tapered and, even so, quite a few stealers were found to be necessary, particularly at the stern. Each plank was securely pinned and glued to the bulkheads and the adjacent plank, working alternately side to side, to prevent distortion of the hull structure. When the glue had thoroughly set, the pins were removed. It is important not to miss any, the pads of the fingers can sustain quite nasty damage when the planking is rubbed down later on if the odd pin is overlooked.

Decks and bulwarks

The hatch coamings were then fitted, followed by the

two circular running tracks for the carronades.

The waterways comprise pre-cut parts fore and aft, with the centre sections being made up from strip material. Colour matching was not difficult, but you do have to remember to look to find the best strips for the job.

The pre-cut ply bulwarks were faced on their inner surfaces before assembly with the hull. Watch the line of vertical pieces that make up the revolving gun doors; the development of the stern bulwark has a longer top edge than that at deck level. Each door was a set of three planks, the outer edges of which were later trimmed to give a gap between each door of about 1mm. A similar procedure was adopted for the doors either side forward. Once this had been done, the remaining, longitudinal facing was carried out.

Before fixing the bulwarks in place, a couple of dry runs are advisable. The instructions recommend that you start at the bows and work back towards the stern, applying the curved stern piece last. Having faced the inner surfaces, I found it easier to centralise the stern piece first, then, matching the sides to it, work towards the front. I then marked the correct height of the underside of the bulwark rails and trimmed the edges accordingly.

The hull was then rubbed down to give a nice even surface ready for the second planking (Fig. 10.3). It is more important to remove any ridges, humps or bumps than it is to attain a high degree of finish. In fact, if you are going to use a contact adhesive for the second planking, a slightly roughened surface will provide a good key.

The second planking

The planking was done in 0.6mm thick sapele strips following the same basic procedure as for the first planking. However, do not be misled into thinking that this means these thinner planks will follow exactly the same line as the first. They will not take any twist at all, and any attempt to try will result in them not laying flat against the surface of the first planking. I found that a taper to 2.5mm width over a length of 180mm at the bows, and to 2.0mm over 80mm at the stern for the first six planks down from deck level, worked out about right. The seventh plank started adjacent to the sixth at stem and stern, but was left to find its own passage along or around the centre part of the hull. The remainder were applied above and below, trimming and tapering to suit.

The outer surfaces of the bulwarks were then planked and the outsides of the carronade gun doors. It is important to ensure that the latter are in line with what had been previously done on the inside surfaces. Ultimately, the rails around the top edge have to be cut in line with the inner and outer port positions.

Finishing the hull

The stem and stern posts, along with the keel, were the next to be fitted. With the hull held firmly between the knees, I used a ¾" *sharp* chisel to gently pare a 5mm wide seating for the stem. Once this had been done, the inner curve of the stem proper was adjusted as necessary to match. Two holes were drilled through the stem before it was glued to the hull so that once the correct position had been attained, it could be permanently pinned. A similar procedure was adopted for the stern post, although it was a case here of slightly adjusting plank thicknesses to present a 5mm wide face. The two-part keel was fitted last, glued and pinned.

The timber heads were prepared and fitted (Fig. 10.4). A piece of card cut as a spacer was used to ensure the correct separation between the pieces. I decided at this juncture to jump ahead a bit to make and fit the gunport frames. Since they were immediately below the bulwark rails, I considered it easier to cut down the position of each gunport side and remove a U shaped piece, rather than leaving the ports until later, when it would have been a case of drilling and creating an aperture. The port frames were then made up *in situ*, ensuring that the top elements were level with the top of the bulwark sides. The two boarding points were treated in the same way.

Fig. 10.3 First hull planking complete with waterways, swivel gun tracks and hatch coamings.

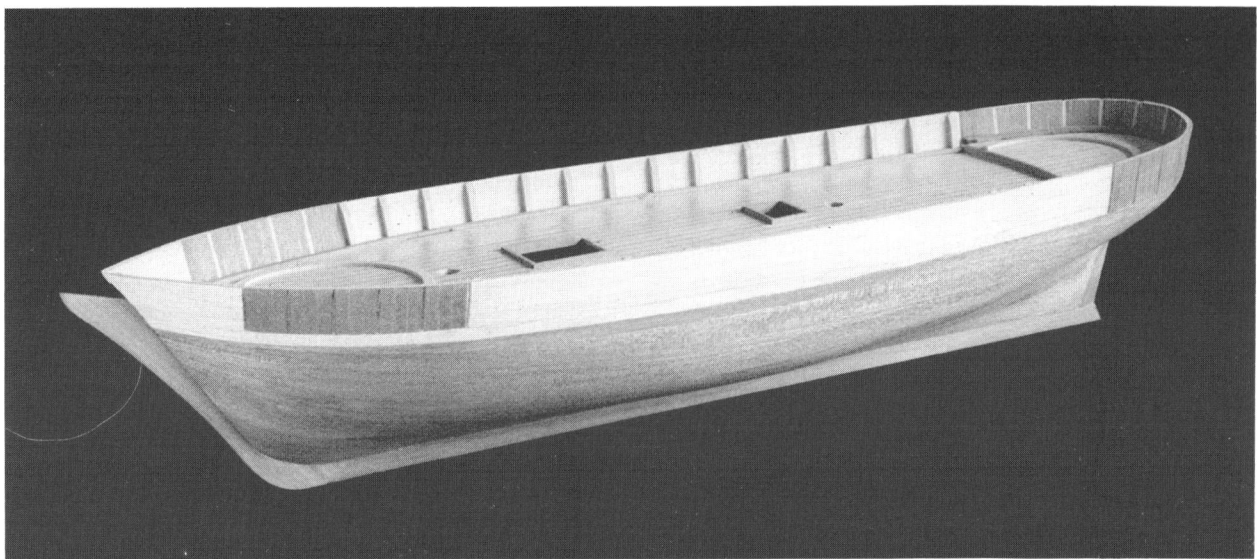

Fig. 10.4 Second planking complete with keel stem posts fitted.

The whole outer surface of the hull was then given a good rub down with progressively decreasing grades of abrasive paper until a good smooth surface was produced.

The rails at the bows and the stern come pre-shaped, while the 'midships sections are made up from strip material. I smoothed off the inner edges before assembly, then used superglue to fix them in place. The bow and stern pieces were put in place first and the intermediate lengths cut to suit. There was still some curve to accommodate with the strips and I found it easier to cut several shorter lengths rather than trying to do it in one hit. Attention was paid to accurately align the inner edges throughout, leaving the more accessible outer edges to work on to get to a fairly constant width.

The main wale or rubbing strake was a pain to do. There is no way that you can take a strip of 4mm wide walnut, bend and twist it to lay flat, and get it to run straight along the desired line. The length between the stem and the front of the raised deck at the stern was OK, but the part aft of that all around the stern I made up by scarfing several pieces together then titivating the upper and lower edges to get the right line. If you put enough pieces in, it means that the width of the wale, after trimming, finishes up just slightly less than the specified 4mm. Upon reflection, I would have done better to use some 5mm from my scrap box, then I could have trimmed to the basic 4mm width.

It then only remained to fit the channels, pin rails and rudder to complete the basic hull construction (Fig. 10.5). However. it was at this stage that I found a design fault; the material specified for the channels was of insufficient width. In fact, if you look at the photographs of the finished model on the box art, you will see that the lanyards between the deadeyes on the lower shrouds

Fig. 10.5 The completed hull with wider than specified channels to avoid interference of shroud lanyards with bulwark rails.

interfere with the outer edge of the bulwark rails. This, of course, should not be and, instead of using 6mm wide strip as advised in the parts list, you really need something in the order of 12mm for the main, and 15mm for the fore channels. So, a little bit of edge-to-edge work is required to increase the width. I found that there was just enough in the kit to accommodate the modification.

The hull was then given a rubbed-in coat of acrylic matt varnish. I had tried brushing a test piece comprising an outer plank fixed with contact adhesive, but I was a bit suspicious of the reaction of the varnish with the adhesive if it seeped through the minimal thickness of the outer planking. A piece of soft cloth to rub in the varnish used less varnish, did the job adequately, and avoided lifting any of the planks. Don't forget, that after rubbing down, some of the planks are somewhat thinner at the edges than the 0.6mm they started out at.

As I have already said, once again we have a kit that does not provide a design, or materials, for a stand. All that was needed was a couple of pieces of 12mm square × 90mm long, shaped and cross slotted to take the keel. I drilled two holes and screwed them to the keel from below. *Lean-to* models are not my favourites!

Fitting out

The inside of the box lid describes pictorially the making of the various deck fittings, galley etc., and there really isn't too much to say about this stage of the construction. The parts list and drawings obviously had to be used in conjunction with the pictures in order to get the type and sizes of material to be used. All the units made up very well and no trouble was encountered until the time came for assembly to the deck. Two discrepancies between drawings and pictures came to light.

The first, and most obvious, was the attitude of the galley. Pictorially, it was shown with the door and port hole facing the port, whereas the drawings showed these features facing starboard. I have to confess that I don't have the faintest idea which is right, the drawing or the picture.

The second problem arose when tying on blocks at deck level. There are two eyebolts just forward of the main mast. One of them has a block strapped to it to take the boom topping lift lanyard. Ah, but which one? The main hull drawings indicate the port side eyebolt and the belaying diagram, the starboard. Again, such limited information that I have on this particular rig did not help solve the problem.

The two carriage-mounted guns are a bit basic, as is their rigging to the sides of the vessel – just a pair of single blocks each side of the carriage. Obviously an area where the more enterprising modelmaker can shine.

The swivel-mounted pieces fore and aft are again somewhat basic. They seem to represent an early type of carronade without recoil slides. The drawings show no rigging at all, although the four rings in the deck around the gun emplacements showed some attempt to acknowledge that there was supposed to be some sort of tackle there. I certainly would not like to be in the vicinity of an unrigged gun, without recoil features, when it was fired!

The completely fitted hull is shown in Figs 10.6 and 10.7.

Fig. 10.6 Deck fittings forward. Note that the double block strapped to the butt end of the bowsprit should be rigged before assembly to the hull.

Fig. 10.7 The fittings towards the stern.

The masts and spars

The bowsprit was made up first (Fig. 10.8). The only modification that I made to the construction was to drill a 1mm dia. hole in the underside of the cap, the top end of the dolphin striker and each end of the support column, so that this rather vulnerable feature could be dowelled with 1mm brass wire for added strength. Note too, that the double block strapped to the butt end of the bowsprit had to be rigged before assembling the bowsprit to the hull – it can't be done properly afterwards.

All masts and spars were tapered by first planing to an octagonal section, followed by spinning and sanding in the chuck of an electric drill. The dowel rods provided in the kit were of African walnut, straight and close grained, and took the plane really well. I made one mast on my small 12v Mantua lathe and, once the right speed and turning tool had been selected, the material was also found to respond well to turning.

When assembling the main mast top and the trestletrees and crosstrees, due consideration has to be given to the considerable rake on the masts. These items should be parallel with the deck.

I also remembered that the fitting of eyebolts and

Fig. 10.8 The bowsprit assembly.

blocks was best done before stepping the masts. Blocks and footropes were added to all spars at this stage as well.

When stepping the masts, ensure that, as mentioned above, the rake on the masts is recognised, together with fore and aft alignment with the bowsprit.

Sail making

Circumstances have decreed that I have had to give very serious thought to the problem of finding an alternative method of sail making. I am not a great believer of putting sails on models, but there are some models where sails really do make a difference, and this is one of them.

The first serious difficulty for one not adept at using a sewing machine is the representation of all the seams that are visible on a sail. A line of stitches produced by a sewing machine is certainly speedy, but I can never seem to get the line straight enough and, unfortunately, when there have to be a series of parallel rows fairly close together, anything less than perfection shows up like a sore thumb.

A dark brown shade of ordinary coloured pencil proved to solve the problem quite well. Snags? Yes, you must use a chisel point and constantly keep it sharpened to a fine edge. Coloured pencils are, by nature, on the soft side and will not produce a thin line for more than about 50cm without attention to the point. It is also best to mark both sides of the sail.

The second problem is the hem all round the edges of the sail. Why have a hem at all? Answer – to stop the edges fraying and again there is an alternative to sewing. Having got your piece of material marked out with the seams and outlines of all the sails, the next step is to apply a band of acrylic matt varnish around the edges of each sail. The band needs to be about 4mm wide and should encroach within the edges of the sail by about 1.5mm. Use enough varnish to ensure that it penetrates through the cloth. When thoroughly dry, each sail can be cut from the cloth and you finish up with a nice 1.5mm reinforcing edge all round.

Finally, the boltropes should be sewn on. This does not require too much needlecraft, more in the way of patience. A simple binding stitch, or blanket stitch, is all that is needed to anchor the rope to the varnish reinforced edge all round the sail.

The standing rigging

The thread provided in the kit for the standing rigging was of extremely good quality. It appeared to have had some sort of treatment, the results of which gave it a degree of stiffness and to lay down the majority of that surface hairiness that attracts the dust as time passes.

The rigging diagrams were also good and, if the sequence is followed as drawn, there should be absolutely no problem with setting up this stage of the rigging. The one minor exception being the lanyards between the lower deadeyes of the fore and main shrouds. The distance indicated between the deadeyes is unusually large and the twist induced in the shrouds when pulling the lanyards up tends to twist these as well. I found that the solution was to coat the thread for the lanyards with white PVA adhesive and leave it to thoroughly dry before attempting to set up the shrouds. This gave the lanyards just enough stiffness to counteract the twist in the shrouds and keep everything reasonably in line. Fig. 10.9 shows the completed standing rigging.

The running rigging

The thread for the running rigging was of a much softer quality than that provided for the standing rigging. Because this led to easy tangling, I considered it prudent to rewind the skein onto a piece of card to avoid any annoying hold-ups in the work to come.

I found that it was best to lash sails on to their respective spars before rigging the latter to the masts. This was particularly important with the gaff sails, since it ensured that the spars involved would be rigged at the correct angle.

All thread used for the running rigging was coated with PVA before use to stiffen it and lay down the surface fibres. This also proved useful for rigging a nice curve on those parts of the rigging that needed to be left a little on the slack side.

The rigging diagrams again proved to be extremely easy to follow and, when working in the sequence depicted, no untoward difficulties were experienced in putting up the many lines on the foremast with its four square sails.

Finishing off

The anchors were rigged, the flag flown, and all the coils of rope made from what was left of the rigging thread.

The anchor rope, coated in PVA, was persuaded into a reasonable curve that looked as if it was hanging naturally. A spot of superglue at the hawse hole kept things in balance and the free ends were then tucked down into the holes in the deck.

I made the flag halliard and assembled the flag off the boat in order to have a better chance of bending and folding the flag into some sort of limp looking shape. Sometimes this works and at other times it doesn't. When it does, the colour of the flag adds something to the model; when it doesn't, I just forget it. A poorly hung flag turns a reasonable model into a toy.

Something in the order of 50 rope coils had to be made up to hang on the belaying pins or lay at the requisite places on the deck. This was a fiddly job and required a lot of patience as well as a steady hand. I always reckon that it is a good idea to remove all rings and watches, then roll up the sleeves, to do this job. Getting the hands in among the rigging is bad enough, but to get it caught up on your watch strap can be disastrous.

A general look over the completed model to find any

Fig. 10.9 The standing rigging.

loose or untrimmed ends of rigging brought the project to an end.

Conclusions

This was an extremely well presented kit, the materials were fine, both in quantity and quality, particularly the standard of rigging thread.

It was a relatively simple and straightforward model to make, and would not overly tax a beginner, provided that care and patience were brought to bear. I am not too sure about the accuracy of some of the rigging, or the way the artillery is set up. Nonetheless, it builds into an attractive model, even if it can't be classed as museum standard.

CHAPTER 11

The Yacht
Britannia 1893

Commissioned by the Prince of Wales, later to become Edward VII, the yacht *Britannia* was launched in 1893 and had a grace and beauty that led to a long string of sailing victories. With a length of 121′6″, it was of wood on steel frame construction.

After the death of Edward VII, the vessel passed into the ownership of George V and following his death in 1936 it was towed into the English Channel and sunk off the Isle of Wight. Mamoli's kit captures the graceful lines of this beautiful yacht and builds into a model 780mm long and 1000mm high (when on the stand). So, as a static model it will require a fairly large area for display.

The Kit

One of the first things that you notice when you open the box is the plan pack. This comprises 5 sheets (10 sides) of excellent drawings and instructions, the latter being in four languages, including English. They come in two distinct sections – general instructions applicable to all models printed on the inside of the plan pack cover, and specific procedures concerned with the vessel in question, integral with the drawings proper. A parts and material list is also given and features a two or three letter code system for identification. This calls for a lot of chopping and changing from one sheet to another and was something that I could have done without. Having said that, all the relevant data was there.

The strip materials were of reasonable, but not the highest, quality and pre-cut parts were adequately presented. The mass of fittings were of extremely high standard and well housed in a plastic moulded tray. For the most part they appeared to have been made specifically for this kit rather than taken from a standard range.

The modelmaker is given the option to make either a static or a sailing model, and wooden and soft metal keel parts are provided to be used according to choice.

Building the hull

The frames are cross-half jointed into a false keel in the conventional manner found in the majority of kits. The pre-cut slots were not all that accurate and therefore not as strong as I would have liked but, nonetheless, they were adequate provided that the glue is left long enough to properly cure. A design aspect that I particularly liked was the extended frame tops which, together with the extremities of the false keel, provided a level and stable seating when the model was deck down on the bench (Fig. 11.1).

The edges of the frames have to be shaped to follow the lines of the hull and the first planking, in lime, can then be applied. Advanced reading of the instructions indicated that the tops of the frames are later removed to deck level and so some care is required to ensure that

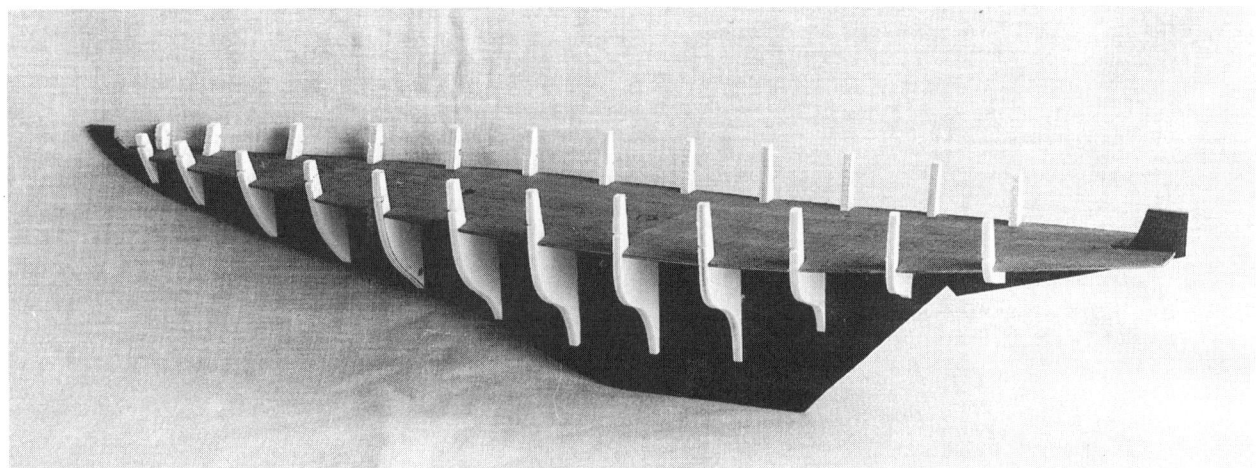

Fig. 11.1 The basic hull framework.

planking in the bulwark area, while glued edge-to-edge, is only clipped to the frames. For the second planking, which is in mahogany, the modelmaker is given the option of applying it either in the conventional fore and aft manner or, for reasons of strength and stability, at 45 degrees to the waterline. Either way, the mahogany strips are fairly course grained and, with a section as small as 4 × 0.05mm, need careful handling if they are not to be broken. A contact adhesive is best for this part of the job and, in particular, I have found that Dunlop Thixofix is one of the better ones. It is a gel, doesn't string and can be easily applied with the tip of the finger without much bother or mess.

As mentioned earlier, you are given another option, this time with regard to the keel material. The kit provides a pair of lead castings for use should you wish to sail the finished model and also wooden pieces if you are building a static model. I chose to use the latter and roughly shaped them to get rid of most of the excess material before gluing them in place on the model. This is most important since the planking and the keel bulb should match and their lines blend to a continuous surface.

The rudder assembly comprises four metal pintles and a cast rudder all hinged on a length of brass rod. The pintles have to be filed to reduce their width in order to match the shape of the hull into which four slots have to be cut. These need to be carefully marked out using the rudder as a guide and each pintle fitted to suit.

The deck is laid in separate planks. I found it easiest to lay the first row on centreline and use this as a guide for the remainder. Again, contact adhesive is probably the best medium to use on these very thin strips, the less viscous PVA tending to warp and lift the edges of the planks. Once the deck has been finished off (Fig. 11.2), the scuppers can be drilled and filed. The instructions refer to seven per side as shown on the assembly drawing. Unfortunately, my assembly drawing had no indication as to their position so my model has seven equi-spaced within the length.

I decided to cut the bulwarks at the prow to take the bowsprit before I fitted the handrails. It is never easy to

Fig. 11.2 The planked hull ready for painting.

drill safely from inside the hull and, in any event, even the smallest drill chuck usually fouls on the deck. Drilling from the outside is also fraught with hazards when the vessel has a sharpish front end. So, a U shaped slot was cut from the top much easier and much safer!

The shaped handrail around the top of the hull is fabricated by laminating five 2 × 1mm strips. Having transferred the shape of the hull to a card or board template, the laminated assembly is glued and pinned to the template and bench while the adhesive is still fluid, and left to harden off overnight (Fig. 11.3). It springs out a bit when released, but the use of cyano gel to fix it to the edges of the hull makes it simple to ease back into shape.

The stand

The framework for the stand is a straightforward cutting and gluing job (Fig. 11.4). However, the two top rails that actually support the hull should be laminated as instructed but not fixed in place until they have been shaped to match the hull contours. However, this turned out to be quite problematical since, in order to seat the

The Yacht *Britannia* 1893

Fig. 11.3 Fabricating the laminated handrail.

hull squarely fore and aft and at the right height with sufficient support on the rails, the rudder would have completely cut through the rear cross frame of the stand. Also, the section of the rails would have been reduced to such small proportions as to be useless. To get round the difficulty, I contoured a cardboard template, transferred the shape to two pieces of thin ply and made a snug fitting platform support which I glued to the top surface of the upper rails. The finished stand does not look too much like the one shown on the box lid, but then it never would have done, even without my modification (Fig. 11.5).

Deck fittings

These details fall into three groups. They are either cast items which only need a little tidying up, skylights that have to be fabricated, or eyebolts to glue into suitably drilled holes.

The skylights are worth a few words. They are fabricated by facing pre-shaped blocks with strip material, framing pieces of glazing material and adding the brass wire protection rails (Fig. 11.6). The kit provides a nice little cast bending jig for the various lengths of railings involved, allowing the modeller to easily reproduce several railings of identical length. A nice touch from Mamoli and an item which will find a permanent place in my tool kit for future use. However, the accurate

Fig. 11.4 The basic stand.

Fig. 11.5 The stand with additional platform to adequately seat the hull in a stable manner.

Fig. 11.6 The fabricated skylights.

marking and drilling of holes required for the railings, through the very fine sections of material involved, is not so easy.

The positions of the 40 eyebolts are marked off by scaling the plan. Choose a drill diameter that provides a fairly tight fit for the shanks of the eyebolts and push them home with the merest touch of superglue. This provides a strong joint to take the tension in the rigging to be applied later (Fig. 11.9).

As stated before, the remainder of the deck fittings are cast items and need minimal attention before fixing in place, again referring to the drawings for proper position. The capstan and anchors are shown in Fig. 11.7. The bowsprit and winch were assembled together, the latter being painted before fixing to the deck (Fig. 11.8). The finished, fitted out hull is shown seated on the modified stand in Fig. 11.10.

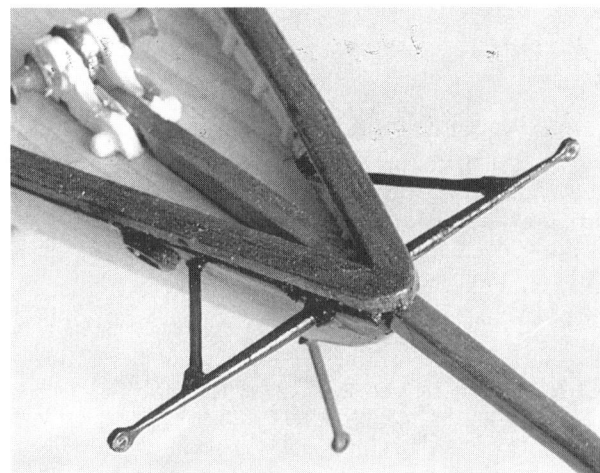

Fig. 11.8 The bowsprit assembly. The winch unit is one of the many cast fittings provided in the kit.

Fig. 11.7 The capstan and anchor layout. Note scuppers at deck level.

The Yacht *Britannia* 1893

Fig. 11.9 The ship's wheel. The deck cleats and eyebolts in the rail must be very securely fixed.

The sails

Full-size plans for each sail make easy work of the marking out and the positioning of all the seams. However, the material provided tended to fray far too readily to attain the small hem sizes designated around the edges of each sail. A considerable amount of machining is needed to sew in all the parallel seams and these really do have to be straight, the separation of the seams is close enough to show up even minor deviations.

The kit provided tubular eyelets for the corners of the sails, thus a suitable size of punch was required for the preparatory hole and also a tool to turn over the tubular portion to form the head on the opposite side of the material. I could not even punch a satisfactory hole in this particular material and after several vain attempts and one spoilt sail, I simply used a needle and thread to fix the sail at the tying off points.

The mast and spars

The mast comprises two main elements both of which have to be tapered from dowel rod (Fig. 11.11). The degree of taper is not very much and it was easy to attain by filing to an octagonal section then spinning to sand the corners off. A similar procedure was adopted for the spars (Fig. 11.12). The positions for several eyebolts were then marked and drilled — it is better to fit them at this stage rather than later after the mast has been stepped.

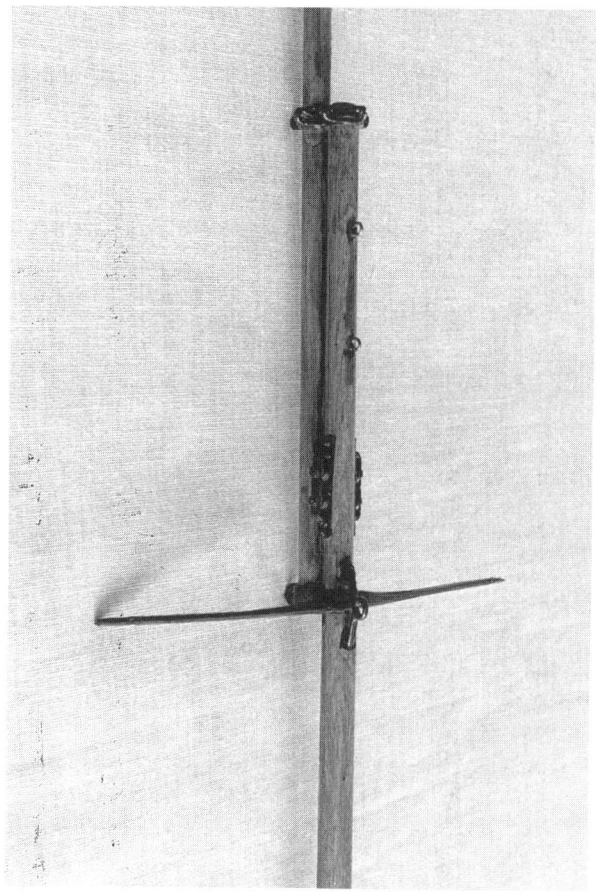

Fig. 11.11 The main mast assembly.

Fig. 11.10 The finished hull. Painted and fitted out stable on modified stand.

The Period Ship Handbook 2

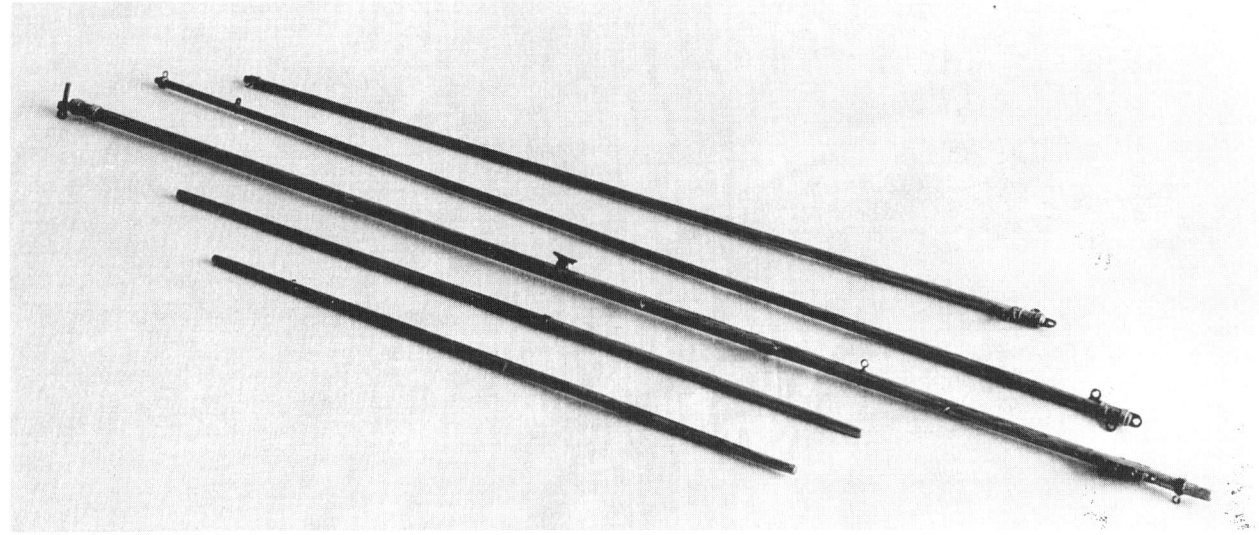

Fig. 11.12 The masts and spars. End fittings, collars etc. are all supplied.

The quality of the cast fittings provided in the kit really showed up at this juncture. Apart from drilling out a few holes they needed little work done on them.

Rigging

Having stepped the mast, the standing rigging was put up. Plaited wire is supplied for this and, while it looks OK it is a bit of a job to get it reasonably taut, so make sure that the eyebolts in the deck are well and truly secured to take the considerable tension on the shrouds. The backstays are a combination of plaited wire and thread and were pulled up much more easily via a pair of double blocks.

It was nice to find that all the rigging blocks were adequately drilled. I can't remember the last kit I built where I didn't have to laboriously open out all the holes to make them big enough for the relevant thread size.

The plans indicate all the rigging, associated blocks and belaying points by a series of sequential numbers — follow the numbers and everything is done in the right order. One point that I would add which, to me, made things even easier, was that it was beneficial to lash the boom and gaff to the mainsail and the sail to the mast rings before any rigging was started. The boom was temporarily tied down to the deck and the gaff to the top of the mast enabling the correct tension to be applied when subsequently rigging the boom topping lifts, the crowsfoot-style gaff lifts and finally the tackle from the boom down to the horse on deck. The various aspects of the rigging are shown in Figs 11.13, 11.14, 11.15 and 11.16.

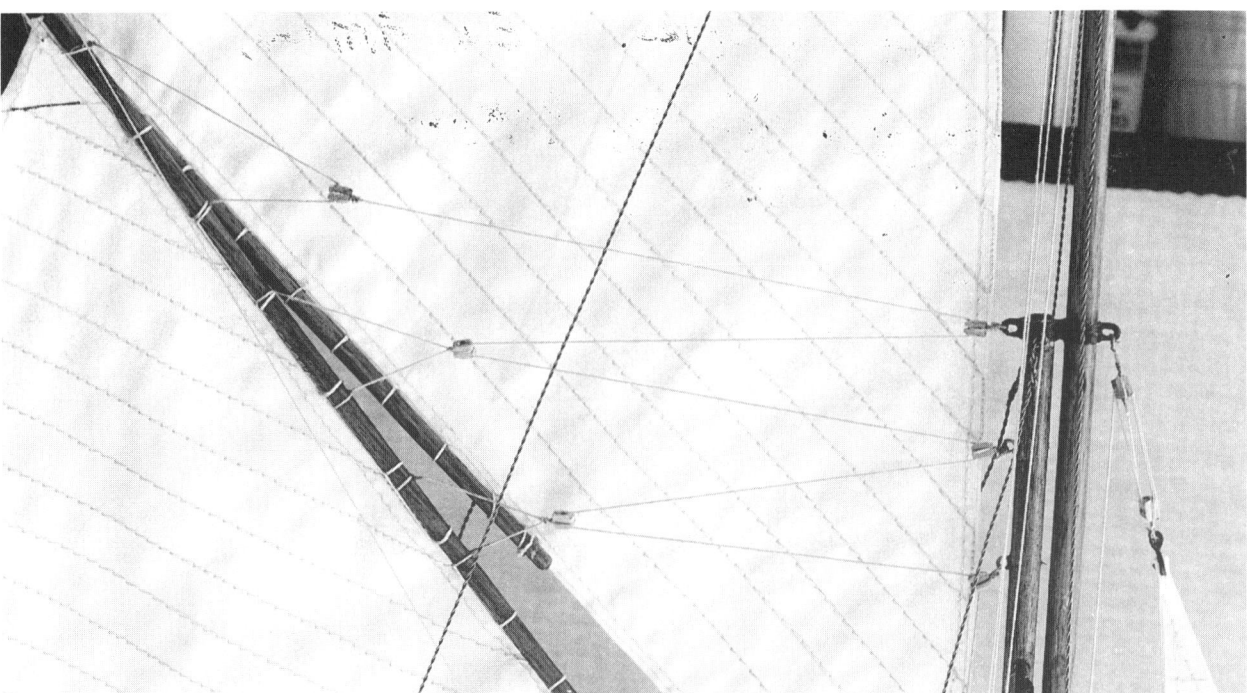

Fig. 11.13 The crowsfoot rigging to upper mainsail spar. Sails are best lashed to spars before setting up.

The Yacht *Britannia* 1893

Fig. 11.14 Rigging at the main mast spreader. Note rings on mainsail and seams sewn on all sails.

Conclusions

The kit makes up into quite an attractive static model. I am not sufficiently qualified to know whether the building of a working model is a viable option, or not. Certainly, the kit provides alternative cast lead keel parts, but I suspect that trimming it for sailing, or whatever one does to get some sort of waterborne performance, would be a bit of a challenge.

However, as a kit for a static model, I found it to be a very pleasant change from the sailing man of war. Some of the finer sections of strip material were a little coarse in grain structure, and it was difficult to machine a scale size hem on the sail material. The fittings were excellent, better than you often find in more expensive kits. The drawings and instructions were quite comprehensive although you are required to do a lot of cross referencing from one sheet to another, but all the information is there to be found.

Quite a lot of thought has gone into the presentation of this kit and, although maybe not for the absolute beginner, the *Britannia* provides many hours of pleasant modelmaking.

Fig. 11.15 The aft end of the bowsprit rigging. The turnbuckles are supplied in the kit but getting the wire rigging taut is not easy.

Fig. 11.16 Rigging to the main boom. Coils of rope should be made up where necessary and fixed adjacent to belaying points.

CHAPTER 12

A Frontiersman Canoe

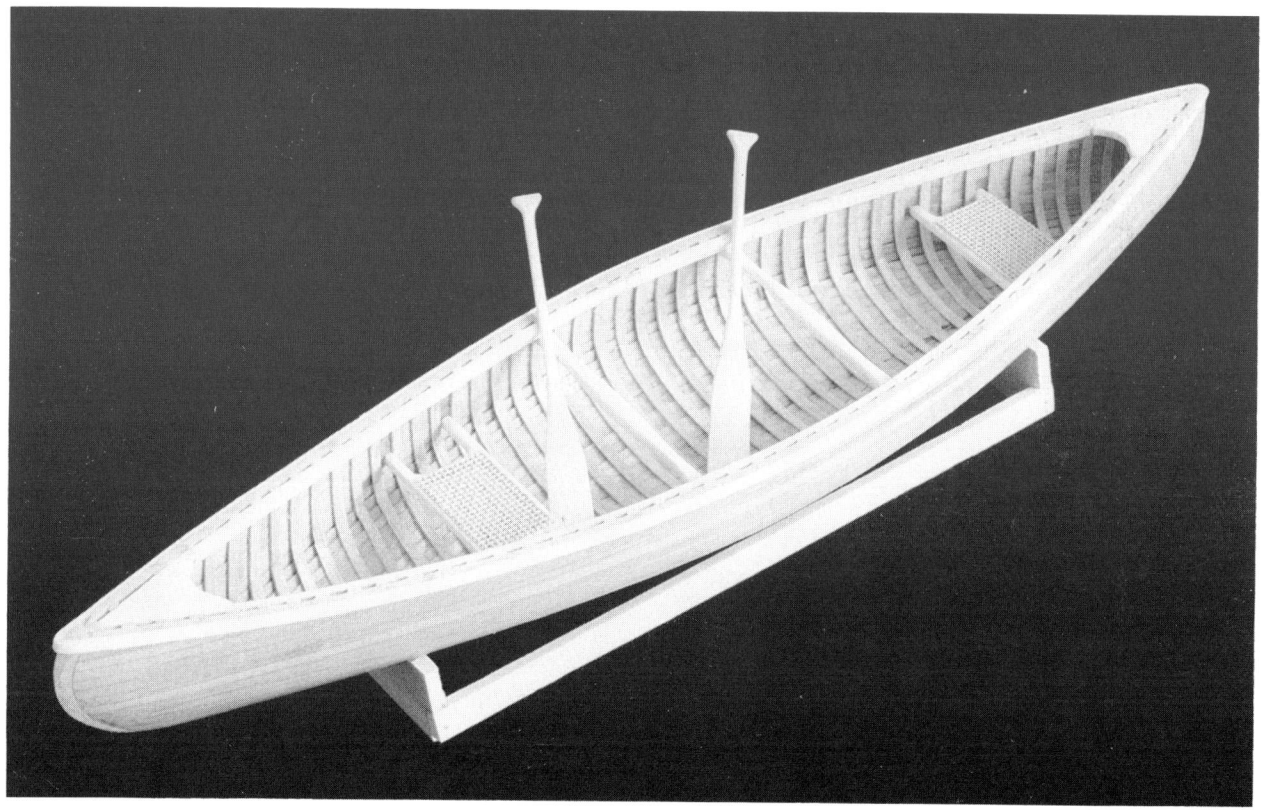

And now for something completely different! The Frontier Trading Company of South Africa has produced a kit for a canoe that builds into a model some 17″ long. The craft is somewhat different to the North American Indian canoe with which we are probably more familiar but nevertheless, as I was to discover, one that lends itself to the modelling techniques that we are conversant with.

The Kit

Obviously a lot of thought has gone into the design and preparation of the kit. All material is held in place with an elastic cord on a concertina folding card arrangement. The wood is of the highest quality. The basic mould, about which the planking of the carcase is done, is your actual proper wood, not ply that you would normally expect to find. I only wish I could find a source of timber of the same type and quality. The instruction booklet is fairly basic, but adequate for what has to be done. There are a number of parts that have to be cut out with a fret saw – no pre-cutting here. However, with this timber there is really no problem. Another plus is the fact that you get materials for a stand, an item so often missing from today's kits.

The main construction

Having got the fret saw out to cut the elements for the basic mould, I decided that I would, in fact, cut all items out to which this particular tool applied.

The only parts that needed special attention were the

seat supports. I would strongly recommend that these two items be separated from the main board on which they are printed, and glued to a piece of scrap ply. Ensure that the adhesive is outside the outline of the actual part, but try to position a small blob between the outlines of the three inner sections that have to be removed. You might get away without doing this if you use a very fine tooth fret saw blade, but there are potential dangers of breaking the part across the two cross pieces. Remember that this is not ply wood!

Having cut out all of the parts, the edges of the mould bulkheads were then filed perfectly square in order to fit snugly against the side faces of the main keel, or strongback, as it is referred to in the instruction manual. This provided the strongest possible glued joint.

Two formers had been cut, around which you have to laminate inner and outer stems. The laminations were cut from a piece of sheet material and pulled and glued around the edges of the formers. It was suggested in the instructions that the laminated strips be held in place by elastic bands. I found this to be inadequate using the bands supplied, and used toolmakers' clamps instead. An equally effective alternative would be to use a strand of brass wire as a tourniquet at each end of the bend. Each former was used to produce two stems. The inner stems were then lightly glued to each end of the strongback and the outer pieces put to one side for later use.

When the glue was completely cured on the mould construction, the planking was started. This utilised strips of timber approximately 5/32" × 1/8", the first strip being placed in line with marks printed on the bulkhead pieces (Fig. 12.1). The strips overlap alternatively, port and starboard, at stem and stern (Fig. 12.2). Initially, until the curve at the bottom of the craft is reached, the section of the planks can be used as provided. At that point, however, a chamfer needs to be planed on one edge in order that adjacent strips fit snugly together without gaps.

Fig. 12.2 The overlap of the planking at the stem. A similar process is involved at the stern but planks overlapping at the stem butt at the stern.

The bottom of the boat requires yet another technique. The ends can no longer be overlapped and you are advised to angle and butt them together along the centreline of the strongback. A better way is to angle the ends to match the plank on the opposite side and continue to plank alternately port and starboard (Fig. 12.3). Take time to cut the angles accurately and the bend in the plank is largely self-supporting.

Once the main body of the planking is complete (Figs 12.4 and 12.5) attention can be given to the top line of the craft. Several shorter lengths of planking material were glued to the top plank either side of the stem and stern posts. These were held in place with crocodile clips, one level at a time. The ultimate shaping of those four levels may be done either at this stage, as recommended in the instructions or, after the removal of the internal mould, when there is a more unrestricted access to the top edges of the craft.

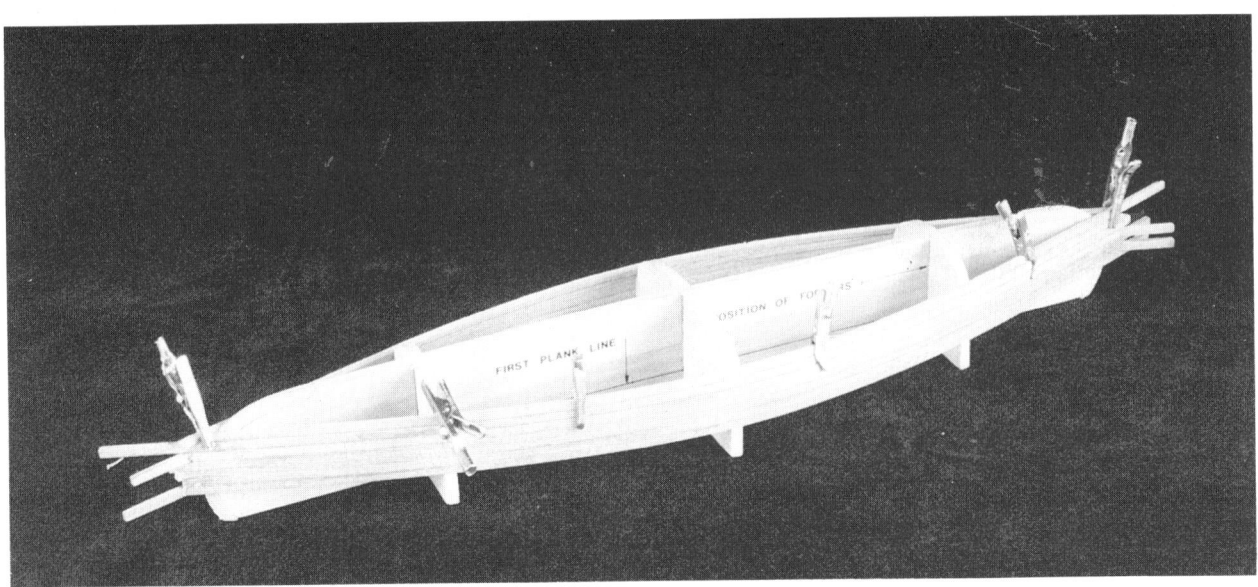

Fig. 12.1 The initial planking down the sides of the craft. Note that the canoe is bottom up in this photograph.

A Frontiersman Canoe

Fig. 12.3 The planking layout adopted for the bottom of the canoe.

The trimming of the planks at each end, to prepare for the fitting of the outer stems, was probably the most painstaking task in the whole project. At the top end, the planks were trimmed to follow the line of the inner stem pieces but, at the lower end, a recess had to be cut to house the thickness of the outer stem. When the shape provided the correct match between inner and outer stems, the latter were glued in place and allowed to thoroughly harden off. Both outer stems were then carved to remove excess material before sanding with the outer surface of the planks to attain a smooth blend (Fig. 12.6).

The removal of the strongback and formers was not quite so easy as the manual implied. Cutting through the strongback with a knife is a bit of a laugh. A blade slim enough to get to the full depth of the boat broke before I had made much impression on the job in hand. A sturdier knife just wouldn't reach into the craft far enough. In the end I used a razor saw to cut through the thickness of the strongback as deeply as I possibly could, then used a pair of pliers to break out the centre section and formers. A pair of electrical side cutters were then used to gradually cut away the remainder. The residual pieces immediately adjacent to the stem and stern posts were then quite easily jiggled free.

Fig. 12.4 The basic planking completed – topside view.

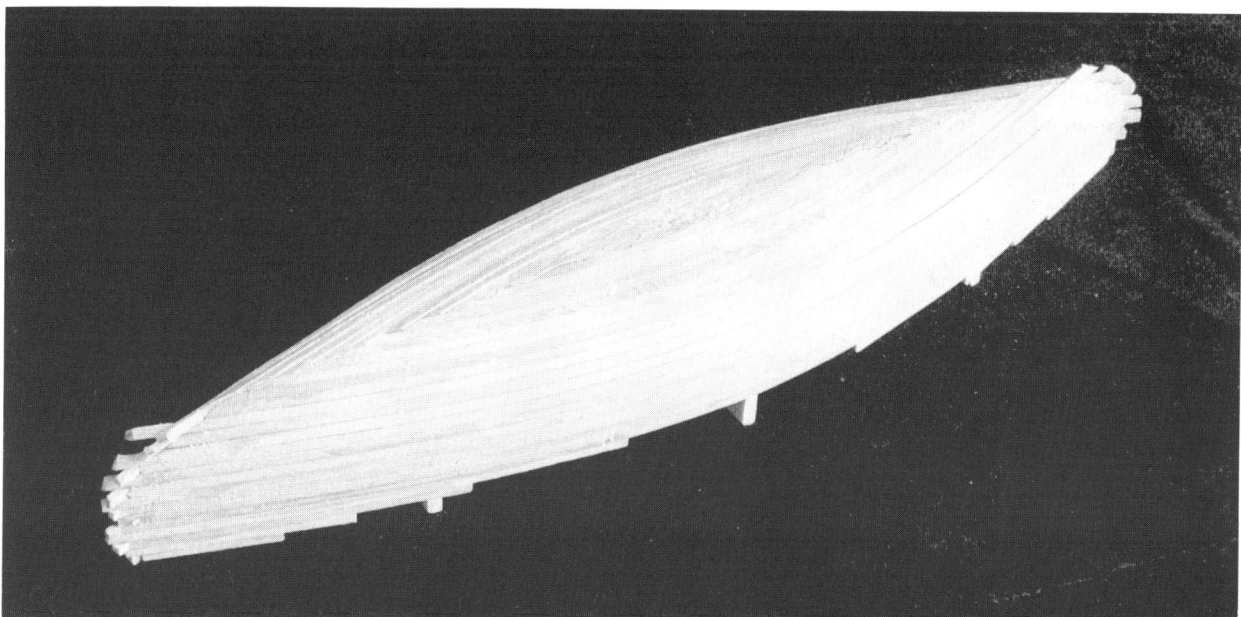

Fig. 12.5 The basic planking completed – bottom side up.

Fig. 12.6 The outer stem fitted and shaped.

Finishing the canoe

How well you have done your planking will determine how much effort you have to put into the finishing the internal surfaces of the canoe. Once the desired smoothness was achieved, the ribs were fitted (Fig. 12.7). These were made from 3mm wide strips cut from sheets of veneer provided. This is not as difficult as might at first appear, the secret being to get all strips the same width, cut from the sheets with a sharp scalpel. I found that a very simple way to ensure that all strips were identical in width was to drive a couple of brass pins into my cutting board spaced just short of the length of the veneer sheet; a further two pins were then placed 3mm off line from the first two just outside the length of the sheet. This permitted the edge of the sheet to sit against the first two pins then, with a steel rule against the second outside pair, the scalpel could be used to cut off the exposed 3mm wide strip.

Fig. 12.7 The inside smoothed and the first rib clipped and glued in place.

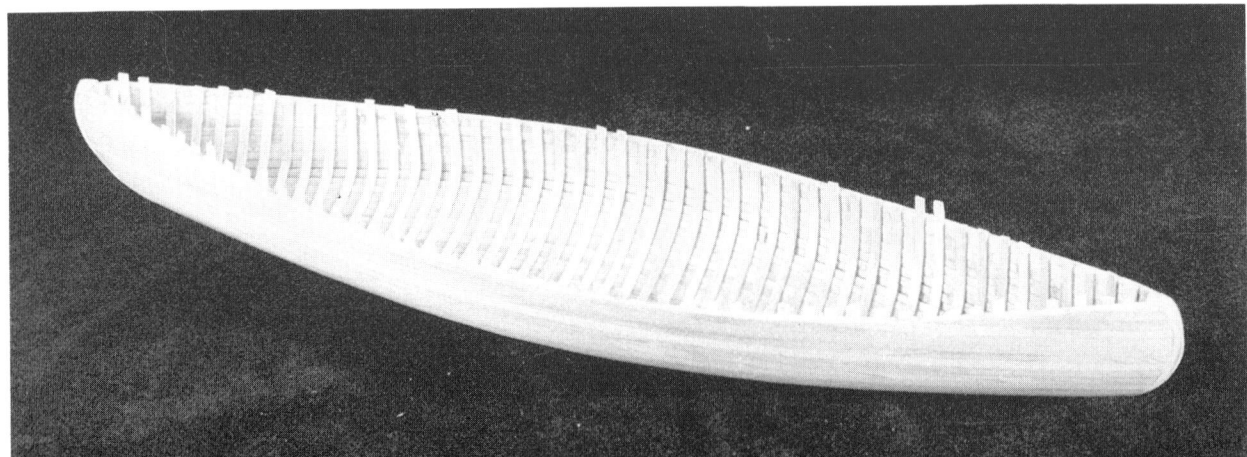

Fig. 12.8 All ribs in place.

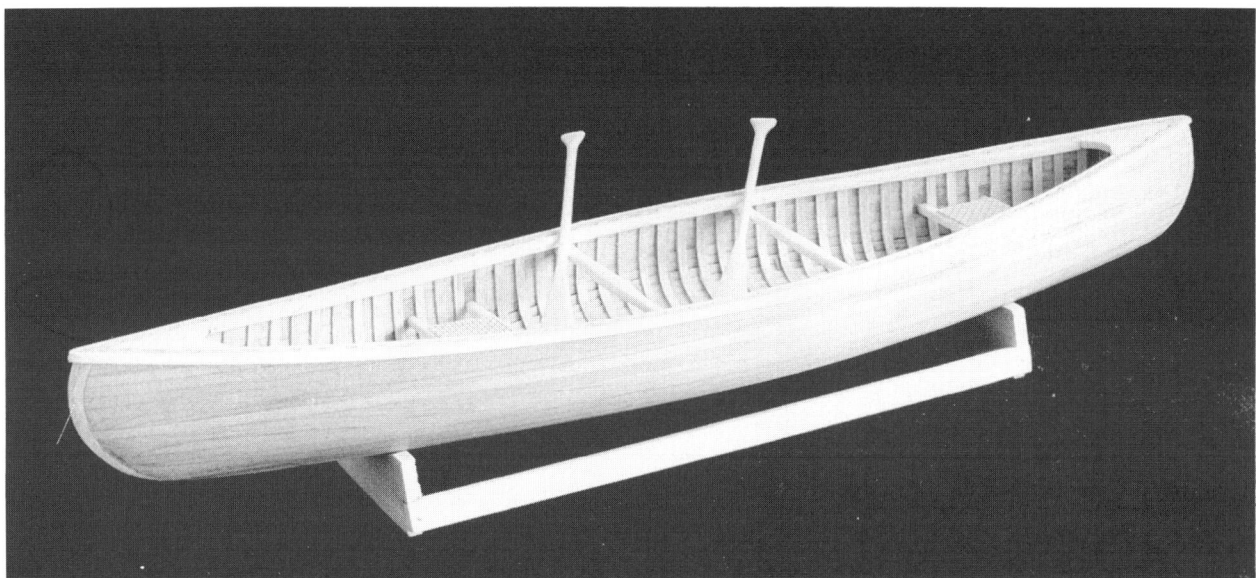

Fig. 12.9 The completed model canoe and stand.

The strips needed to be steamed to soften the fibres to permit the ribs to sit tight against the inside of the craft. The ribs, apart from a few in the centre, all follow compound curves that not only have to conform to the sectional shape of the canoe (Fig. 12.8) but also have to twist to maintain the required 5mm separation. Without steaming, this is almost impossible. A quick boil in the electric kettle is more than enough to do the trick. A dozen at a time allows you working time to get them fitted before moving on to the next batch.

The two triangular shaped deck pieces were next to be put in place, followed by the inner gunwale strips. Again, a few crocodile clips were found best to hold the required curve while the adhesive set. The outer strips were then added using a similar procedure. A final rub down was then given and the completed shell given three coats of acrylic satin varnish. It only remained to make up the seats, thwarts and paddles to complete the craft (Fig. 12.9). Parts for a very basic but practical stand were provided on which to rest the canoe.

Conclusions

First impressions were deceptive. This kit, certainly, is not a weekend project, or one for the inexperienced modelmaker. It makes up into a very acceptable and attractive model which would grace both the domestic and competition environment. It certainly has the potential, if made with care, to catch a judge's eye at exhibition. The timber provided is excellent, although there are no drawings apart from the sketches given in the basic instruction booklet. If you want a shorter term project with a subject completely different, this might just fill the bill.

CHAPTER 13

The Rate System

The seventeenth century saw the first really serious attempts to establish the ground rules for the design and gunning of ships for the Royal navy. Up until that time, much was left to the craftsmanship of the shipwrights who, by the traditional handing down of the craft, knew what was required. It was also the case that the obviously successful earlier designs were used as a basis for the new. Nothing wrong in that, provided those people concerned recognised, and remembered, what was significant in those designs.

With the requirement for an ever-increasing number of guns, and the consequent more critical effect this had on the design and manning of ships, it was seen necessary to lay down some sort of standardisation. This was done, not only in respect of the dimensional aspects of the vessel, but also in rigging and fitting out. Thus, men who were moved around from ship to ship would not be *lost* in terms of handling guns and rigging, and standardisation was seen to have the potential to improve overall ship handling efficiency.

Vessels were graded according to the number of guns carried and, in the time of James I, there were four *Ranks*. The first rank encompassed ships with 45 to 55 guns. The second rank vessels had 38 to 42 guns. The third rank ships had 26 to 34 guns. All smaller craft fell into the fourth rank. This system prevailed until the 1650s when vessels were reclassified into six *Rates*.

In the 1670s, Samuel Pepys, as Secretary of the Admiralty, was instrumental in introducing the 1677 Establishment, the intention of which was to provide standardisation and uniformity to the fleet. Again, this Establishment had a man/gun basis. After a series of further Establishments in 1685, 1703, 1716, 1743 and 1745, radical reform of the whole Navy under the Anson administration signalled the demise of the Establishments.

THE RATES AND NUMBER OF GUNS CARRIED

Designation	1651	1660–1690	After 1690
First Rate	60	100	100
Second Rate	50–60	80–100	80–100
Third Rate	40–50	64–80	64–80
Fourth Rate	30–40	40–50	50–60
Fifth Rate	16–24	30–40	Up to 46
Sixth Rate	Up to 16	Up to 28	Up to 28

The above table is very basic, there were transitional periods wherein the number of guns varied for a particular class of vessel.

From about 1755, the classification of ships changed somewhat and the *type* of vessel became more significant. The 100-gun ship was still referred to as a first rate and similarly the 80 98-gun ships, second rates. Below that, there was now the 74, 64, 50 and 44-gun ships, with 40, 38, 36, 32, 28, 24 and 20/22-gun frigates. Finally, there were the sloops, brig-sloops and various smaller craft.

CHAPTER 14

More Modelmaking Techniques

Bow and stern blocks

Most kits provide block material for building up the bows and stern immediately fore and aft of the first and last bulkhead or frame. Sometimes, instead of a block, there is a series of laminated pieces of sheet material. Either way, they have to be shaped to take the run of the planking. This can be quite a hazardous process, both to the model and the fingers, if a large proportion of the surplus material isn't removed before fixing the block/laminations to the hull.

If you are working with laminations, make them up into a block first and finish the faces that are to contact the bulkhead and false keel. Similarly, prepare blocks in the same manner.

Hold these pieces in place and mark the outline of the adjacent bulkhead on one face and that of the false keel on the other. Now remove the surplus, parallel to the ship's centreline in one plane, and square to it in the other on the bench before gluing the block in place. This saves a lot of tedious and potentially dangerous work on the actual model.

The final shaping with file or coarse glasspaper should be constantly checked by using a strip of planking material to check that you are attaining the right run for the planking. For the stern end particularly, where there might well be some internal curved work to do, pieces of large dowel wrapped in the glasspaper offer a simple solution to getting into some of the more awkward corners.

Remember too, that the thickness of the stern post normally matches the combined thickness of the false keel and the port and starboard planking. Thus the thickness of the false keel adjacent to the stern post should be reduced at the same time as the stern blocks are being shaped.

Gratings

Making gratings from the parts normally supplied in a kit is not what would be considered a difficult job. Nevertheless, it is surprising just how many modelmakers get them wrong. There is a right and a wrong way for the ledges and battens to lay. OK, it may take a keen eye to spot whether you have got it right, but not such a keen eye to notice if some of the gratings on your pride and joy are correct whereas others are not. The variation rather tends to stand out. Certainly, in a competition it is the sort of thing the judges may well look for when assessing marks for accuracy.

So, which way round should they be? The ledges run across the vessel, or athwartships. The top surface of the ledges have grooves across them into which the battens sit running fore and aft. Therefore when looking down on the top of the grating, it is the battens running fore and aft that are seen in their entirety.

As for making these items, I usually follow a set procedure that always seems to work very well. The actual grating part is made up first from the comb jointed pieces normally provided in the kit. A dab of adhesive on the finger run along the flat surface of each piece will usually deposit just enough into the slots without too much ooze taking place. The pieces would have been cut just a little overlength and, when the glue has dried, the grating assembly is then trimmed down to proper size. The rotary sander is ideal for this operation and I ensure that the outer dimensions of the grating are such that I finish up with a full batten on the two sides and a full ledge fore and aft.

Framing the grating is done in two stages. First, I glue the fore and aft parts of the frame to their respective ledges and let the adhesive completely set. The ends are then sanded down flush with the outside battens. Again, the rotary sander makes for an easier life, but careful work with a file and sandpaper block works just as well.

The second stage is to fit the port and starboard frame pieces against the battens. When set, these are then trimmed off flush with the outer faces of the fore frame and after frame respectively.

Alternative sail making

Many of the foregoing chapters describing the techniques used for making the various models have featured the making of sails more as a dressmaker's task. It occurred to me that perhaps not everybody has the talent, or indeed the desire, to wield the needle and thread to the degree of expertise needed to produce a really fine suit of sails. So, what are the alternatives? The obvious one, and I make no bones about subscribing to it myself, is to get someone with the necessary ability to make them for you. However, what do you do if this avenue is not open to you? Circumstances forced the issue in my own case, and I had to give very serious thought to the problem. I am not a great believer of putting sails on models, but there are some models where sails really do make a difference. For instance, I never think a Thames Barge looks right without being fully rigged. So, being obliged to make sails for one particular project, I sat down and analysed the problems.

The first serious difficulty for one not adept at using a sewing machine is the representation of all the seams that are visible on a sail. A line of stitches produced by a sewing machine is certainly speedy, but I can never seem to get the line straight enough and, unfortunately, when there have to be a series of parallel rows fairly close together, anything less than perfection shows up like a sore thumb. Then I remembered that Artenaval, the Portuguese kit producer, provided material pre-printed with the seams. So, why not do something similar? Accordingly, I took some spare sail material and experimented with several marking media. The contrast of drawing ink was too great and you could never guarantee that it wouldn't run, and the ordinary lead pencil was not the right colour. What did fit the bill was an ordinary coloured pencil. A dark brown shade proved to solve the problem quite well. Snags? Yes, you must use a chisel point and constantly keep it sharpened to a fine edge.

Coloured pencils are, by nature, on the soft side and will not produce a thin line for more than about 50cm without attention to the point. It is also best to mark both sides of the sail.

a) DRAW OUTLINE OF SAIL AND SEAMS ONTO CLOTH WITH CHISEL POINTED COLOURED PENCIL

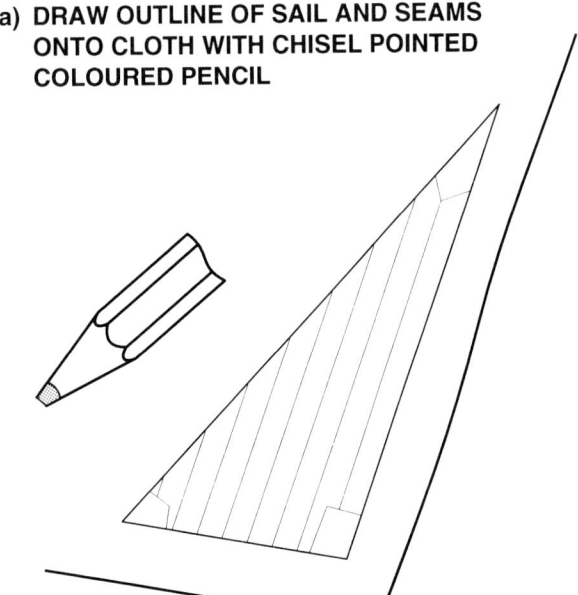

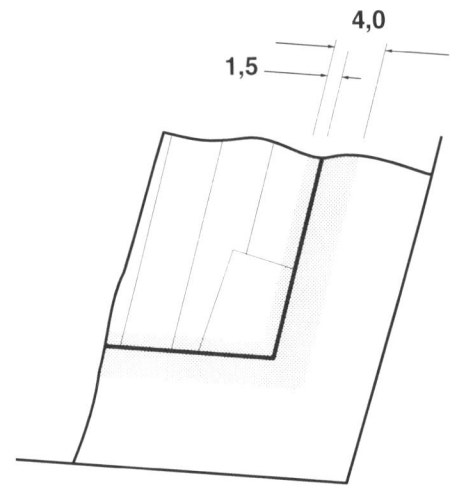

b) BRUSH ON BAND OF ACRYLIC MATT VARNISH ALL ROUND EDGE OF SAIL

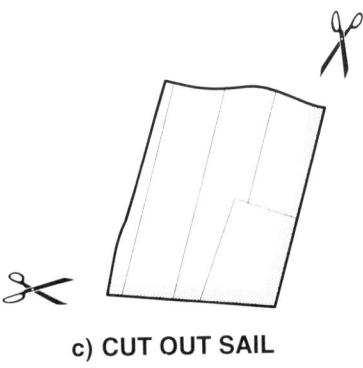

c) CUT OUT SAIL

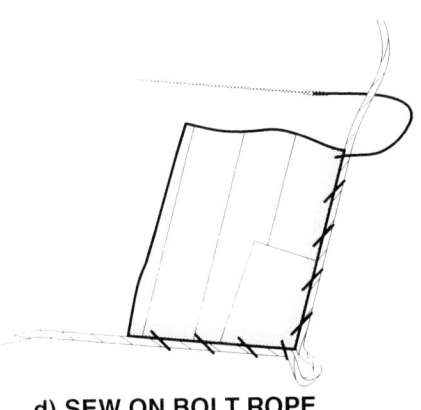

d) SEW ON BOLT ROPE.

The second problem is the hem all round the edges of the sail. Try as I might, I could not produce the folded hem required at a suitable width. Even had I been able to tack an acceptable hem, the original problem of machining it straight cropped up again. So, I went back to basics and asked myself if a hem was really essential. Why have a hem at all? The obvious answer is, to stop the edges fraying. Surely, there must be another way and, after a few trials and, I might add, errors, I came up with the following solution.

Having got your piece of material marked out with the seams and outlines of all the sails, the next step is to apply a band of acrylic matt varnish around the edges of each sail. The band needs to be about 4mm wide and should encroach within the edges of the sail by about 1.5mm. If boltropes are not to be put on, the corners of the sails should also be reinforced. Use enough varnish to ensure that it penetrates through the cloth. When thoroughly dry, each sail can be cut from the cloth and you finish up with a neat 1.5mm reinforced edge all round, with corners that can be pierced for eyelets and/or blocks.

Finally, if specified, the boltropes should be sewn on, using as fine a needle as possible. This does not require too much needlecraft, more in the way of patience. A simple binding stitch, or blanket stitch, is all that is needed to anchor the rope to the varnish reinforced edge all round the sail. Don't forget to look to see if there are loops to leave at the corners.

This method of sail making is only OK for models built to a scale of say, no bigger than 1/48, provided that you take care with the thickness of your drawn lines. However, it does solve the problem if your sewing skills, like mine, are virtually non existent. It eliminates that difficult task, even for the expert, of producing a very narrow width of tucked hem round the edges and those close parallel seams.

CHAPTER 15

The Planking of Period Ship Models

What it's all about?

I remember overhearing on one occasion some rather destructive comment concerning the planking on a kit-built model. The line of planking was not accurate, the planks ran the full length of the hull and the wales had been put on afterwards. These remarks were entirely true but, for all that, the work was neat and the model had obviously had quite a bit of time spent on it. But it was the totally deflating comment, about not being a true modelmaker unless you scratch built and did the planking properly, that somewhat riled me. Here was a young man, with not too much experience, being put down by the sneering words of a senior modeller who should have known better.

I later asked the so-called expert if he had a thickness device for making his planks and, on getting a negative reply, asked how he managed to get all the different thicknesses correct for planking his 17th-century Third Rate. It turned out that apart from the wales, all his planks were the same thickness. I have to admit to a certain amount of pleasure in commenting that he had missed a golden opportunity to do the job properly.

The purpose of this little preamble? Merely to demonstrate that the vast majority of modelmakers compromise to some degree as to accuracy and authenticity of what they build. If you can put your hand on your heart and say that you have done the best you can within your facilities and capabilities, then you can view your finished model with justified pride. Some criticism can usually be levelled at even the best of modelmakers but, provided that it is constructive, rather than like that in my introductory story, then it should be looked upon as one of the ways we all participate in the never-ending learning process.

I am in no way attempting to present the definitive treatise on the subject of the planking of the man of war; there are several excellent works, written by far better qualified people, already published. What I am trying to do here is to identify the options for modelmaking, and present some workable compromises that will lend themselves equally to the more experienced modeller and beginner alike. All the drawings are of typical arrangements rather than of specific vessels or types. It is anticipated that the modeller will have done the research necessary to identify the specifics relating to the ship model under construction.

So, what are the limits within which you make your compromise when it comes to planking? At the lower end of the scale, some of the simpler kits provide for very basic covering of the hull with strip material that hardly deserves to be called planking. At the top end, you have the scratch-built model that has been correctly framed, onto which planks of correct width, thickness and length are properly fixed. From this, it can be seen that one thing leads to another, and you can't just consider planking in isolation. Thus, the whole model is usually something of a compromise and, as such, will always be open to the critical remarks of the so-called *expert*.

If you are going to scratch build, then obviously you have a far wider range of options available to you. Nonetheless, some very basic decisions have to be made. Should you intend to partially plank (dockyard style), in accordance with the methods and dimensions of your chosen period, then certainly you will need to frame to the same specification, including the correct disposition and size of beams for the deck planking. This is really the ultimate type of project for the period ship modelmaker and, to see exactly what is achievable, I recommend that you take a look at the photographs of the completed frame model of the *Egmont* in Peter Goodwin's *The Construction and Fitting of the Sailing Man Of War 1650 1850*. This must be one of the finest examples of the coming together of painstaking research and brilliant craftsmanship.

OK, so you feel that the facilities you have available or, maybe your modelmaking skills, do not lend themselves to you being able to go that far, but you still want to produce something that *looks* right on the outside. This usually means totally planked and decked, allowing for some compromise on the inner frame construction which, of course, will not be seen on the finished model. This calls for careful planning because you have to remember that much of the planking will have butt joints set at frames. So, some drawing work is necessary to determine the planking layout in order to conveniently position your compromise frames. Do not forget that the deck planking also followed laid down patterns, and this too must be taken into consideration at this stage in order to position beams.

Finally, we come to models produced from kits in all their various degrees of quality. Here, in the majority of cases, the compromise is often one of simulation. The number of frames and their position is usually a function of *kit* design rather than one of pure ship design, and you will be lucky if frames come at the correct position for accurate plank lengths and joints. A further problem lies in the thickness and type of material used for the frames – 6mm ply is hardly adequate for pinning the ends of two butt-jointed planks. Then, of course, many kits use the double-planking method where the first planking is perhaps lime, which is subsequently planked over with thin strips of say, mahogany or walnut. With care, this method will often permit the second planking to simulate, quite accurately, the true shapes and sizes of the original planks. With single-planked hulls, the only chance you have of producing a result that looks anything like what it should, is to use a sharp scalpel to lightly mark the true ends and joints of the planks.

The scratch-built option

The ship of war was planked both internally and externally and if you are going to build a proper dockyard model, there is much detail to recognise in both of these areas in terms of plank sizes and the way that they were jointed. If your ambitions run to creating such a model, the best advice that I can offer is to do your research well in order that you identify the pattern of planking and its fixing, the types of joints employed, and the widths and thicknesses of the timber used. Again, I would refer you to Peter Goodwin's work on the subject as an excellent guide to everything that is pertinent, and then on to the detail of your specifically chosen subject.

I am going to start the discussion with the scratch-built, externally planked model, the only internal planking being that above deck level (Fig. 1). I also have to assume that the basic structure, or frame, has been so constructed as to provide supports for the required joints at the right places.

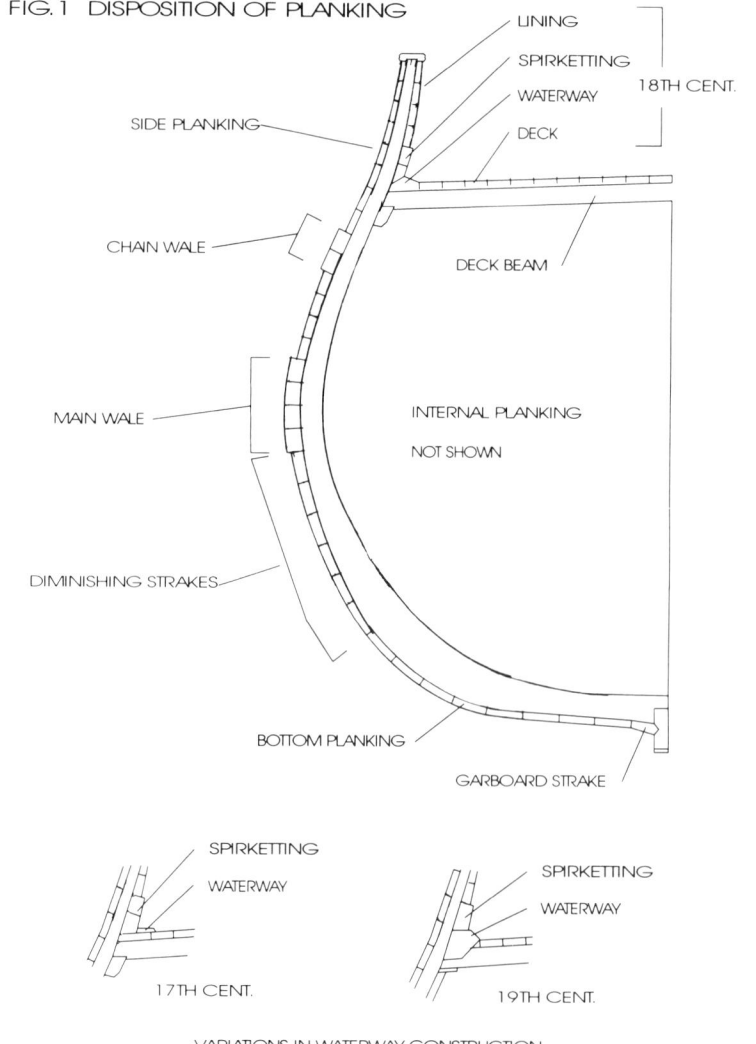

FIG. 1 DISPOSITION OF PLANKING

VARIATIONS IN WATERWAY CONSTRUCTION

The Planking of Period Ship Models

Whether you work with the frame housed on a jig or whether you work with it in your lap, the procedure for planking is the same. The first step is to correctly mark on the outside of the hull the position of the main wales and chain or channel wales, if applicable. The latter were identified as being the wales to which the chains from the shrouds were fixed. The wales were the thickest of the hull planking and were designed to be effective fore and aft stiffeners. Note that the line of the wales was not parallel to the decks but aligned to the sheer of the hull. This accounts for the fact that some of the gunports fore and aft have to be cut into the top line of the wales, the gun decks normally being parallel to the waterline.

Wales were usually planked using the top and butt or anchor stock systems. The proportions of these two systems are outlined in Fig. 2. The length of the planks varied according to the Rate of the ship and the main wales were usually two strakes wide. The proportions governing the long and short angles of the planks remained constant irrespective of the Rate of vessel.

The channel wales may also have been laid using the top and butt or anchor stock methods, but many were wrought in plain parallel planking. This is another instance where your research pays dividends. The timber thickness used for these wales was 75% of that used for the main wales irrespective of the planking method employed.

The garboard strake was that row of planks immediately adjacent to the keel and would be shaped along its lower edge to fit into the keel rabbet. Its width was a function of the moulded keel depth — usually two-thirds. However, it was not rectangular in section, being thicker on the edge that tucked into the keel. Its upper edge was normally only half as thick as the lower. For the most part, the garboard strake would be straight planking but there were variations. Thus, should you wish to produce a model having this depth of authenticity, your research should reveal such detail.

The diminishing strakes were so called due to the fact that their thickness diminished between the bottom edge of the main wale and the top edge of the bottom planking. In the seventeenth century, these strakes were normally rectangular in cross-section, but later the section was in

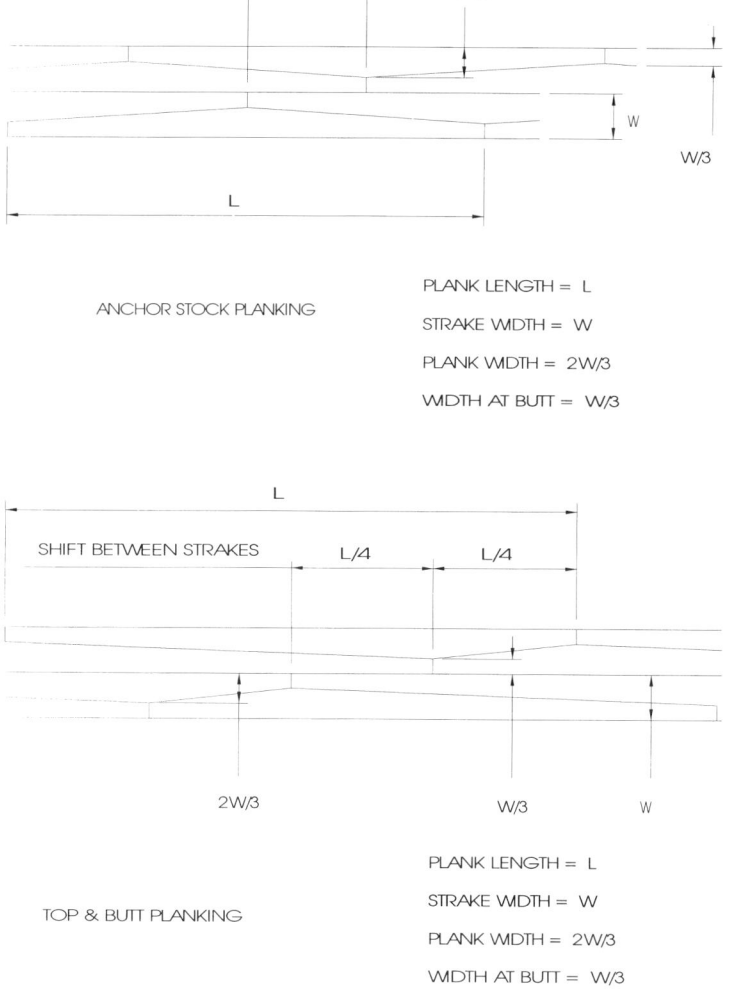

FIG.2 STYLES OF PLANKING

ANCHOR STOCK PLANKING

PLANK LENGTH = L
STRAKE WIDTH = W
PLANK WIDTH = 2W/3
WIDTH AT BUTT = W/3

TOP & BUTT PLANKING

PLANK LENGTH = L
STRAKE WIDTH = W
PLANK WIDTH = 2W/3
WIDTH AT BUTT = W/3

fact tapered. This variation in thickness between the top and bottom edges was controlled by simple arithmetical formulae based on the thickness of the main wale and the number of strakes being applied. Depending on the period, top and butt or parallel planking was used.

The bottom planking was that area between the garboard strake and the bottom of the diminishing strakes. In the majority of cases this was laid with parallel planks with square butts, but some variations were employed after the late eighteenth century. It was in this section, particularly, that the use of stealers and dropstrakes were found necessary at bows and stern. These were short lengths of plank let into the edges of two others adjacent to the stem or stern post to avoid excessive bending of a plank on its width. A drop strake was a similar application where the short plank was let into the top edge of the plank in question.

The side planking was the thinnest of the planking but, even so, its dimensions were still governed by rules relating to the thickness of the channel wales.

The internal planking comprised, for the purpose of this discussion, the waterways, the spirketting and the lining. Fig. 1 shows the arrangement of this planking and the variations that can be found during various periods. The procedures for applying the spirketting could be quite complex since this too, was a feature that provided longitudinal stiffening of the vessel. The position of joints had to be arranged in accordance with the position of gunports and, jointing between adjacent planks was usually necessary. The lining was that planking from the top of the spirketting to the rails.

Deck planking also had procedures and proportions which the modelmaker should recognise. In the main, the gun decks carried the thickest of the planking; the heavier and greater the number of guns, the thicker the planks were. Generally, decks were laid with either a three butt or four butt shift where there were three or four planks respectively between butt joints on the same beam (Fig. 3). A margin plank was laid adjacent to the inner edge of the waterway, its purpose being to house the ends of those planks as they met the curvature of the ship's side fore and aft (Fig. 4). The rules controlling this joggling of planks was quite precise. The end of the plank was not to be reduced to less than half its width and the taper so caused should always be more than twice the full plank width.

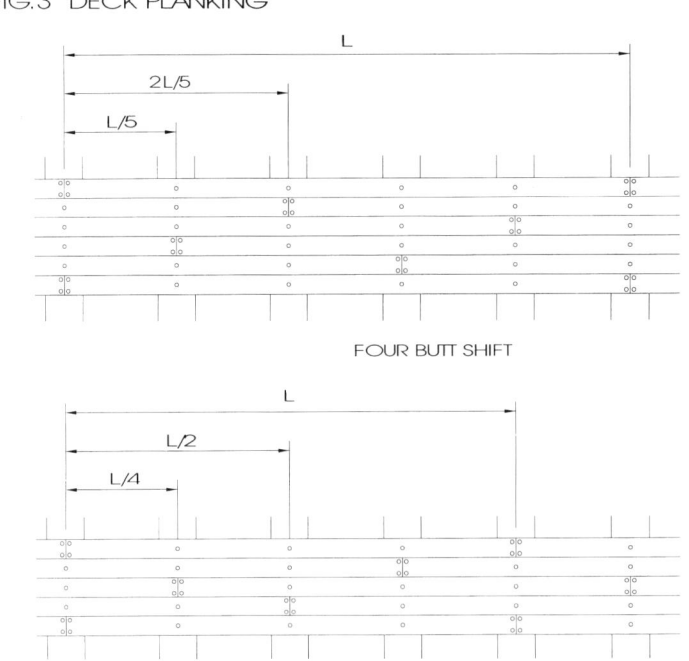

FIG.3 DECK PLANKING

FOUR BUTT SHIFT

THREE BUTT SHIFT

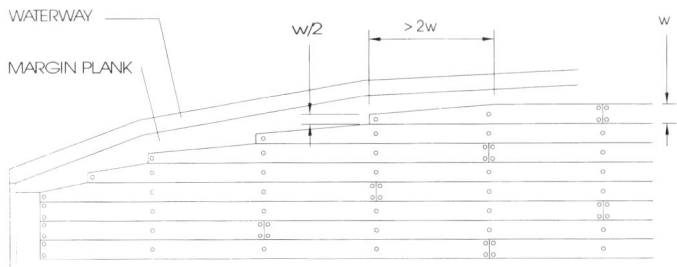

FIG.4 JOGGLING INTO THE MARGIN PLANK

As you can see from the foregoing, making a model to this degree of accuracy is not a project to be undertaken without a lot of thought. As a modelmaker, you are always going to come up against the inevitable compromise, so it is most important to establish just what it is you are trying to accomplish right from the start. Producing a good looking model with everything in the right place and to correct scale is one thing, but constructing it in true shipyard fashion, planked and framed correctly, with all the right planking systems, is quite something else.

Then, having made that decision, what materials are you going to use? Good old English oak or elm, maybe? Just remember that you can't get scale wood with scale grain so, what do you do? You buy an alternative that works well, bends well and looks something like the original. Yes, another compromise.

Maybe the bottom of the hull was coated in white stuff. After all that time spent properly applying the bottom planking, do you really want to cover it all up with paint? Probably you will succumb to yet another compromise and let the world see your lovely woodwork.

The message is, establish your specification and stick to it. There will always be an *expert* who will tell you that you should have done this or that, but if you have fulfilled your set aims to the best of your ability, you will attain the best sort of satisfaction from your labours.

The kit-built option

Here you are largely confined to building the *looks good* model. The main structure is a kit-based design that usually has no bearing on a true ship's frame. The carcase is frequently a false keel, into which is slotted a number of bulkheads having the correct sectional shape for their position along the keel. The kits that allow you to produce something like the appearance of true planking are those that are double planked. That is, the carcase is first planked with say, lime strips, followed by a further layer of planking in perhaps walnut or mahogany. However, don't expect the kit drawings to give details of the correct planking methods — for that, you have to do your own research. What the kit provides is the *opportunity* to do something a bit special, over and above the stem to stern strips normally seen on kit-built models. The requirements are basically the same as for the scratch-built model in terms of what you actually see; it is the application that is different.

The basic compromise is to apply the second planking in such a way as to simulate the authentic planking system. The fact that you have a total surface, onto which you apply the visible planking, obviates the need for frames in the right place. Many kits specify 0.5mm or 0.6mm thick strips for the second planking. This, of course, makes for fairly easy cutting, although if you want to simulate anchor stock, or top and butt planking, the grain structure of such materials needs the application of very sharp tools in a direction that doesn't guide the cutting edge off course.

The next important target is to make sure that this second planking is totally adhered to the first. Contact adhesive is OK provided that you can be sure that the total surface is firmly fixed. If you want to be absolutely certain that you have attained the best joint possible, then a PVA adhesive is perhaps the better choice. It will take a little longer, but you don't want the ends of planks lifting when you later come to drill holes to simulate the plank fixings. Splits will inevitably occur, running from the hole out to the end of the plank.

Another feature of the kit construction will almost certainly be the *laid on* wale. Instead of the wale timbers being thicker than the rest, they will merely be an added strip or so to the surface of the main planking. This is not really a problem provided that you recognise the line of the wale when you do the second planking. The secret is to plank the wale position first with plain parallel planking, simulate the adjacent side planks and diminishing planks as required, then apply the correct form of planking for the wale as a third layer of planking.

In many ways, this simulation process is more demanding than building from scratch, but it does allow the modeller who builds from kits, for whatever reason, the opportunity to do something a little bit special. I have seen some kits made up into superb models using this sort of technique. The few times that I have used the method, the materials in the kit have been adequate both in quantity and quality, with few recourses to the scrap box.

So, what can you do if the kit in question is only single planked? The short answer is, not a lot! The best that can normally be done is to plank the hull as per the kit instruction, then mark the butt joint positions with a scalpel or similar sharp edge. I have never attempted to mark top and butt or anchor stock planking in this way and would hesitate to recommend so doing. Bearing in mind the finished shape of the hull, I can visualise the edge of the blade going everywhere except on line.

Even though it would not be historically correct to portray the planking with all butt joints, it does add something to the model. It is essential that all planking is well glued, edge-to-edge, and allowed to dry out thoroughly before starting on the marking. In fact, a rubbed in coat of matt varnish will also prove of value as it seems to steady the tip of the blade to advantage.

Before leaving this particular type of kit, I feel that a few words regarding the shaping of the planks is in order. The instructions, in all probability, will indicate planking strips that take in the complete length of the hull. This means that virtually all of the planks will need to be tapered fore and aft and stealers fitted. The best indication as to the amount of tapering to be done is to measure the distance from keel to rail on the biggest frame or bulkhead and divide this length by the width of the planking strips provided. This will give you the number of planks that will be required. If you now measure the distance at other key bulkheads and divide those distances by the number of planks, you will obtain

133

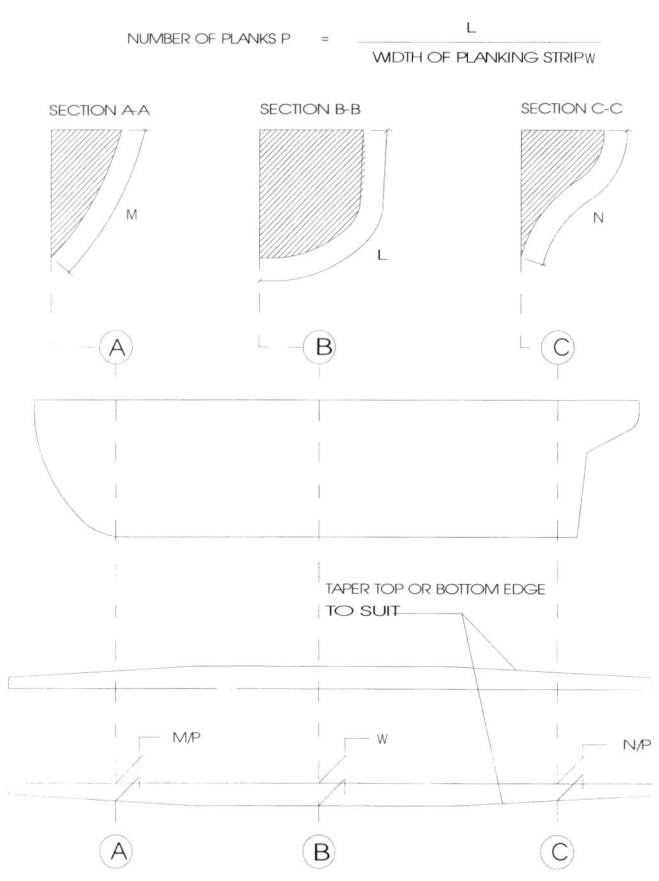

FIG.5 DETERMINING PLANK TAPERS FOR SIMPLE PLANKING

$$\text{NUMBER OF PLANKS P} = \frac{L}{\text{WIDTH OF PLANKING STRIP W}}$$

the width of the plank at those particular points (Fig. 5).

Shape only the top or bottom edge of the plank to suit the model in hand to give the taper, offer it up and adjust accordingly. Stealers will come into play where the lines of the hull take the strips into a severe sideways bend condition. Kits usually describe stealers as wedge-shaped pieces tapering to a sharp point. This, of course, is totally inaccurate, but then so is the basic planking system. If done carefully, you can still finish up with a neat covering to the hull, and a nice looking model, but it won't be shipshape and all that stuff!

Fastenings

There were several types of plank fastenings, the most common probably being the trennal and the bolt. The trennal or tree-nail was basically a wooden dowel, tight fitting, and often supplemented by a wedge driven into a slot cut across its outer end. The bolt was an unthreaded copper or iron rod, headed at one end and hammered over a washer, or rove, at the other.

In many cases, the wedged trennal and the bolt head were made underflush to the surface of the planking and caulked over. This helps the kit builder considerably, since all that needs to be done is to cleanly drill through the top planking and fill the hole with filler. Use a sharp drill and ensure that the hole position is adequately centred using the point of a scriber or even a sharp pencil. This is another operation that is best done after applying a good rubbed in coat of matt varnish. The value of the well stuck plank also becomes apparent at this stage.

At 1/48 scale, a hole 1/32" dia or 0.8mm is just right to simulate the real thing, which was about 1.5" dia. Once the filler has set, the whole surface can then be scraped and sanded to the required finish. For smaller scales, marking the position with the point of a sharp pencil will often suffice. Incidentally, should you wish to leave bolt heads exposed, it is possible to buy 10mm black pins which provide a very acceptable effect.

As far as fixing when applying the first layer of planking is concerned, the pin and glue method is the one usually adopted. Any bend in the plank should be produced with an over-bend (see later comments on bending). This serves two purposes; first it avoids stressing the glued joint and, secondly, it enables the pins to hold the plank in place without being driven fully home. The latter is quite important since, before sanding down the surface of the first planking, it is advisable to remove all the pins and having the heads standing proud helps enormously. Don't forget also, that when using these small sections of timber, splitting can be a very real problem therefore all pins should be inserted into pre-drilled holes. Pins can be pushed home with a pusher if you can get the hang of using one correctly. I still favour the lightweight hammer where I can see the pin all the time.

Plank bending

I think that every modelmaker has his or her own favourite method of bending planks. If you have found a method that suits the way you work, produces the results you want and hasn't hurt your pocket too much, there isn't a lot more to be said. However, I am not going to use that statement to get me off the hook, but I have to confess that having found a satisfactory method for myself many years ago, I have little experience of the sophisticated and expensive equipment that can be obtained. Unless you make a lot of models, and do a lot of bending, there are some relatively cheap and easy to use compromises (that word again).

Much, of course, depends on the section and type of timber to be bent as to the degree of force, or pressure, that is required to achieve an adequate bend. Some of the thinner and softer woods will succumb readily to simple pressure between thumb and forefinger, and all that is needed is to work your way back and forth along the planking strip until the right curve has been induced. I always tend to overbend initially, so that by the time the plank has been glued and generally handled to get position, the natural regression towards straightness in the fibres has brought the curve back to what is required. This is important, particularly if you are applying the outer planking to a double-planked hull and fixing by means of adhesive only – the last thing you want is for the timber to uncurl and fight the adhesive. Having said that, whatever means of fixing you are employing, the system can be adversely stressed and the joint weakened if the wood tends to move. It's something like a cold joint in soldering – not very good!

The next upward rung on the bending ladder is probably the plank nipper. *Amati* produce a typical example of this simple device and, quite frankly about 90% of all the bending I do employs this tool, either in the wet or dry state. It does, however, have one disadvantage; it marks the planking strip severely on the inside of the bend. Under normal circumstances, this doesn't matter too much, since the inside of the bend is not seen. But, be careful, because if for some reason or another you find yourself in the position of having to do a bit of excessive rubbing down when finishing the hull, those marks will show up or, in extreme cases, break the plank. So, the advice is to use gentle pressure at fairly frequent intervals to get your bend.

For thicker, or more stubborn materials, a hot soak will very often help. This can be done in conjunction with the plank nipper if necessary. As far as equipment goes, I found that a 3-pint electric jug kettle is just the thing – it is totally adequate to cover the length of most bends. Fill with water, stick a few strips down the spout opening, and boil up. The length of time you leave the strips in the jug obviously depends on circumstances, but the concentrated heat and steam in such a kettle seems to keep times to a minimum. A word of warning. Do not use the one from the kitchen that boils the water for tea or coffee, buy one for specific use in your workroom. The heated and soaked timber leaves considerable stains and deposits. Make sure that you buy the 3-pint size and, taller and slimmer is better than short and squat. You will find that the cost is considerably less than for formal bending equipment.

Summing up

Making model boats is all about enjoyment. The better the model, both in terms of technical accuracy and standard of workmanship, the greater the enjoyment experienced. Do the best with what your skills and pocket will allow then, in addition to enjoyment, you will get satisfaction. We all learn something with every successive model and it is this that provides the inspiration to build the next one, where that new knowledge can be put to work and provide even more enjoyment.

I repeat the message. Decide at the outset what it is you are trying to achieve in building your model, then stick to that specification. Much of the satisfaction is in achieving that goal. If you feel that you could have done better in some area or another – and it will be most unusual if you don't – then raise your sights to a more difficult target for your next model.

Conclusion

At the end of the original *Period Ship Handbook I* suggested that there could never be a finite end to such a book, since the very next model made could well be the source of yet another chapter. How right that statement turned out to be!

With ten vastly different models in this later selection, I certainly have learned new skills, made new friends and contacts, and have had many hours of satisfying pleasure.

I sincerely hope this book will help you to enjoy the same experiences.

Bibliography

Bellabarba, S. & G. Osculati.	*The Royal Yacht Caroline 1749.*	Conway Maritime Press.
Chapman, F. H. af.	*Architecture Navalis Mercatoria.*	Stockholm, Sweden, 1768 and reprinted Rostock 1962–84
Gardiner, R.	*The First Frigates.*	Conway Maritime Press.
Goodwin, Peter.	*The Construction and Fitting of the Sailing Man of War 1650–1850.*	Conway Maritime Press.
Hahn, Harold M.	*Ships of the American Revolution and Their Models.*	Conway Maritime Press.
Julier, Keith 1992.	*The Period Ship Handbook.*	Nexus Special Interests.
Lavery, Brian.	*The Arming and Fitting of English Ships of 1600–1815.*	Conway Maritime Press.
Lees, John.	*The Masting and Rigging of English Ships of War 1625–1860.*	Conway Maritime Press.
Roding, J. H., Hamburg, Germay 1793–98.	*Allgemeines Worterbuch der Marine.*	Reprinted Amsterdam 1969

Index

Abrasive paper 10
Adhesives 10
Anchors 20, 32, 43, 52, 60, 112
Armed pinnace circa 1803 53

Balustrading 70
Belaying 51
Bitts 43, 68
Block shaping 125
Boats 24, 32, 44
Boltropes 59, 126
Bowsprit 15, 26, 46, 50, 84, 89, 106, 112
Braces 52
Britannia 1893 109
Bulwark rails 41
Bulwarks 68, 84

Cable 32
Canoe 117
Capstan 22, 32, 44, 112
Caravel, 15th century 65
Caroline, Royal Yacht 13
Carronade 103
Chainplates 23, 48, 79, 87
Channels 22, 41, 104
Cleats 44, 58, 77
Clinker construction 96
Collar, mainstay 49
Crosstrees 27, 106
Crowsfeet 27, 32

Deadeyes 22, 29
Drawings 11, 35, 54, 66, 76, 84, 93, 102, 109, 117

Euphroe blocks 32, 50

Fid 47
Figurehead 19
Finishes 10
Fittings 37, 43
Footropes 48

Frame assembly 14, 36, 54, 66, 76, 84, 95, 102, 109, 118
Frame edge shaping 14, 36, 66, 84, 109

Gammoning 28
Gratings 21, 125
Gun carriage 22, 37, 57, 88, 105
    tackle 22, 61
Gunports 15, 26
Gunport lids 42
Gunwales 76, 97

Hatch coamings 102
Hatches 68
Head timbers 20
Headrails 19, 41
Hearts 50
Holly, clinker-built rowing boat 93

Instruction manual 13, 35, 54, 66, 76, 84, 93, 102, 109, 117

Jeers 51
Jib-boom 46, 89
Jib-boom saddles 46

Kit quality 11, 35, 54, 66, 76, 84, 93, 102, 109, 117
Kit selection 11
Knees 98

Lancha Bombadeira, Portuguese bomb ship 83
Lanterns 23
Lateen yard 59, 71
Le Hussard, hermaphrodite brig 101

Masts 27, 46, 57, 71, 78, 89, 106, 113
Materials 13, 35, 54, 66, 84, 93, 102, 109, 117
Oars 59, 91, 98
Ornamentation 18, 19, 40, 56

Paddles 121

Painting 45, 56, 77, 87
Pendants 52
Pin rails 30, 43
Plank bending 135
Planking 14, 15, 36, 38, 54, 67, 76, 84, 96, 102, 103, 110, 118, 129
Pumps 20

Quarter galleries 16, 40

Rails 49, 55, 111
Rate System 123
Ratlines 30, 50
Renommée, frigate 35
Rigging 28, 50, 61, 71, 81, 89, 107, 114
Rowlocks 97
Rudder 17, 57, 69, 110
Rudder hinges 17, 69

Sail lacing 62
Sails 11, 59, 71, 81, 89, 107, 113, 125
Shrouds 22, 29, 50, 57, 89, 104
Sir Winston Churchill, three-masted schooner 75
Staircase 21

Stand 15, 43, 62, 69, 76, 86, 89, 110, 121
Stays 30, 50, 51, 52
Stirrups 48
Stove 22
Stunsail boom 48
Stunsail boom irons 48

Tabernacle 56
Thole pins 58
Thwarts 56, 98, 121
Tiller 57, 63
Tools 9, 10, 13, 66, 94, 117
Tops 27, 47
Trestletrees 47, 106
Tubs 60

Varnish 10, 126

Wales 38, 104, 130
Winches 77
Windlass 68
Woldings 59

Yards 28, 48, 79, 89